THE UNIVERSITY IN CHAINS

◆

THE RADICAL IMAGINATION SERIES
Edited by Henry A. Giroux and Stanley Aronowitz

THE UNIVERSITY IN CHAINS
Confronting the Military-Industrial-Academic Complex

HENRY A. GIROUX

Paradigm Publishers
Boulder • London

Copyright © 2007 by Paradigm Publishers

Published in the United States by Paradigm Publishers, 3360 Mitchell Lane, Suite E, Boulder, Colorado 80301 USA.

Paradigm Publishers is the trade name of Birkenkamp & Company, LLC, Dean Birkenkamp, President and Publisher.

Library of Congress Cataloging-in-Publication Data

Giroux, Henry A.
    The university in chains: confronting the military-industrial-academic complex / by Henry A. Giroux.
        p. cm.
    Includes bibliographical references and index.
    ISBN 978-1-59451-422-7 (hardcover : alk. paper)—ISBN 978-1-59451-423-4 (pbk. : alk. paper) 1. Education, Higher—Political aspects—United States. 2. Higher education and state—United States. 3. Education, Higher—Aims and objectives—United States. 4. Militarism—United States. I. Title.
    LC89.G53 2007
    378.73—dc22

                                                            2007010323

Printed and bound in the United States of America on acid-free paper that meets the standards of the American National Standard for Permanence of Paper for Printed Library Materials.

Designed and Typeset by Straight Creek Bookmakers.

11   10   09   08   07   1   2   3   4   5

For Susan, without end

For Zygmunt Bauman, with great admiration

To the memory of Grizz

◇

Contents

◇

Acknowledgments

I want to thank Susan Searls Giroux, Sophia McClennen, Doug Morris, Donaldo Macedo, and Christopher Robbins for providing me with a number of critical insights and suggestions that otherwise would not have been in *The University in Chains*. While I am solely responsible for the book, their critical input was invaluable in helping me think through various ideas that I take up and develop. I also want to thank Howard Zinn, Stanley Aronowitz, Jasmin Habib, Ira Shor, Olivia Ward, Nasrin Rahimieh, Peter Mayo, Giles Gherson, Joseph A. Massad, David Theo Goldberg, Brian McKenna, Nick Couldry, John Comaroff, Doug Kellner, Zygmunt Bauman, Lewis Gordon, Lawrence Grossberg, Roger Simon, Carol Becker, Ken Saltman, Paul Street, Max Haiven, and Scott Stoneman for their critical input. Grace Pollock, my invaluable graduate assistant of the last three years, did an excellent job in editing the manuscript and in helping me research the book. My administrative assistant, Maya Stamenkovic, "saved" my sanity on numerous occasions with her research and administrative skills. She outdid herself in the help she provided me in finishing this book. I also want to thank my long-term editor and good friend, Dean Birkenkamp, who has been a great critic and supporter of my work. His advice on how to organize this book changed the project significantly and helped produce a much better book. I want to thank Christine Arden, once again, for her superb copyediting. Grizz, my canine companion of ten years, died in 2006, but shared his remaining warmth and love for half the time I was finishing the book. I will miss him terribly. For inspiring my hope for the future, thanks go to my three boys, Jack, Chris, and Brett—so dear to my heart and yet so far away. Our new canine housemate, Kaya, has been a great joy to have these last few months and brings a smile to my face every time I open the door and see her joy and love. Having her lie under my desk while I finished the book surely helped make the task easier. And, of course, I want to acknowledge all of those university professors, students, and educators who are on the frontlines of one of the most important struggles of our time—taking risks to make learning matter and the future better. Once again, I also want to thank my incredible partner, Susan, who never fails to inspire me with her warmth, sparkling intelligence, great love of music, and utterly seductive presence. Finally, I hope Ellen Willis would have been proud of this book. I will miss her generosity, worldliness, warmth, and razor-sharp intelligence. An earlier version of Chapter 3 appeared in *College Literature* and is used with permission.

◇

Introduction

Challenging the Military-Industrial-Academic Complex After 9/11

> The undiminished presence of suffering, fear and menace necessitates that the thought that cannot be realized should not be discarded.
>
> —*Theodor Adorno*

What is the task of educators at a time when the forces of democracy appear to be in retreat and the emerging ideologies and practices of militarization, corporatism, and political fundamentalism bear down on every aspect of individual and collective experience? How one answers this question will have a grave impact not only on higher education but on the future of democratic public life. There are no simple solutions. Hence it becomes crucial, particularly for educators, to provide alternative democratic conceptions of the meaning and purpose of higher education and its relationship to the larger political order, assessing the corporatist and militaristic tendencies within both the university and the wider society. *The University in Chains* argues that both the academy and democracy are in peril, that a fundamental assault has been launched on the academy's unfulfilled legacy of democratic education and its present and future role as a democratic public sphere. But the rigid ideological, economic, and religious chains that are now engulfing higher education so as to eliminate critical thought, noncommodified and nonmili-

1

tarized forms of knowledge, intellectual engagement with important social issues, and interdisciplinary social formations represent more than an attack on democracy. Such assaults also suggest an attack on politics itself—that is, on those forms of teaching, exchange, dialogue, and social relations that refuse to "methodically eliminate speaking and acting human beings."[1] To propose that the university is in chains is not to suggest it has been taken over in toto by anti-democratic forces; nor is the metaphor meant to imply that the university is no longer a site of contestation and struggle. Nor am I suggesting that the question of what the university is and the possibilities it holds for academic labor, students, and public life should not be open to question in light of the changing conditions that now influence educational institutions. What is at stake here are the urgency and uniqueness of the threat the university now faces as a counterinstitution whose ability to not only foster a substantive democracy but also critically negotiate its role in a variety of contexts has been weakened considerably, if not utterly compromised, in the last twenty years. *The University in Chains* is a direct response to the growing forces at work in the creation of the national security state and its frontal assault on education, civil rights, and dissent, fully in tune with a post-9/11 America that is becoming increasing militarized and policed. How we address the interlinking crisis of the academy with the crisis of democracy may, under present circumstances, go beyond the important questions raised in Jacques Derrida's *Eyes of the University* and Bill Readings's *The University in Ruins.*[2] Other than problematizing what the university might be or analyzing how the university has been transformed within a globally sanctioned neoliberal discourse of excellence and efficiency, there is too little in these discourses about either the historical relations between the academy and the forces of militarization or what the academy has become in light of the predominance of such complex and shifting forces. *The University in Chains* makes a case for reclaiming higher education as a democratic public sphere and counterinstitution, one that enables teachers and students to engage in a culture of questioning, a pedagogy of critical engagement, and a democratic politics of civic responsibility. In part, this suggests connecting higher education to educational projects that enable the development of social movements, public spheres, and groups of critical citizens that are able not only to challenge the ascendancy of a number of dangerous anti-democratic tendencies in the United States but also to address what the democratic role of higher education might be within a post-9/11 world. This is an awesome responsibility, yet higher education can play a key role in reclaiming the frayed relationship between education and democracy, knowledge and engaged citizenship, and learning and an informed citizenry.

The crisis in American democracy has been heralded and exacerbated by the nation's growing insecurity about its place in the world, the hollowing out of the state as a provider of crucial social supports, the rise of "the millennial military state,"[3] the pernicious effects of negative globalization, the atomization of everyday life, and the growing violence that has come to mark not only the wars abroad but also the wars at home. The ensuing fears, insecurities, and hardships have not (yet) sparked massive collective resistance to the authoritarian ideologies, practices, and conditions that fuel them so much as an increasing skepticism—or even overt hostility—toward democratic politics, higher education, and critical thought itself. Fewer and fewer Americans seem willing to defend those vital institutions and habits of mind that are crucial to a substantive democracy, especially the idea of the academy as a public good and a crucial democratic public sphere. Cynicism about politics and skepticism about education have become mutually reinforcing tendencies that have resulted from the larger decoupling of the university from the obligations of civic responsibility, public service, and community life. Not only the American public but many educators have lost a meaningful language for linking schooling to democracy, convinced that education is now about job training, competitive market advantage, patriotic correctness, and a steady supply of labor for the national security state. Critical thought is under assault in all public spheres, but especially higher education, as right-wing ideological zealots and Christian fundamentalists legitimate a rampant anti-intellectualism and a rigid moralism fueled by a deep bias against appeals to reason, dissent, dialogue, and secular humanism. Reproducing a blind obedience to power, religious fundamentalists and their ideological counterparts on the Right spread across college campuses promoting a form of patriotic correctness that labels critical thought as either un-American or Satanic, while displaying a rigid intolerance toward all criticisms of state power and government domestic and foreign policies.[4]

An incessant assault on critical thinking, a trampling of civil liberties by right-wing politicians, a manufactured public culture of in/security that serves to mystify all-too-real vulnerabilities, and an all-embracing commitment to free-market fundamentalism that undermines the purposeful social relations in which university educators work, if not the very concept of the social itself, have undercut the possibility for thinking anew about how vital social institutions can be defended as public goods. Moreover, as socially conscious visions of equity recede from public memory, unfettered brutal self-interest and greed combine with retrograde social policies to make security and safety a top domestic priority, fueling a panic-driven culture of fear and an increasingly powerful military-industrial-academic complex. Patriotic correctness, consumerism, and militarization have become the most powerful trilogy of forces now shaping education, redefining the meaning of citizenship, and establishing the contours of an authoritarian social order. As the spaces for producing engaged citizens are stripped of their critical capacities, commercialized, and militarized, a culture of consent, fear, terror, and paranoia emerges to further fuel the growing authoritarianism of U.S. society.[5]

The struggle for the university as a democratic public sphere and as a site of resistance against the growing forces of militarism, corporatism, and right-wing political fundamentalism demands a new understanding of what it means to view the university as a "place to think in relation to other places where thought takes place"[6]; to take seriously the relationship between learning and the formation of engaged, thoughtful citizens; and to prevent the university from being further compromised by those anti-democratic forces and ideologues who view empowering knowledge, critical thinking, and an educated citizenry as a form of subversion, or worse.

Given the seriousness of the current attack on higher education by an alliance of diverse right-wing forces, it is difficult to understand why the majority of liberals, progressives, and left-oriented educators has become relatively silent or tacit apologists in the face of this assault. The current threats to democracy demand the most concrete response, urgent but deliberative and careful. Urgency entails not only responding to the crisis of the present—increasingly shaped by the anonymous presence of neoliberal capitalism, militarism, and a number of other anti-democratic tendencies—but also connecting to the future that we make available to the next generation of young people. Democracy cannot work if citizens are not autonomous, self-reflective, and independent—qualities that are indispensable for citizens, and students, if they are going to make vital judgments and choices about participating in and shaping decisions that affect everyday life, institutional reform, and governmental policy. If higher education is to be a crucial sphere for educating citizens equipped to understand others (and with a self-consciousness about the limits of such understanding), to exercise their freedoms in concert with larger concerns over social justice, and to ask questions regarding the basic assumptions that maintain human dignity and govern democratic political life, academics will have to assume their responsibility as citizen-scholars, take critical positions, and relate their work to larger social issues. Against the encroaching forces of militarization, corporatism, and ideological intolerance, educators have the difficult task of matching their sense of engaged scholarship with a meaningful and critical pedagogy, one that enables students to engage in debate and dialogue about pressing social problems and to believe not only that civic life matters but that they can make a difference in shaping it.

The powerful regime of forces that increasingly align higher education with a reactionary notion of patriotic correctness, market fundamentalism, and state-sponsored militarism presents difficult problems for educators and requires a profoundly committed sense of individual and collective resistance from all of those who are willing to fight for a future that does not reduce the university to a place of commerce, a research site for the Pentagon, or a training ground for staffing innumerable intelligence agencies. As the twenty-first century unfolds, higher education faces both a legitimation crisis and a political crisis. As a handmaiden of the Pentagon and corporate interests, it has lost its claim to independence and critical learning. Turning its back on the public good, the academy has largely opened its doors to serving private and governmental interests and in doing so has compromised its role as a democratic public sphere. And yet, in spite of its current embattled status and the inroads made by corporate power, the defense industries, and the neoconservative Right, higher education remains uniquely placed to prepare students both to understand and to influence the larger educational forces that shape their lives. The university is one of the few remaining public spaces capable of raising important questions about the mutually informing relationship among higher education, critical pedagogical practices, and the promise of a substantive democracy.

The University in Chains argues that higher education represents one of the most important spheres in which the battle for democracy is currently being waged. It is the site where the promise of a more just future emerges out of those visions and pedagogical practices that combine hope and moral responsibility with the productivity of knowledge as part of a broader emancipatory discourse. In an effort to connect strategies of resistance to a discourse of critique and possibility, this book examines the increasing attacks on higher education after 9/11 being waged on multiple fronts by the forces of militarization, corporatization, and various groups of right-wing fundamentalists who regard critical thought itself as a threat to the dominant political order. In particular, right-wing political power views higher education as a reproductive site in which the dual formulations of command and obedience trump liberal notions of dialogue, critique, and civic engagement. The first chapter examines the growing relationship between diverse forces that make up the national security state and higher education. Building upon President Eisenhower's warning about the rise of the military-industrial complex and Senator William Fulbright's concern about the more expansive *military-industrial-academic complex,* this chapter situates the development of the university as a "hypermodern militarized knowledge factory"[7] within the broader context of what I call the "biopolitics of militarization" and its increasing influence and power in American society after the tragic events of September 11, 2001. Highlighting and critically engaging the specific ways in which the forces of militarization are shaping various aspects of university life, Chapter 1 focuses on the growth of militarized knowledge and research, the increasing development of academic programs and schools that serve military personnel, and the growing influence of the CIA on college campuses. It concludes by offering some suggestions both for resisting the rising tide of militarization and for reclaiming the university as a democratic public sphere.

The second chapter focuses on the increasing corporate influence on higher education and the currently fashionable idea of the university as a "franchise" largely indifferent to deepening and expanding the possibilities of democratic public life and increasingly hostile to the important role the academy can play in addressing matters of "public welfare [and] service, and specifically how we bring citizens into public life."[8] Operating as both a training ground for future employees and a storefront for business corporations, the university is now part of an unholy alliance that largely serves dominant state, military, and business policies while decoupling vital aspects of academic knowledge production from democratic values and projects.[9] The analysis in Chapter 2 focuses not only on how corporatization affects the governing structure of the university but also on how it redefines faculty, students, and adjuncts as either entrepreneurs, customers, or clients. The result is a reshaping of the structure of the university, the content of courses, and the broader culture of higher education. As the university is stripped of its role as a democratic public sphere and viewed as a market niche, faculty are seen as contract employees, and students become important only in the logic of profit margins. Under the instrumentalized model of higher education, faculty are increasingly being stripped of their autonomy and critical capacities, silenced in the governance process, and reduced to roles that either operate in the service of training or position them as conduits for grant money. Students, by extension, are now viewed as future employees or customers, increasingly indentured by financial debt and forced into careers that have less to do with public service than with providing the financial incentives to enable them to pay back student loans. But more important, as the university is modeled after the wisdom of the business world, corporate interests not only play a more visible and powerful role in shaping university policy, curricula, and labor practices but also contribute to "the sweeping shift towards non-tenure-track academic labor [that] has been one of the most worried-over trends in American higher education."[10]

The third chapter argues that higher education in the United States, in spite of its international renown, is currently being targeted by a diverse number of right-wing forces, which have hijacked political power and have waged a focused campaign to undermine the principles of academic freedom, sacrifice critical pedagogical practice in the name of patriotic correctness, and dismantle the university as a bastion of autonomy, independent thought, and uncorrupted inquiry. Ironically, by adopting the vocabulary of individual rights, academic freedom, balance, and tolerance, private advocacy groups, such as the American Council for Trustees and Alumni, and individuals, such as David Horowitz, are waging a campaign designed not merely to counter dissent but to destroy it and, in doing so, to eliminate all of those remaining public spaces, spheres, and institutions that nourish and sustain a democratic civil society. Education for these right-wing groups is passive, accommodating, and quiet. It rewards mimicry rather than cultural production and is entirely adverse to Theodor Adorno's insistence that "Thinking is not the intellectual reproduction of what already exists. . . . Its insatiable aspect, its aversion to being quickly and easily satisfied, refuse the foolish wisdom of resignation. . . . Open thinking points beyond itself."[11] Chapter 3 suggests that there is much more at stake in the current assault on the university than the issue of teaching the right books—a battle call reminiscent of the culture wars of the previous decades,[12] the utterly dishonest call for balance, or the more recent assault on academic freedom. There is also the concerted attempt by right-wing extremists and corporate interests to strip the professoriate of any authority, render critical pedagogy as merely an instrumental task, eliminate tenure as a protection for teacher authority, and remove critical education as the foundation for any viable notion of civic courage, engaged citizenship, and social responsibility.

The fourth chapter raises questions about how the university might be defended as a democratic public sphere. At stake here is making visible the notion that the attack on the university is an assault that deprives young people of a meaningful future and renders undischarged human possibilities, the obligations of civic responsibility, and the very idea of the informed citizen moot, if not dangerous. The chapter is a call for educators and others who care about young people and the promise of a substantive democracy to address what is new in the assaults on higher education. It also serves as a reminder of what happened to higher education during the McCarthy period and as an inducement to critically examine the consequences for academic freedom when people did not speak up to defend the university against the forces of right-wing authoritarianism, political corruption, and media-induced panics. Combining a language of critique and possibility, this concluding chapter offers some tentative theoretical, pedagogical, and practical suggestions for countering the anti-democratic forces attempting to rewrite the academy as a space that both undercuts the presence and purposeful education of critically thinking, speaking, and acting human beings and positions the university as a site that is losing its claim as a democratic public sphere. Most important, the chapter attempts to recover and renew the university's role in pursuing a future that makes good on the promises of genuine global democracy, creating the institutional and pedagogical conditions that enable and unleash in faculty, students, and the university those undischarged possibilities that embrace a future that greatly transcends the violent and debased totalizing narratives of terror, war, racial injustice, ecological abuse, state violence, and privatization that define the present.

The University in Chains attempts to contribute to the undoing of the suffocating relationship between higher education and the anti-democratic forces of militarization, corporatism, and patriotic correctness. What is unique about this book is that it addresses the crisis of higher education from the interrelated registers of three fundamentalist assaults—militarization, patriotic correctness, and corporatism—and in doing so makes clear both why the university is in chains and why this is such an important problem for the public to acknowledge and critically engage, especially those of us who believe in the democratic possibilities of higher education as well as in democracy itself. It is no longer enough to deal with the crisis of higher education merely through expressions of indignation or modes of analysis that focus on the current threats as isolated and separate rather than operating in tandem. This book takes up the challenge of understanding the combination of forces laying siege to higher education and points to what it might mean to speak and act thoughtfully in defense of the university as a democratic public sphere.

Notes

1. Elisabeth Young-Bruehl, *Why Arendt Matters* (New Haven: Yale University Press, 2006), p. 39.

2. See Jacques Derrida, *Eyes of the University* (Stanford: Stanford University Press, 2004); Bill Readings, *The University in Ruins* (Cambridge, MA: Harvard University Press, 1996).

3. The concept of the millennial military state is taken from Stephen John Hartnett and Laura Ann Stengrim, "War Rhetorics: The National Security Strategy of the United States and President Bush's Globalization-Through-Benevolent-Empire," *South Atlantic Quarterly* 105:1 (Winter 2006), p. 180.

4. I have taken up the issue of religious fundamentalism in Henry A. Giroux, *The Terror of Neoliberalism* (Boulder, CO: Paradigm Publishers, 2005). See also Kevin Phillips, *American Theocracy* (New York: Viking, 2006); Michelle Goldberg, *Kingdom Coming: The Rise of Christian Nationalism* (New York: Norton, 2006); and Gary Wills, "A Country Ruled by Faith," *New York Review of Books* (November 16, 2006), pp. 8–12.

5. On the culture of fear, see Zygmunt Bauman, *Liquid Fear* (London: Polity, 2006); and Corey Robin, *Fear: The History of a Political Idea* (New York: Oxford University Press, 2004). On the issue of militarization, see Gore Vidal, *Perpetual War for Perpetual Peace* (New York: Nation Books, 2002); Chalmers Johnson, *The Sorrows of Empire: Militarism, Secrecy, and the End of the Republic* (New York: Metropolitan Books, 2004); Andrew J. Bacevich, *The New American Militarism* (New York: Oxford University Press, 2005); Carl Boggs, *Imperial Delusions: American Militarism and Endless War* (Boulder, CO: Paradigm Publishers, 2005); and Noam Chomsky, *Failed States: The Abuse of Power and the Assault on Democracy* (New York: Metropolitan Books, 2006). On the rise of authoritarianism in the United States, see Henry Giroux, *Against the New Authoritarianism* (Winnipeg: Arbeiter Ring, 2005). And on the relationship between totalitarianism and the manufactured crisis of total terror, see Hannah Arendt, *The Origins of Totalitarianism*, rev. ed. (New York: Shocken, 2004, originally published in 1951).

6. Roger Simon, "The University: A Place to Think?" in *Beyond the Corporate University*, ed. Henry A. Giroux and Kostas Myrsiades (Lanham, MD: Rowman & Littlefield, 2001), p. 46.

7. John Armitage, "Beyond Hypermodern Militarized Knowledge Factories," *Review of Education, Pedagogy, and Cultural Studies* 27 (2005), p. 221.

8. Jeffrey J. Williams, "Franchising the University," in *Beyond the Corporate University*, ed. Henry A. Giroux and Kostas Myrsiades (Lanham, MD: Rowman & Littlefield, 2001), p. 15.

9. Doug Henwood, *After the New Economy* (New York: The New Press, 2005).

10. John Gravois, "Tracking the Invisible Faculty" (December 15, 2006), available online at http://chronicle.com/weekly/v53/i17/17a00801.htm.

11. Theodor W. Adorno, *Critical Models: Interventions and Catchwords* (New York: Columbia University Press, 1998), pp. 291–292.

12. This issue is critically analyzed in Susan Searls Giroux, "Playing in the Dark: Racial Repression and the New Crusade for Diversity," *College Literature* 33:3 (Fall 2006), pp. 93–112. See also Henry A. Giroux and Susan Searls Giroux, eds., "The Assault on Higher Education," a special issue of *College Literature* 33:3 (Fall 2006).

◆

1

Arming the Academy

Higher Education in the Shadow of the National Security State

Terror becomes total when it becomes independent of all opposition; it rules supreme when nobody any longer stands in its way. If lawfulness is the essence of non-tyrannical government and lawlessness is the essence of tyranny, then terror is the essence of totalitarian domination.

—*Hannah Arendt*

A nation that continues year after year to spend more money on military defense than on programs of social uplift is approaching spiritual death.

—*Martin Luther King Jr.*

Remembrance of Warnings Past

As part of his farewell address on January 17, 1961, President Dwight David Eisenhower recognized that in the aftermath of World War II and at the dawn of the Cold War, the United States faced a dire menace abroad in the form of the Soviet Union and a less visible but equally dangerous threat within its own borders, which he memorably referred to as "the military-industrial complex."[1] Eisenhower viewed the military-industrial complex as an outgrowth of a growing and sinister relationship among government agencies, the military, and the defense industries, and he believed that it made a mockery out of democratic values while undermining the foundation of democratic institutions and civic society.[2] According to Eisenhower, the conditions for the production of violence, the amassing of huge profits by defense industries, and the corruption of government officials in the interest of making war the organizing principle of society had created a set of conditions in which the very idea of democracy, if not the possibility of politics itself, was at stake. Democracy was in the midst of becoming armed and in the process had entered into a new relationship in which the military and the war industries were bound together in a pact to militarize society and make the armed forces the center of both economic and political life.[3] The nature of power in American life was undergoing a deep and fundamental shift. President Eisenhower, in retrospect, was far more prescient than even he may have realized when he warned:

> This conjunction of an immense military establishment and a large arms industry is new in the American experience. . . . In the councils of government, we must guard against the acquisition of unwarranted influence, whether sought or unsought, by the military-industrial complex. The potential for the disastrous rise of misplaced power exists and will persist. We must never let the weight of this combination endanger our liberties or democratic processes. We should take nothing for granted. Only an alert and knowledgeable citizenry can compel the proper meshing of the huge industrial and military machinery of defense with our peaceful methods and goals, so that security and liberty may prosper together.[4]

Eisenhower's attack on the military-industrial complex was a dead-on prophecy, and because of it he has been rightly regarded as a statesman of heroic proportion.[5] Yet what is often generally unknown about his speech is that he also warned about the rise of the "military-industrial-academic complex," though he deleted the phrase before he delivered his talk.[6] He did insist, nevertheless, that Americans had to be vigilant about the federal government's potential for dominating the nation's research universities:

> Today, the solitary inventor, tinkering in his shop, has been overshadowed by task forces of scientists in laboratories and testing fields. In the same fashion, the free university, historically the fountainhead of free ideas and scientific discovery, has experienced a revolution in the conduct of research. Partly because of the huge costs involved, a government contract becomes virtually a substitute for intellectual curiosity. For every old blackboard there are now hundreds of new electronic computers. The prospect of domination of the nation's scholars by Federal employment, project allocations, and the power of money is ever present and is gravely to be regarded.[7]

Later in the decade, Senator William Fulbright took seriously Eisenhower's alarming distrust of the military-industrial complex and extended its political and theoretical reach. He did so by situating Eisenhower's comments onto a more expansive Hobbesian terrain by coupling the emerging power of an overly strong military-industrial complex with the province of higher education—including the latter's long-standing commitments to academic freedom, civic engagement, and "pure" research guided by intellectual curiosity or social needs rather than by commercial or military interests. Recognizing that major universities had come increasingly to depend on Pentagon contracts, grants, and funds for their research laboratories, Fulbright retrieved Eisenhower's cast-off phrase, the "military-industrial-academic complex," to warn against the creeping influence of the federal government and a for-profit arms industry over America's major research universities.[8] Fulbright's comments were blunt and to the point: "In lending itself too much to the purposes of government, a university fails its higher purpose."[9]

Unfortunately, Eisenhower and Fulbright's predictions about the fundamentally anti-democratic nature of the military-industrial complex and its efforts to annex the university went unheeded as the Cold War unfolded and the university's relationship with larger society underwent fundamental changes. No longer seen as an autonomous repository of truth, neutrality, disinterestedness, pure research, and professionalism, higher education became, in the words of Clark Kerr, chancellor of the University of California at Berkeley in the 1950s and early 1960s, "a multiversity," one that actively embraced multiple constituencies and forms of patronage provided by the federal government, military, and corporate interests.[10] Kerr welcomed such a change, even as it enshrined a more practical and commercial role for higher education and fundamentally altered and instrumentalized the internal workings of universities. As Rebecca S. Lowen points out in her brilliant study of Stanford as an exemplar of the new Cold War university,

> the postwar university was a wholly new institution, one that was uniquely responsive to the society of which it was now very much a part. Kerr recognized the significance of the cold war to American universities. Such military technologies as ballistic missiles, guidance systems, hydrogen bombs, and radar required the expertise of highly trained scientists and engineers. By the early 1960s the federal government was spending approximately $10 billion annually on research and development.... Universities and university-affiliated centers received annually about one-tenth—or $1 billion—of these federal research and development funds.... These universities, in turn, depended on federal patronage for over fifty percent of their operating budgets.[11]

As the university's relationship to the larger society changed in the postwar period, there was a decisive transformation in the way in which higher education traditionally operated. Lowen captures this change when she writes:

> Large laboratories staffed with myriad researchers having no teaching duties and working in groups with expensive, government-funded scientific equipment became common features of the leading research universities after World War

II. As the organization and funding of science changed, so did the kinds of knowledge produced and taught. Universities made room for new fields of study, such as nuclear engineering and Russian studies, which bore obvious relevance to the nation's geopolitical concerns.[12]

During the 1960s, especially with the massive student resistance directed against the Vietnam War, the possibility of a powerful military state undermining the reality and promise of higher education as a democratic public sphere generated various protests on college campuses, which aimed at keeping the military and intelligence agencies as far away from university campuses as possible.[13] Distrust of the military and government intelligence agencies reached a high point in 1975, when Senator Frank Church headed a Senate committee that investigated the Watergate break-in and uncovered numerous government abuses including secret CIA funding of student organizations, the agency's attempts to overthrow the democratically elected government of Chile, and clandestine plots to assassinate Fidel Castro.[14] Once the Vietnam War ended, the dissenters went home and a fog of historical and social amnesia descended over the country, paving the way for an eventual return of the repressed, as the military-industrial-academic complex gained greater momentum from the late 1980s to the present—a momentum whose power is largely unchecked and whose perniciousness is unjustly ignored.[15]

While the rise of the military-industrial complex and its influence on higher education were of great concern during the 1960s and '70s, they seem to have dropped off the map as we enter into the first decade of the new millennium. As Andrew J. Bacevich, former West Point graduate and Vietnam veteran and current director for the Center for International Relations at Boston University, insists, "Few in power have openly considered whether valuing military power for its own sake or cultivating permanent global military superiority might be at odds with American principles"[16] as well as with the democratic values and public spirit that should be at the heart of higher education. The idea that "military is to democracy as fire is to water"[17] has been ignored by almost all major politicians under the Bush presidency, and one consequence is that a creeping militarism has materialized into a full-fledged coup, fueled by a war on terror and the military occupation of Iraq and Afghanistan, and resulting in endless cases of kidnapping, torture, abuse, and murder.[18] Noam Chomsky has amply charted the rise of the United States as a warfare state and its implications for the rest of the world given America's refusal to renounce war as a central tool of its foreign policy. He writes:

> By now, the world's hegemonic power accords itself the right to wage war at will, under a doctrine of "anticipatory self-defense" with unstated bounds. International law, treaties, and rules of order are sternly impressed on others with much self-righteous posturing, but dismissed as irrelevant for the United States—a long-standing practice, driven to new depths by the Reagan and Bush II administrations.[19]

In the Shadow of the Military-Industrial-Academic Complex

While there has been an increasing concern among academics and progressives over the growing corporatization of the university, the transformation of academia into what John Armitage calls the "hypermodern militarized knowledge factory"[20] has been largely ignored as a subject of contemporary concern and critical debate.[21] Such silence has nothing to do with a lack of visibility or the covert attempts to inject a military and security presence into higher education. The militarization of higher education is made obvious, not only by the presence of over 150 military-educational institutions in the United States designed to "train a youthful corps of tomorrow's military officers"[22] in the strategies, values, skills, and knowledge of the warfare state, but also, as the American Association of Universities points out, by the existence of hundreds of colleges and universities that conduct Pentagon-funded research, provide classes to military personnel, and design programs specifically for future employment with various departments and agencies associated with the warfare state.[23]

Rather than being the object of massive individual and collective resistance, the militarization of higher education appears to be endorsed by liberals and conservatives alike. The National Research Council of the National Academies published a report called *Frameworks for Higher Education in Homeland Security*, which argued that the commitment to learning about homeland security is an essential part of the preparation for work and life in the twenty-first century, thus offering academics a thinly veiled legitimation for building into undergraduate and graduate curricula intellectual frameworks that mirror the interests and values of the warfare state. Similarly, the Association of American Universities argued in a report titled *National Defense Education and Innovation Initiative* that winning the war on terrorism and expanding global markets were mutually informing goals, the success of which falls squarely on the performance of universities. This group argues, with a rather cheerful certainty, that every student should be trained to become a soldier in the war on terror and in the battle over global markets, and that the universities should do everything they can "to fill security-related positions in the defense industry, the military, the national laboratories, the Department of Defense and Homeland Security, the intelligence agencies, and other federal agencies."[24] And in a surprisingly candid statement completely at odds with Eisenhower and Fulbright's warnings, as well as with the fundamental mission of land-grant institutions, the report states:

> To maintain our leadership amidst intensifying global competition, we must make the best use of talented and innovative individuals, including scientists, engineers, linguists, and cultural experts. The same is true for winning the war on terrorism. The nation must cultivate young talent and orient national economic, political, and educational systems to

offer the greatest opportunities to the most gifted American and international students.[25]

It gets worse. Major universities have appointed former CIA officials as either faculty, consultants, or presidents. For instance, Michael Crow, a former agent, is now president of Arizona State University, and Robert Gates, the former director of the CIA, was the president of Texas A&M, until named in 2006 as the secretary of defense under the George W. Bush administration. While it is difficult to predict how their CIA background might have affected their role in running their respective universities, English Professor Cary Nelson offers a telling story of visiting the University of California's San Diego campus as part of a team evaluating the literature department. Upon meeting the provost, a former CIA employee, Nelson was asked "if it were true the literature department would only hire communist faculty?"[26] Professor Nelson burst out laughing until he realized the provost was not kidding. Hardly a laughing matter: One wonders how such a provost, with his Cold War mentality still unthawed, dealt with tenure decisions involving faculty whose research advances progressive social interests. Equally alarming is the fact that more and more universities are cooperating with intelligence agencies with few objections from faculty, students, and other concerned citizens.[27] In the aftermath of the terrorist attacks of September 11, 2001, many academics, to the contrary, are enthusiastically offering their services for the plethora of expert personnel positions sought by the sixteen federal intelligence agencies and programs that employ over 100,000 personnel.[28] The *Wall Street Journal* claims that the CIA has become a "growing force on campus,"[29] while a November 2002 issue of the liberal magazine *The American Prospect* published an article by Chris Mooney calling for academics and the government intelligence agencies to work together. As he puts it, "Academic-intelligence relationships will never be problem free. But at present, the benefits greatly outweigh the costs."[30] Such collaboration seems to be in full swing at a number of universities. For example, Pennsylvania State

University, Carnegie Mellon, the University of Pennsylvania, Johns Hopkins, and a host of others have surprisingly expanded the reach and influence of the national security state by entering into formal agreements with the Federal Bureau of Investigation (FBI) in order to "create a link between leading research universities and government agencies."[31] Graham Spanier, the president of Penn State, argues in a statement pregnant with irony, that the establishment of the National Security Higher Education Advisory Board, which he heads, "sends a positive message that leaders in higher education are willing to assist our nation during these challenging times."[32] FBI Director Robert S. Mueller III is more precise about what is expected from this partnership. He writes: "As we do our work, we wish to be sensitive to university concerns about international students, visas, technology export policy, and the special culture of colleges and universities. We also want to foster exchanges between academia and the FBI in order to develop curricula which will aid in attracting the best and brightest students to careers in the law enforcement and intelligence communities."[33] Behind such stated concerns lies the harsh reality of a national security state that harasses foreign students, limits the ability of U.S. scholars to work with colleagues in "enemy" countries such as Cuba and Iran, and denies visas to international graduate students and intellectuals getting work in the United States, particularly those critical of U.S. policies. Spanier's commentary and Mueller's frankness, coupled with a long history culminating in the current military-industrial-academic complex, read like a page out of George Orwell's *1984*, countering every decent and democratic value that defines higher education as a democratic public sphere.

In a post-9/11 world in which the war on terrorism has exacerbated a domestic culture of fear and abetted the gradual erosion of civil liberties, the idea of the university as a site of critical dialogue and debate, public service, and socially responsible research appears to have been usurped by a patriotic jingoism and a market-driven fundamentalism that conflates the entrepreneurial spirit with military aggression in the interests of commercial success and geopolitical power. Faculty now flock to the Department of Defense, the Pentagon, and various intelligence agencies either to procure government jobs or to apply for grants to support individual research in the service of the national security state. As corporate money for research opportunities dwindles, the Pentagon fills the void with billions of dollars in available grants, stipends, scholarships, and other valuable financial rewards, for which college and university administrators actively and openly compete. Indeed, the Department of Homeland Security is flush with money:

> [It] handles a $70 million dollar scholarship and research budget, and its initiatives, in alliance with those of the military and intelligence agencies, point towards a whole new network of campus-related programs. [For instance,] the University of Southern California has created the first "Homeland Security Center of Excellence" with a $12 million grant that brought in multi-disciplinary experts from UC Berkeley, NYU, and the University of Wisconsin–Madison. Texas A&M and the University of Minnesota won $33 million to build two new Centers of Excellence in agrosecurity.... The scale of networked private and public cooperation is indicated by the new National Academic Consortium for Homeland Security led by Ohio State University, which links more than 200 universities and colleges.[34]

While the new collaboration between the national security state and higher education may produce little debate and even less resistance, the post-9/11 resurgence of patriotic commitment and uncritical support on the part of faculty and administrators toward the increasing militarization of daily life run the risk of rendering the academy complicit with a larger set of institutional (if not quite public) commitments to war, violence, fear, surveillance, and the erosion of civic society more generally.

As higher education comes under the powerful influence of military contractors, intelligence agencies, right-wing think tanks, and for-profit educational establishments pushing militarized knowledge and values, the interests of a militarized state and economy begin to coincide too closely with higher education. As a result, the academy is increasingly stripped of its democratic commitments and values, which are clearly jeopardized as its civic mission is relegated to the interests of the military-industrial complex. Under such circumstances, democracy succumbs to the ideology of militarization and becomes synonymous with the dictates of a national security state. Some of the basic elements of such a state were outlined in the September 2002 *National Security Strategy of the United States* (NSSUS) and have become operative as part of the Bush administration's post-9/11 policy of militarization both at home and abroad. Stephen John Hartnett and Laura Ann Stengrim distill the report's five overarching themes as follows:

> First, the NSSUS offers *a doctrine of preemption,* by which the United States claims the right to strike against foes wherever and whenever it feels threatened. Second, the NSSUS proposes *a millennial military state* where waging war is the chief and perpetual function of the federal government. Third, the NSSUS wraps points 1 and 2 in *a promise of benign universalism,* an apparently generous offer to spread U.S. goods, capital, institutions, and values far and wide. Fourth, ... the NSSUS links U.S. national security, global economic growth, and the fate of foreign governments to their enthusiasm for *evangelical capitalism.* Fifth, even while explicitly attempting to avoid this charge, the NSSUS makes broad claims about rogue states in a world of evil, that, when coupled with President Bush's post-9/11 speeches, hint at a form of conflict observers from both Left and Right have called *a clash of civilizations.*[35]

As the reality of extreme violence becomes central to both political and everyday life and the militarization of society begins "to loom so large in its field of vision and strategic action,"[36] it becomes all the more important for higher education to be defended as a vital public sphere crucial for both the education of critical citizens and the defense of democratic values and institutions. Given the current threat posed by the national security state to higher education's democratically informed civic mission, I want to engage the question of what the role of higher education might be when "the government has a free hand to do whatever it wants in the name of national security"?[37] More specifically, I want to offer an alternative analysis of the fate of democracy and the role of higher education, one that refuses to simply serve the expressed needs of militarization, neoliberalism, and the national security state, all of which appear to be pushing the United States toward a new form of authoritarianism.[38] In what follows, I first want to situate the development of the university as a "hypermodernized militarized knowledge factory" within the broader context of what I call "the biopolitics of militarization" and its increased influence and power within American society after the tragic events of September 11, 2001. Second, I will highlight and critically engage the specific ways in which this militarization is shaping various aspects of university life, focusing primarily on the growth of militarized knowledge and research as well as the growing influence of the CIA on college campuses. Finally, I will offer some suggestions both for resisting the rising tide of militarization and for reclaiming the university as a democratic public sphere.

Biopolitics and the Reworking of Power and Disposability

Within the last few decades, matters of state sovereignty in the new world order have been retheorized so as to provide a range of relevant insights about the relationship between power and politics, the political nature of social and cultural life, and the merging of life and politics as a new form of biopolitics, one that not only redefines "classic notions of sovereignty as the power of life over death"[39] but increasingly defines who actually lives and who dies. Central here is the task of reformulating the meaning of contemporary politics and how it currently functions to regulate matters of life and death—issues intimately related both to the articulation of community, social citizenship, and the public good and to the regulation, care, and development of human life. Under the new biopolitical regime, the body is understood primarily as an object of power, but it is a body that is social and multiple, scientific and ideological. Biopolitics points to new relations of power that are more capacious, concerned not only with the body as an object of disciplinary techniques that render it "both useful and docile" but with a body that needs to be "regularized," subject to those immaterial means of production that produce ways of life that enlarge the targets of control and regulation.[40]

The concept of biopolitics, while revealing different tensions for its major theorists, registers a number of distinctive characteristics that mark contemporary politics in the United States. First, politics is no longer exclusively defined through a notion of sovereignty and power in which the spheres of the economic, social, and political are viewed as separate and largely unrelated. That is, political struggle is no longer confined either to the production of economic labor or to the state's role in "legislating norms and preserving order in public affairs, but must also bring into play the production of social relationships in all aspects of life."[41] And as both Giorgio Agamben and Michel Foucault argue, the traditional separation between the realm of politics and the complex set of relations that constitute what it means to be a living human being is no longer acceptable.[42] Politics is now defined in more ample terms and its axis of meaning is inextricably linked to matters of life and death, largely mediated through the prism of disposability, fear, and "security as the sole task and source of [state] legitimacy."[43] Modern politics, as Jean Comaroff argues, "reveals how modern government stages itself by dealing directly in the power over life: the power to exclude, to declare exceptions, to strip human existence of civic rights and social value."[44] State violence and totalitarian power, which historically have been deployed against marginalized populations—principally black Americans—have now, at least in the United States, become the rule for the entire population, as life is more ruthlessly regulated and increasingly placed in the hands of military and state power.

Second, politics can no longer be reduced to participation in elections, access to and distribution of material and cultural resources, or even the regulation and disciplining of the body. On the contrary, politics is increasingly about the power of modern states to impose a state of exception, to condemn entire populations as disposable, and to make life and death the most crucial and relevant objects of political control.[45] As violence, insecurity, and fear empty public life of its democratic possibilities and the warfare state is transformed into a garrison state, life and death lose their distinctive meanings as a measure of what it means to live in a genuine democracy. Instead, life for many people becomes unpredictable, put on short notice, and subject to the vicissitudes of outsourcing, privatization, and a social Darwinism in which the losers vastly outnumber the winners. As fear is privatized, shifting from the promise of the state to protect its citizens to an emphasis on the "dangers of personal safety," life replicates art in the form of bad Reality TV, legitimating the inevitability of crumbling social bonds, the dismantling of the social state, and the neoliberal mantra of having to face alone the ever growing misfortunes caused by systemic problems, now designated as "an unavoidable fate."[46] Like the consumer goods that flood American society, immigrant workers, refugees, the unemployed, the homeless, the poor, and the disabled are increasingly viewed as utterly expendable, relegated to a frontier-zone of invisibility created by a combination of economic inequality, racism, the collapse of social safety nets, and the brutality of a militarized society, all of which "designates and constitutes a production line of human waste or wasted humans."[47]

Biopolitical mediation of life and death takes on a heightened significance as the state not only consolidates its power over all spheres of life but also increasingly exercises its sovereignty "in the power and capacity to dictate who may live and who may die."[48] Examples of both the state of exception and the exercise of sovereign power are nonetheless made visible at times, as when the American government installs torture as integral to its military and clandestine operations, exposed in the public disclosure of the abuse and torture of prisoners at Abu Ghraib, Guantanamo Bay in Cuba, Bagram Air Base in Afghanistan, and numerous other detention centers around the world.[49] As Neil Smith points out, "these prisons are a global embarrassment for the United States,"[50] particularly when a highly respected organization such as Amnesty International labels Guantanamo "the gulag of our times."[51] They are shamelessly visible in the sickening massacre that took place in Haditha in Iraq,[52] and in the politics of "disappearing" reminiscent of the Latin American dictatorships of the 1970s in which human beings are subjected to the outsourcing of torture by the U.S. government under a policy known as "extraordinary rendition." This policy, signed by President George W. Bush, authorizes the CIA not only to set up detention facilities outside of the United Sates in which to detain, interrogate, and torture alleged terrorist suspects and sympathizers, without any benefit of a court of law, but also to abduct and transport such suspected terrorists to third countries such as Syria and Egypt that engage in human rights abuses, including torture.[53] Known-innocent individuals who have been subjected to this barbaric policy include Maher Arar, a Syrian-born Canadian citizen detained at J.F.K. Airport in September 2002 and taken to Jordan and Syria where he was tortured;[54] Khaled el-Masri, a Kuwait-born citizen with German nationality, who was abducted while vacationing in Macedonia and transported to an American-run prison where he was beaten and kept in solitary confinement for five months.[55] Both men were eventually released. Completely cleared of any terrorist connections by the Canadian government, Arar was eventually given a formal government apology and a compensation package worth millions. Despite the Canadian government's decision to clear Arar of any connection to terrorism, the U.S. government refused to remove his name from its terrorist watchlist.

A biopolitics of disposability and exclusion is also evident in the existence of secret CIA prisons known as "black sites"[56] and in the abrogation of basic civil rights enacted by the passage of the Military Commissions Act of 2006, which allows people named as "enemy combatants" to be imprisoned and charged with crimes without the benefit of a lawyer or the right of *habeas corpus.* Of course, selective acts of disposability are far from new in the United States and can be traced back to the country's founding, a long history of slavery, well-documented attacks on civil liberties, and the ruthless exercise of government power against left-wing dissidents. Such a history is evident in the repressive and deadly attacks waged by the government against critics of U.S. foreign and domestic policy during the red scare of the Wilson era, the McCarthy period of the 1950s, the ruthless and illegal harassment of anti-war activists during the Vietnam War, the widespread investigations and disruptions aimed at dissident political organization under the FBI's Counter Intelligence Program (Cointelpro) from 1956 to 1971, and the actual killing of African-American activists and Black Panther Party members Fred Hampton and Mark Clark in Chicago in the late 1960s.[57]

The politics of disposability today is more capacious in its reach and lethal in its assault on multiple conditions necessary to both individual liberty and sheer survival. Today, disposability works in a dual sense in that it not only legalizes acts of torture and abuse committed against those who are "disappeared" from traditional legal protections but also disposes of the crime by granting immunity to its perpetrators.[58] The biopolitics of disposability was on full display in the aftermath of Hurricane Katrina, which laid bare the racial and class fault lines that mark an increasingly damaged and withering democracy and revealed the emergence of a new kind of politics, one in which entire populations are rendered officially outside the registers of political and moral concerns, an unnecessary burden on state coffers, now consigned to fend for themselves. Katrina provided images from the other Gulf crisis, capturing the despair and suffering of hundreds of thousands of poor black, brown, and infirm and elderly people who were abandoned for weeks without food or water, without any place to wash or go to the bathroom, without relief from the scorching sun. The world watched in disbelief as CNN broadcasted images of bloated, decomposing bodies floating in the waters flooding New Orleans along with startling footage of dead people, mostly poor African-Americans, left uncollected in the streets, in yards, on porches, and in hospitals, nursing homes, and collapsed houses. Clearly, the Bush administration's response to the tragedy of Hurricane Katrina reveals a set of biopolitical commitments that disregard populations rendered "at risk" by global neoliberal economies, embracing instead an emergent security state founded on fear, class privilege, and updated notions of racial purity.[59] Under such circumstances, punishment rather than compassion defines exclusion, eviction, and disposability as the inevitable by-products of a set of biopolitical commitments in which "death's presence in life [becomes] more ubiquitous and consequential than ever."[60]

From Militarism to a Biopolitics of Militarization in a Post-9/11 World

In the current historical conjuncture, biopolitics has taken a deadly turn as "war has gone from an instrument of politics, used in the last resort, to the foundation of politics, the basis for discipline and control."[61] Increasingly, military power and policies are being expanded to address not only matters of defense and security but also problems associated with the entire health and social life of the nation, which are now measured by military values, spending, discipline, loyalty, and hierarchical modes of authority.[62] Even so, biopolitics as a theoretical construct occupies a complex and shifting terrain that cannot be reduced to a monolithic conception. There is a tendency, consistent with Giorgio Agamben's notion of biopolitics, for the state to disappear into "the state of exception" and politics into "bare life."[63] Under such circumstances, as Jacques Ranciere points out, the complexity of politics, agency, and resistance disappears as "[p]olitics is ... equated with power, a power that is increasingly taken as an overwhelming historicoontological destiny from which only a God is likely to save us."[64] The reach of the influence and power of biopolitics not only extends to producing abject human deprivation, meaningless suffering, and social exclusion but also includes a framework for resistance and a multidimensional counterpolitics. Rendered *dialectically,* biopolitics does not limit power to an all-encompassing mode of domination and reduce agency to a life of meaningless suffering. On the contrary, a biopolitics of resistance associates the call for a sustainable life with collective struggles that connect bodies to human rights, dignity, and human life as well as to a redemptive politics that makes the promise of a democratic political order possible. But as the citizen has increasingly assumed the role of informer, soldier, and consumer willing to enlist in or conscripted by the totalizing war on terror, biopolitics has taken a sinister turn in the United States as it is increasingly being shaped by the forces of empire, violence, and militarization. As biopolitics is reduced to the imperatives of homeland security and as war becomes the major structuring force of society—a source of pride rather than alarm—it becomes all the more crucial to understand how a "mature democracy is in danger of turning itself into a military state."[65] The increasing militarization of American society raises serious questions about what kind of society the United States is becoming, and, as Achille Mbembe asks, "What place is given to life, death, and the human body? How are they inscribed in the order of power?"[66]

After the events of 9/11, the United States shifted from a militarized state to a militarized society. The consequences of this transformation can be explained, in part, with reference to a broad, though hardly steadfast, distinction between militarism and militarization. Militarism, as John Gillis argues, "is the older concept, usually defined as either the dominance of the military over civilian authority, or more generally, as the prevalence of warlike values in a society."[67] Militarism is often viewed as a retrograde concept because it characterizes a society in which military values and beliefs reside exclusively in a ruling group or class; it is also derided for its anti-democratic tendency to either celebrate or legitimate a hierarchy of authority in which civil society is subordinate to military power. Militarism makes visible the often contradictory principles and values between military institutions and the more liberal and democratic values of civil society. Militarism as an ideology has deep roots in American society, though it has never had enough force to transform an often faltering, often illiberal democracy into a military dictatorship.

Militarization, on the other hand, suggests less a complete break with militarism—with its celebration of war as the surest measure of the health of the nation and the soldier-warrior as its noblest expression—than an intensification and expansion of its underlying values, practices, ideologies, social relations, and cultural representations. Michael Geyer describes militarization as "the contradictory and tense social process in which civil society organizes itself for the production of violence."[68] Catherine Lutz amplifies this distinction, defining militarization as

> an intensification of the labor and resources allocated to military purposes, including the shaping of other institutions in synchrony with military goals. Militarization is simultaneously a discursive process, involving a shift in general societal beliefs and values in ways necessary to legitimate the use of force, the organization of large standing armies and their leaders, and the higher taxes or tribute used to pay for them. Militarization is intimately connected not only to the obvious increase in the size of armies and resurgence of militant nationalisms and militant fundamentalisms but also to the less visible deformation of human potentials into the hierarchies of race, class, gender, and sexuality, and to the shaping of national histories in ways that glorify and legitimate military action.[69]

The conceptual distinction has more gravitas in a post-9/11 society in which military "power is the measure of national greatness, and war, or planning for war, is the exemplary (and only common) project."[70] To be sure, the process of militarization has a long history in the United States and is varied rather than static, changing under different historical conditions.[71] While militarization is a deeply historical and contingent process, taking many different forms across history and culture, it became the mechanism of first choice under the administration of George W. Bush and Dick Cheney. Enthralled with military symbols and power, the U.S. government has worked tirelessly to further solidify "America's marriage of a militaristic cast of mind with utopian ends . . . as the distinguishing element of contemporary U.S. policy."[72] Indeed, Bush's "militaristic cast of mind" translates into policies that blur the line between military and civilian functions, divert funding from social programs for the poor to those that support the wars on terror and national security interests, and increasingly rely upon violent, anti-political solutions to solve both domestic and foreign problems. These new policies reveal "that the fields of politics and violence . . . are no longer separated," even as the Bush government insists that it acts in the interests of spreading democracy.[73] We live at a time when "military metaphors and military ways of doing things have become so much a part of our lives that we barely recognize"[74] the merging of politics and violence. As society becomes militarized, the collapse of any distinction between the two becomes common sense just as the discourse of war, used to solve political conflicts abroad, is employed metaphorically in the multiple wars against drugs, crime, homelessness, obesity, poverty, and a number of other social problems.[75] As a powerful structuring principle of society, militarization increasingly provides the model for organizing many public schools. Military-like discipline and zero-tolerance policies now provide the conceptual tools for turning many schools, urban ones in particular, into fortress-like institutions, largely controlled, regulated, and monitored by armed guards and characterized by lock-downs, invasive surveillance techniques, and the erosion of student rights. Another example of the militarization of American society is evident in the ongoing criminalization of social problems, with the result that the traditional distinctions between social services and the criminal justice system are blurring.[76] Instead of offering poor and disenfranchised youth decent jobs, the militarized state threatens them with incarceration. Instead of providing the homeless with decent shelter and food, the state issues them fines and then arrests them for failure to pay. Instead of providing people with decent health care, the state passes legislation that makes it more difficult to file for bankruptcy when medical bills outstrip income and easier to end up in a criminal court. Instead of treating economic migrants with dignity, the government supports policies and practices advocated by right-wing militia groups. The growth of the military model in American life has played a crucial role in the paramilitarizing of the culture, which provides both a narrative and a legitimation "for recent trends in corrections, including the normalization of special response teams, the increasingly popular Supermax prisons, and drug war boot camps."[77] In the paramilitaristic perspective, crime is no longer seen as a social problem. Crime is now viewed as both an individual pathology and a matter of punishment rather than rehabilitation. Moreover, as Nikhil Singh points out:

> Crime and war now blur in a zone of indistinction ... [and] the prison is the perfect foil for the kind of order that utopian neoliberalism seeks: a depoliticized order where political conflict is forever banished by the threat of absolute constraint. This helps to explain why the concept of criminality and a science of policing loom so large in its field of vision and strategic action. The criminal, the barbarian, and the terrorist represent actors who lack self-control, who are incapable of inhabiting liberal subjectivity and who therefore must be confronted with illiberal means (either through extermination or through the deprivation of their freedom).[78]

As the matrix for all relations of power, war in all of its actual and metaphorical modalities spreads the discourse and values of militarization throughout a society that has shifted, as Hardt and Negri argue, from "the welfare state to the warfare state."[79] What is new about militarization in a post-9/11 world is that it has become normalized, serving as a powerful pedagogical force that shapes our lives, memories, and daily experiences, while erasing everything we thought we knew about history, justice, solidarity, and the meaning of democracy.[80] But military thinking does more than normalize the language and practices of "the military as the organizers of violence"[81] and war, it undermines the memories of democratic struggles and possibility; it also punishes dissent. In a post-9/11 world in which politics is seen as an extension of war, the realm of public debate is reduced to an impoverished vocabulary of moral certainties and absolutes, leaving little room for challenging a growing militarization of public life.

As society is increasingly contoured through war, it becomes more difficult for the American public to understand, translate, or challenge how the discourse of militarization at home results in enormous amounts of suffering abroad. As politics is reduced to the rhetoric of war, patriotic posturing, and spectacularized violence, immediacy replaces context, and distance undercuts the reality of the horrible consequences of militarization with its endless and barbaric production of violence, human suffering, despair, and death. Militarization, with its rigid certainties, ritualistic reverence for authority, distrust of dissent, and celebration of violence, prevents the establishment of a direct link among the discourses of fear, hostility, and aggression, the militarization of society, and the practical realities of waging war abroad.[82]

As democratic politics is neutralized and the state makes security its most cherished goal, state policy and terrorism begin to mimic each other and, in the end, begin to "form a singly deadly system, in which they justify and legitimate each others actions."[83] Under such circumstances, the formation of a critical citizenry and the call for a genuine participatory democracy become unpatriotic and thus subject to charges of treason or dismissed as unchristian in an ideologically charged American political culture that defines the relationship of the United States to the rest of the world largely around a Manichean division between good and evil.[84] What happens when militarism provides the most legitimate framing mechanism for how we relate to ourselves, each other, and the rest of the world? One consequence is the development of what C. Wright Mills once called "a military definition of reality,"[85] which is now largely accepted as common sense by most people in American society. As Andrew J. Bacevich argues in *The New American Militarism*, too few have pondered what the consequences might be for American democracy when it accepts the possibility of a war on terrorism that has no foreseeable end, no geographical borders, and an ill-defined enemy. Similarly, too few people seem willing to ponder the question of what happens to civic virtue when armed force becomes the most important expression of state power, and military establishments become the most trusted and venerated institutions in American society.

Kevin Baker claims that the military "has become the most revered institution in the country,"[86] whose importance is repeatedly accentuated by manufactured moral panics about threats from "evil doers" and by endless terror alerts that are designed to legitimate Bush's notion of a "war without limits" as a normal state of affairs. Under such circumstances, private insecurities and public fears translate into a kind of "war fever" in which "[w]ar then becomes heroic, even mythic, a task that must be carried out for the defense of one's nation, to sustain its special historical destiny and immortality of its people."[87] The spread of war fever, intensified through a deadly dose of fear, carries with it not only a kind of paranoid edge, endlessly stroked by government alerts and repressive laws used "to create the most extensive national security apparatus in our nation's history,"[88] but also a cheap celebration of a kind of macho politics that refuses to recognize that "[t]he poison that is war does not free us from the ethics of responsibility."[89] This type of macho politics also reproduces a masculinity that finds its highest expression in the kind of celluloid brutality, violence, and carnage that characterizes standard Hollywood fare.[90] Cultural critic Jonathan Rutherford argues that the militarization of masculinity is part of America's current revival, with the fascination for war shaped by an older frontier spirit. Such sentiments hark back to a dark atavistic period in the European past under the shadow of fascism and reaffirm the emboldened message that the warrior spirit revives an authentic manliness in which "war makes man."[91] Bacevich extends this insight and insists that

> [t]oday as never before in their history Americans are enthralled with military power. The global military supremacy that the United States presently enjoys—and is bent on perpetuating—has become central to our national identity. More than America's matchless material abundance or even the effusions of its pop culture, the nation's arsenal of high-tech weaponry and the soldiers who employ that arsenal have come to signify who we are and what we stand for.... To state the matter bluntly, Americans in our own time have fallen prey to militarization, manifesting in a romanticized view of soldiers, a tendency to see military power as the truest measure of national greatness, and outsized expectations regarding the efficacy of force. To a degree without precedent in U.S. history, Americans have come to define the nation's strength and well-being in terms of military preparedness, military action, and the fostering of (or nostalgia for) military ideals.[92]

The new ethos of militarization no longer occupies a marginal place in the American political landscape, and it is reinforced daily by domestic and foreign policies that reveal a country obsessed with war and the military values, policies, and practices that drive it.[93] For instance, the military budget request for 2007 totals $462.7 billion, and as noted by Christopher Hellmen, a respected military budget analyst from the Center for Arms Control and Nonproliferation, when "adjusted for inflation [the 2007 military budget] exceeds the average amount spent by the Pentagon during the Cold War, [and] for a military that is one-third smaller than it was just over a decade ago."[94] Moreover, the 2007 military budget request does not include supplemental funding for the wars in Iraq and Afghanistan, which for 2006 alone was $115 billion and from September 11, 2001, to the end of 2006 was more than $445 billion.[95] The U.S. military budget is "almost 7 times larger than the Chinese budget, the second largest spender ... almost 29 times as large as the combined spending of the six 'rogue states' (Cuba, Iran, Libya, North Korea, Sudan and Syria) who spent [U.S.$]14.65 billion [and is] more than the combined spending of the next 14 nations."[96] An indication of how intensively the United States privileges the military over nonmilitary sectors of society—a central dimension of the process of militarization—can be found in comparing federal expenditures on the military and education before and after 9/11. For example, in 2000, the United States allocated approximately $24 billion to K–12 education and $280 billion to the Department of Defense; in 2003, federal expenditures on all levels of schooling totaled $102.8 billion while $379.3 billion was designated for the military.[97] Such immense levels of defense spending by the federal government have grave implications for expanding a U.S. war machine that uses massive resources "devoted to the monopolistic militarization of space, the development of more usable nuclear weapons, and the strengthening of its world-girdling ring of military bases and its global navy, as the most tangible way to discourage any strategic challenges to its preeminence."[98] The projection of U.S. military force and power in the world can be seen in the fact that the United States owns or rents 737 bases "in about 130 countries—over and above the 6,000 bases" at home.[99] Not only does the United States today spend "approximately as much as the rest of the world combined on its military establishment"[100]—producing massive amounts of death-dealing weapons—but it is also the world's biggest arms dealer, with sales in 2006 amounting to "about $20.9 billion, nearly double the $10.6 billion the previous year."[101]

What is clear in light of these figures is that militarization is not just a legitimating ideology for the state's coercive power, it is also a source of economic power for U.S. military industries, and, unfortunately, a source of employment for significant portions of the labor force. Such high levels of military funding, spending, and arms exporting both fail to guarantee security at home and give too much political power to the global producers and merchants of arms such as Lockheed Martin, Boeing, Raytheon, and

General Dynamics. Moreover, both major political parties have a stake in high military spending, and as reported in the *New York Times,* "the billions that have been supporting the industry are expected to continue unabated, and perhaps even increase."[102] Chalmers Johnson argues that U.S. imperial ambitions are driven by what he calls "military Keynesianism, in which the domestic economy requires sustained military ambition in order to avoid recession or collapse."[103] Among the consequences of "military Keynesianism" are massive waste, incompetence, and an egregious lack of oversight. For instance, in 2001 the Pentagon's own inspector general admitted that the department could not account for $2.3 trillion in spending. At the same time, "a congressional investigation reported that inventory management in the army was so weak it has lost track of 56 airplanes, 32 tanks, and 36 missile launchers."[104] And a 2006 Senate Arms Committee report stated that "[t]he American military has not properly tracked hundreds of thousands of weapons intended for Iraqi security forces and has failed to provide spare parts, maintenance personnel or even repair manuals for most of the weapons given to the Iraqis."[105] In 2005, the U.S. Inspector General's office reported that nearly $9 billion allocated for Iraqi reconstruction projects could not be accounted for and was considered lost.[106] Besides spending that cannot be explained, the Pentagon has given priority to costly weapons projects at the expense of providing decent medical care for returning wounded soldiers and "appropriate body armor for the troops, and plates for the Hummers in Baghdad."[107] In some cases, soldiers in Iraq and Afghanistan have purchased additional body armor with their personal funds. According to journalist George Monbiot, the U.S. federal government "is now spending as much on war as it is on education, public health, housing, employment, pensions, food aid and welfare put together."[108]

It gets worse. As Pentagon spending reaches record levels, the machinery of war diverts money from crucial domestic programs such as health care, child care, food programs, educational opportunities for low-income working families, and housing assistance for the elderly and the poor. By starving the social state through tax cuts for the very rich, welfare schemes for major corporations, and the allocation of billions of dollars to fund a costly war in Iraq and an imperial foreign policy, American militarism exacts a high price from democracy while simultaneously wasting valuable resources. For example, David Leonhardt, a reporter for the *New York Times*, estimates that as of January 2007 the war in Iraq has cost the American taxpayer $1.2 trillion, a figure that is hard to imagine unless you begin to address what this amount of money could finance in solving real social problems. Leonhardt provides an eye-opening comparison that points to both financial waste and moral indifference. He writes:

> For starters, $1.2 trillion would pay for an unprecedented public health campaign—a doubling of cancer research funding, treatment for every American whose diabetes or heart disease is now going unmanaged and a global immunization campaign to save millions of children's lives. Combined, the cost of running those programs for a decade wouldn't use up even half our money pot. So we could then turn to poverty and education, starting with universal preschool for every 3- and 4-year-old child across the country. The city of New Orleans could also receive a huge increase in reconstruction funds. The final big chunk of the money could go to national security. The recommendations of the 9/11 Commission that have not been put in place—better baggage and cargo screening, stronger measures against nuclear proliferation—could be enacted. Financing for the war in Afghanistan could be increased to beat back the Taliban's recent gains, and a peacekeeping force could put a stop to the genocide in Darfur. All that would be one way to spend $1.2 trillion. Here would be another: The war in Iraq.[109]

The biopolitics of militarization—driven by the colonial fantasies of global empire, an incessant focus on homeland security, the political benefits of promoting and exploiting a culture of fear, and corporate profiteering made from the war on terror—not only finds expression in bloated military budgets and dangerously high levels of arms production, it also permeates the entire realm of culture. According to William Greider, the new American biopolitics of militarization "is heading, in ad hoc fashion, toward the quasi-militarization of everyday life."[110] The esteemed historian Tony Judt goes further, connecting the growing militarization of everyday life to both a frontal attack on democracy and the residue of older forms of fascism. Judt insists that there is a precedent in twentieth-century Western history for a country whose government exploits

> national humiliation and fear to restrict public freedoms: for a government that makes permanent war as a tool of state policy and arranges for the torture of its political enemies; for a ruling class that pursues divisive social goals under the guise of national "values"; for a culture that asserts its unique destiny and superiority and that worships military prowess: for a political system in which the dominant party manipulates procedural rules and threatens to change the law in order to get its own way; where journalists are intimidated into confessing their errors and made to do public penance. Europeans in particular have experienced such a regime in the recent past and they have a word for it. That word is not "democracy."[111]

Cultural politics is no stranger either to modern authoritarian regimes or to the central role an aesthetics of militarization plays in promoting the enduring attraction if not "rehabilitation of fascist ideas and principles."[112] The intersection of war, violence, and the spectacle have become standard fare in American culture, appearing not only in all manner of commodities, Hollywood films, and news programs but also as part of a virtual reality fueled by high-tech weapons of war that mimic a postmodern aesthetic in their prioritizing of the visual and performative over the real, all the while reinforcing the importance of recognizing and making visible the degree to which the cultural machinery of militarization occupies an influential and powerful place in American life. Militaristic values, identities, and symbols permeate every aspect of American society, produced, distributed, and affirmed through numerous sites of pedagogy in the wider culture. Instead of being displayed on blackboards, limited to classroom desks and taught from lecterns, the new public pedagogy of militarization is written in digital formats, represented on the Internet, portrayed in various screen cultures, videogames, advertisements, and television programs such as *24*, and promoted and inscribed in hundreds of commodities, representations, and images that circulate through the new electronic media technologies. Whether in the form of George W. Bush imitating Tom Cruise's role in the film *Top Gun* or the news media's endless replay of the bombing of Baghdad as "shock and awe" and the toppling of Saddam Hussein's statue, or the television images of soldiers framed against the setting sun in Afghanistan, "war has once again become a grand pageant, performance art, or a perhaps temporary diversion from the ennui and boring routine of everyday life."[113] Representations of masculinity now seem inseparable from both a hardened indifference to human suffering and an infatuation with the aesthetic of over-the-top violence. Screen culture consistently legitimates violence, the criminalizing of social problems, and masculinity as an extension of the warrior mentality. One popular television program, *Dexter*, comes close to legitimating vigilante violence by portraying the main character less as a ruthless killer who murders people he deems to be criminals than as a complicated, likable, and reasonable American everyman with a tortured past. On the other hand, Jack Bauer, the central character of the television drama *24*, makes a case in each episode for torture, murder, and shredding the Constitution. In both television dramas, hyper-violence provides the organizing optic for representing a particular notion of militarized masculinity while legitimating the fascistic assumption that violence is the only reasonable solution to all sorts of problems ranging from everyday crime to the threat posed by terrorists (almost always people of color). Though both characters overidentify with violence—and, in Bauer's case, with the military code of honor—such excesses take on either a type of tragic ethical grandeur or are spruced up as the highest expression of patriotic duty. More disturbing, these modern-day Jack the Ripper and Adolf Eichmann types are portrayed as "warm human beings—loving, caught in the emotional dilemmas of ordinary people."[114]

This militarizing aesthetic, which occupies the center of public pedagogy—or what Raymond Williams once called "the educational force of our whole social and cultural experience ... the whole environment, its institutions and relationships [that] actively and profoundly teaches"[115]— leaves no one exempt and few untouched by its onslaught of messages, ideas, values, and ideologies. For instance, the line between entertainment and war disappears as the U.S. Department of Defense competes with the best of videogame culture with its free and widely popular online videogame website *America's Army,* an effective recruiting tool that currently has more than 5 million registered players, making it one of the "top five on the web."[116] Game designers now seek out the military, and the result is the emergence of a "'military-entertainment complex' [that has] sprung up to feed ... the military's desire to bring out ever-more-realistic computer and video combat games [as part of] an arm of media culture geared toward preparing young Americans for armed conflict."[117] Since African-Americans make up about 21 percent of the enlisted personnel in the armed forces, the military has made a concerted effort to convince black urban youth that it understands hip-hop culture, professional sports, street culture, and videogames. Not surprisingly, the most pernicious and insidious recruitment efforts have taken place in poor urban and rural neighborhoods. As Max Schmookler observes:

> [I]n the fall of 2003, the military's "Take It To The Streets" campaign used hip-hop culture to lure black and Latino youth, seen as having few, if any, other options for "upward mobility," into uniform. Teams of recruiters cruised the streets in specially outfitted Hummers, stopping to hold impromptu basketball shoot-outs and push-up contests, serve up personalized dog tags and distribute Army brand

jerseys, hats, wristbands and headbands. Yet, even with spotlights at MTV's Spring Break, BET's Spring Bling, various NAACP functions, and dozens of other venues with a high proportion of African Americans, the numbers of black recruits have declined substantially since the beginning of the Iraq war.[118]

As part of a larger attempt to maintain recruitment quotas, especially by focusing on the most disadvantaged youth, the Army has enhanced recruiting by using marketing tools and in doing so has appropriated the culture, language, lifestyles, and aesthetics of the groups they are targeting. As Army recruiter Colonel Thomas Nickerson put it, "You have to go where the target audience is.... Our research tells us that hip-hop and urban culture is a powerful influence on the lives of young Americans. We try to develop a bond with that audience. I want them to say, 'Hey, the Army was here—the Army is cool!'"[119] Of course, what the colonel fails to point out is that unlike videogames, the masculine lure of painted-yellow Hummers, and hip-hop music, war is neither a fashion nor a sport, and who wins or loses is measured less in the pursuit of pleasure and fun than in the all-too often tragedy of mangled bodies, posttraumatic illnesses, amputated limbs, body bags, and ruined lives. According to many of the Army's recruiting ads, joining up is about getting a free college education, traveling all over the world, and learning to use high-tech weapons that mimic videogame culture. If teenagers are going to be recruited to go to a war that, in itself, is based on lies, deception, and incompetence, it seems more than reasonable for them to be told the truth about what to expect once they join the ranks of the military. As *New York Times* columnist Bob Herbert points out, what is disturbing about such recruiting practices is that what they leave out is not only utterly deceptive but morally indefensible. He writes, "There was no mention of combat, or what it's like to walk the corridors and the grounds of the Walter Reed Army Medical Center in Washington, where you'll see a tragic, unending parade of young men and women struggling to move about despite their paralysis or with one, two or three limbs missing."[120]

As recruitment goals become more difficult to achieve given the unpopularity of the misbegotten war in Iraq, army recruiters will up the ante by touting the prospective benefits provided for the young men and women willing to risk their lives as part of the "Army of One," but they will say nothing about a Bush administration that has consistently attempted to cut "budgets for myriad programs intended to protect or improve the lives of veterans and active duty soldiers."[121] Needless to say, recruiters will also ignore the horrendous revelations revealed in the *Washington Post* about wounded soldiers brought back from Iraq and Afghanistan to be treated at the Walter Reed Army Medical Center only to find themselves in rooms that "included mold, rot, mice and cockroaches."[122] Surely, no one will mention a military bureaucracy that has been not simply indifferent to the needs of the wounded soldiers and their families but also in some cases has impeded their recovery. Instead of receiving much-needed quality care in return for their sacrifices, the wounded soldiers were given roach bombs and mouse traps for their rooms and subsisted "on carry-out food because the hospital cafeteria" was too far away to actually use.[123] The call to "support the troops" does not merely ring hollow in this case; it also belies how fraudulent such rhetoric actually is when human life is treated so cheaply by this administration. Bob Herbert puts it well in claiming that

> [r]eal-life human needs have never been a priority of this administration. The evidence is everywhere—from the mind-bending encounter with the apocalypse in Baghdad, to the ruined residential neighborhoods in New Orleans, to the anxious families in homes across America who are offering tearful goodbyes to loved ones heading off to yet another pointless tour in Iraq. . . . In the old days, these troops would have been referred to as cannon fodder. However you want to characterize them now, the casually unfair treatment is an expression of the belief that they are expendable. . . . The

outpatient fiasco at Walter Reed is just one aspect of a vast superstructure of suffering.[124]

The militarization of popular culture also extends to the Internet, where the Army recently launched its own profile on *MySpace.com*, a hugely popular social networking site. Though created as recently as 2003, the site now has as many as 21.1 million visitors in any given month. Other attempts to recruit young adolescents can be seen in the Pentagon's sponsorship of the "Professional Bull Riders, the Professional Rodeo Cowboys' Association, NASCAR, [and] their use of specially engineered video games, and snazzy television commercials."[125] High school students are particularly sought after by the Pentagon. Under a little-publicized aspect of the Bush administration's No Child Left Behind Act of 2002, any secondary school that received federal money had to allow military recruiters on school grounds or lose the funding. Even more disturbing is the fact that the law requires high schools to provide a host of personal information about students, including their names, addresses, and phone numbers. Using a marketing company called BeNOW, the Pentagon has created one of the largest private databases on youth in the country, consisting "of 30 million 16–25-year-olds, including name, address, email addresses, cell phone numbers, ethnicity, social security numbers and areas of study. This database is updated daily and distributed monthly to the Armed Services for recruitment purposes."[126] Military recruiters, under pressure to fill quotas, often target certain schools and particular students for recruitment, and they do not hold back in their efforts. A *Boston Globe* inquiry in 2004 found that "Officers call the chosen students repeatedly, tracking their responses in a computer program the Army calls 'the Blueprint.' Eligible students are hit with a blitz of mailings and home visits. Recruiters go hunting wherever teens from a targeted area hang out, following them to sporting events, shopping malls, and convenience stores."[127] Overly aggressive tactics to get young people to enlist are not the only ways in which military recruiters step over the line.

They also harass and commit serious crimes. For instance, a report by the Associated Press revealed that more than 100 young women in 2005 were preyed upon sexually by military recruiters. The six-month investigation found that "[w]omen were raped on recruiting office couches, assaulted in government cars and groped en route to entrance exams [and that at] least 35 Army recruiters, 18 marine Corps recruiters, 18 Navy recruiters and 12 Air Force recruiters were disciplined for sexual misconduct or other inappropriate behavior with potential enlistees in 2005."[128]

Such charges are particularly serious in light of the increasing presence of military recruiters on middle- and secondary-school campuses in the United States. Taking seriously the U.S. Army recruiting motto, "First to contact, first to contract," Army recruiters are making their presence felt at every level of schooling. Hany Khalil, an organizing coordinator at United Peace and Justice, who opposes the presence of the military in the nation's public schools, claims that military recruiters "have unrestricted access to kids in the schools, cafeterias and classrooms. They even brought Humvees onto campuses to make the prospect of going to war seem sexy and exciting."[129] Targeting youth of color and working-class youth has been especially successful through the expansion of its Junior Reserve Officers Training Corps (JROTC) programs in high schools and its Middle School Cadet Corps (MSCC) program at the K–8 schools.[130] In Chicago, "When moving up to high schools ... graduating eighth-graders can choose from 45 JROTC programs, including three full-time Army military academies, five 'school-within-a-school' Army JROTC academies and one JROTC Naval academy."[131] The militarization of middle- and secondary-school culture is characterized not only by strategies and tactics that involve serious improprieties, such as helping high school students cheat in order to pass exams and even to misrepresent drug tests, but also by a constant presence of military personnel in such schools. Karen Houppert provides a vivid image of how extensive this presence has become by commenting on the wide range of activities encouraged in the Army's rules of engagement for recruiters. She writes:

Recruiters are told to dig in deep at their assigned high schools, to offer their services as assistant football coaches— or basketball coaches or track coaches or wrestling coaches or baseball coaches (interestingly, not softball coaches or volleyball coaches)—to "offer to be a chaperon [*sic*] or escort for homecoming activities and coronations" (though not thespian ones), to "deliver donuts and coffee for the faculty once a month," to participate visibly in Hispanic Heritage and Black History Month activities, to "get involved with local Boy Scout troops" (Girl Scouts aren't mentioned), to "offer to be a timekeeper at football games," to "serve as test proctors," to "eat lunch in the school cafeteria several times each month" and to "always remember secretary's week with a card or flowers."[132]

The attractiveness of military culture resonates outside of the schools both in popular websites, sports events, music programs, and videogames organized around military values and in the dominant media culture in which Hollywood films and television shows, such as *Pearl Harbor, JAG, Over There, Saving Private Ryan,* and *Flags of Our Fathers,* perpetually legitimate a romanticized view of soldiers as warriors and war as the highest expression of a nation's honor. And if the message is lost in television dramas such as *Band of Brothers* and Hollywood films such as *Blackhawk Down,* it is endlessly broadcast by the "Foxified" media in "news" brought to us by former generals, embedded reporters who double as Pentagon stenographers, and not remotely funny fake-news programs with fraud reporters paid by the Bush administration to act like journalists.[133] For instance, David Barstow and Robin Stein reported in the *New York Times* that "at least 20 federal agencies, including the Defense Department ... have made and distributed hundreds of television news segments ... records and interviews," many of which "were subsequently broadcast on local stations across the country without any acknowledgment of the government's role in their production."[134] The Pentagon in recent years has embraced the myth-making possibilities of Hollywood, and the importance of cultural politics, by setting up a special department to negotiate with major studios, giving them the opportunity to gain access to military technology to create "realistic" films at a discount rate in exchange for allowing the military to be involved with film production. It appears that the national entertainment state is being refigured as the national entertainment-military state.[135]

Romanticizing the military does more than legitimate military culture; it also enforces a reactionary form of patriotism that pays off in special favors as it silences public dissent. Hence, it should come as no surprise that the Bush administration aligns itself with corporate media such as the Sinclair Broadcast Group, which showed their Republican Party spirit a few years ago by not allowing their sixty-two television stations to air an April 30, 2004, special edition of *Nightline* in which the program's host, Ted Koppel, committed the allegedly unpatriotic act of reading the names and showing the faces of the then 721 U.S. soldiers who had died in Iraq.[136]

Conservative think tanks and public intellectuals funded by ultra-right-wing millionaires such as Richard Mellon Scaife, Lynde and Harry Bradley, John Olin, Joseph Coors, and others continue to play an important role in the ongoing militarization of American society. Right-wing corporate, religious, and social groups have put together an array of pedagogical institutions and intellectuals who staff them as part of a reactionary conservative countereducation machine.[137] For instance, the American Heritage Foundation, the American Enterprise Institute, the Cato Institute, and the Project for the New American Century, among others, have played a crucial role in supporting the wars in Iraq and Afghanistan, in pursuing a politics of oil designed to subordinate the Middle East to U.S. interests, and in advancing the expansion of an imperial presidency under George W. Bush. These foundations have produced policy papers that promote an aggressive interventionist foreign policy, favoring preemptive military strikes, open-ended war, a heavily funded military apparatus, the pushing aside of global alliances, and a willingness to ignore international law. One particularly influential report, *Rebuilding America's*

Defenses, produced by the Project for the New American Century in 2000, is often cited as providing the blueprint for George W. Bush's foreign policy, including the war in Iraq. The chauvinism that informs this report is clearly legible and sums up a central feature of neoconservative empire-building in its claim that "[t]his report proceeds from the belief that America should seek to preserve and extend its position of global leadership by maintaining the preeminence of U.S. military forces," fight and win multiple wars, ensure that the United States remains the principal power in the world, and do everything possible to make certain that its political and economic principles are universally embraced.[138] Maureen Dowd captures the spirit of this type of militaristic jingoism by pointing out that the "neocons had grandiose plans to restore trumpets, morality and spine to foreign policy, to establish America as a hyperpower with a duty to export democracy—by force and on its own."[139] Unfortunately, the neoconservatives were so high on imperial power, their drug of choice, that they never saw the contradiction between the principles of democracy and the brutality of imposing it with bombs and guns, packaged for CNN, Fox, and the world in the aesthetic of "shock and awe."

On the domestic front, neoconservatives, Christian evangelicals, and market fundamentalists have supported new methods of security and policy measures such as the Patriot Act and the Military Commissions Act of 2006 in an ongoing effort to undermine fundamental civil liberties and stifle dissent in the media, universities, and most other public spheres capable of holding authority accountable. Such groups have worked incessantly to promote a culture of in/security and political accommodation in the United States as part of a broader set of commitments to militarization and war fever. Second-generation neoconservatives such as William Kristol, Charles Krauthammer, Richard Pearle, and others have argued relentlessly that force is the best arbiter of democracy, and as Robert Kagan succinctly put it, "Military strength alone will not avail if we do not use it actively to maintain a world order which both supports and rests upon American hegemony."[140] Another cultural warrior mobilized by militaristic fantasies is former Republican House Speaker Newt Gingrich, who has insisted that Congress declare World War III and serve notice on the American people "that the U.S. will use all its resources to defeat our enemies—not accommodate, understand, or negotiate with them, but defeat them."[141] One of the most influential Christian evangelicals in America, Jerry Falwell, has succinctly argued that "God is pro-war," tempering this seemingly sacrilegious commentary from a man of the cloth with the qualification that "[t]he Bible tells us war will be a reality until Christ returns."[142] What all of these individuals share is a belief in militarization as a religion,[143] and a conviction that the American way of life embodies a number of universal truths to be imposed on the rest of the globe, justified in an older colonial rhetoric of the "right and duty to spread democracy."[144]

Cynthia Enloe has argued that "[t]hings become militarized when their legitimacy depends on their association with military goals."[145] Such associations are becoming increasingly visible in American society and provide a measure of the degree to which militarization is spreading throughout the social order. But such associations are not easy to acknowledge, especially when they become so normalized that they no longer occupy the social margins. In addition, it becomes more difficult to address how the objects of everyday life are being militarized when, as often happens, public criticism of militarization is viewed as un-American or an act of disloyalty. Hence, it is not surprising that militarization now shapes the production of commodities such as toys, clothing, high fashion, and automobiles, often with little critical comment.[146] Consider the Hummer, the military-style SUV that projects an aura of hyper-militarized masculinity and paranoid fantasy. The degree to which a kind of pathologized militarization has become sutured into everyday life is even more evident in the concept vehicle called the Synus, pioneered by the Ford Motor Company and displayed at the 2005 North American International Auto Show. This car, though not yet in production, represents for Ford a legitimate integration of aesthetics and function in an age when security has become a pressing personal as well as social need. The description provided for the Ford Synus speaks for itself:

> As the population shifts back to big cities, you'll need a rolling urban command center. Enter the Synus concept vehicle, a mobile techno sanctuary sculpted in urban armor.... Short and slim for easy city manoeuvring, it looks bank-vault tough on the outside—with intimidating and outrageous styling that even features a vault-style spinner handle in back with a deadbolt door latching. When parked and placed in secure mode, Synus deploys protective shutters over the windshield and side glass. Small windows on the flanks and roof are non-opening and bullet-resistant.... The interior can transform into a mini-home theater with multi-configuration seating and a multi-media work station, all controlled by a Wi-Fi laptop. Use the 45-inch flat-screen LCD from Sharp for Internet research, DVD viewing or any screening needs. Plus, you can monitor your surroundings in real time as seen by the rear-mounted cameras.[147]

The unprecedented militarization of U.S. society is now effectively tamed with the language of consumerism, designed to mobilize the desires of a besieged middle class with covertly racist tropes and assumptions willingly deployed in the ongoing "permanent war" against presumed criminals, immigrants, barbarians, and terrorists who pose a grave threat to American security. In the Ford Motor Company pitch for the militarized Synus car, militarization, in/security, and the demonization of urban space easily fuse in an attempt to indulge the border-crossing fantasies and adventures of those who dare to negotiate the cities of the future. The not-so-hidden consumer attraction of this car with its blatant appeal to patriarchal-masculine traditions, a fortress mentality, and uncompromising sense of certainty about friend and enemy reinforces the racist presumption that the only safe public sphere is one that is controlled, homogenized, and white, and that there are commodities available to protect privileged classes from the pathologies of the "dark" urban centers. The expanding war economy and its search for domestic markets reveal the degree to which militarization takes for granted that the war on terrorism is being waged both abroad and at home. The latest consumer trends now flawlessly align themselves with relations of power that accentuate a growing authoritarianism and "a deepening ethos and practice of human violence against other humans" in a militarized culture in which "terrible acts of violence are stripped away as barbarism winds up integrated into the structures and norms of modernity itself."[148]

The Militarized Knowledge Factory: Research, Credentials, and the CIA

As in other spheres of American civic life, higher education is being militarized through a variety of government agencies, appeals, and practices. One approach centers on the collusion among the Pentagon, war industries, and academia in the fields of research and development. War industries not only provide large grants to universities but also offer job opportunities to their graduates while simultaneously exercising a subtle, though influential, pressure in shaping the priorities of the programs and departments crucial to their corporate interests. Companies that make huge profits on militarization and war such as General Electric, Northrop Grumman, and Halliburton establish through their grants important ties with universities while promoting a philanthropic self-image to the larger society.[149] John Armitage has argued that as the university becomes militarized it "becomes a factory that is engaged in the militarization of knowledge, namely, in the militarization of the facts, information and abilities obtained through the experience of education."[150] The priority given to such knowledge is largely the result of the vast sums of research money now given to shape the curricula, programs, and departments in universities across the country. The scale, sweep, range, and complexity of the interpenetration between academia and military-funded projects are as extensive as they are disconcerting. Nicholas Turse explains:

> According to a 2002 report by the Association of American Universities (AAU), almost 350 colleges and universities conduct Pentagon-funded research; universities receive more than 60% of defense basic research funding; and the DOD is the third largest federal funder of university research (after the National Institutes of Health and the National Science Foundation).... [T]he Department of Defense accounts for 60% of federal funding for university-based electrical engineering research, 55% for the computer sciences, 41% for metallurgy/materials engineering, and 33% for oceanography. With the DOD's budget for research and development skyrocketing, so to speak, to $66 billion for 2004—an increase of $7.6 billion over 2003—it doesn't take a rocket scientist to figure out that the Pentagon can often dictate the sorts of research that get undertaken and the sorts that don't.[151]

Along with the money that comes with such defense-oriented funding is a particular set of assumptions about the importance of ideas, knowledge, and information and their relevance to military technologies, objectives, and purposes. One gets a glimpse of such assumptions, as Turse points out, in the objectives put forth by Department of Defense research centers:

> The credo of the Army Research Laboratory (ARL) in Adelphi, Maryland, for instance, is "delivering science and technology solutions to the warfighter" which it strives to do by "put[ting] the best and brightest to work solving the [Army's] problems" by employing "a variety of funding mechanisms to support and exploit programs at universities and industry." The Space and Naval Warfare Systems Command (SPAWAR) is also high [on the list of] "University relationships" that provide it with "an excellent recruitment resource for high-caliber graduate and undergraduate students.[152]

In the post-9/11 world, one of the few sites from which money flows is the military war machine, and the grants and research funds needed to essentially buy off the best universities are not trivial. In 2003, for example, Penn State received $149 million in research and development awards while the Universities of California, Carnegie Mellon, and Texas received $29.8 million, $59.8 million, and $86.6 million, respectively—and these are not even the top beneficiaries of such funds.[153] So, has the Pentagon and the Department of Defense gotten what they paid for? The outcome of such investments can be glimpsed in the type of knowledge and areas being researched. For instance, the Department of Defense along with a number of other departments and agencies financially backing the militarization of knowledge support two main areas of weaponry: space-based armaments and so-called Future Combat Systems. The space weapons being researched in universities around the country include "microwave guns, space-based lasers, electromagnetic guns, and holographic decoys," while the future combat weapons include "electric tanks, electro-thermal chemical cannons, [and] unmanned platforms."[154] High-tech weapons of death have become so commonplace that major newspapers and magazines do feature stories on them, offering up reports on issues such as future robot armies, the building of killer Micro Air Vehicles (weapons designed as bugs), and a "ray gun that shoots a beam that makes people feel as if they will catch on fire."[155] Research for such weaponry is, in part, carried out at universities such as MIT, which gets 75 percent of its funds for its robotics program from the Department of Defense. How these funds shape research and development and the orientation of theory toward the production of militarized knowledge is evident in MIT's design and production of a kind of Robo-Marine called "the Gladiator," which is a tactical unmanned ground vehicle containing an MT40G medium machine gun, surveillance cameras, and slots for launching paint balls and various smoke rounds, including "tear gas, or stingball and flashbang grenades."[156] One Pittsburgh paper called it "a remote-controlled 'toy,' [with] some real weapons," with "containers for hand grenades that can be used for clearing obstacles and creating a footpath on difficult terrain for soldiers following behind. It also features what looks like organ pipes to produce smoke, and it has a mount on top for a medium-size machine gun or multipurpose assault weapon."[157] Critical commentary apparently not included. In fact, the Gladiator is designed for military crowd-control capabilities, reconnaissance, surveillance, and direct-fire missions. Carnegie Mellon University received a $26.4 million Defense Department grant to build six Gladiator prototypes. The University of Texas receives funding from the Department of Defense for its Applied Research Laboratories, which develops in five separate labs everything from Navy surveillance systems to "sensing systems to support U.S. ballistic missile targeting."[158] MIT, one of the largest recipients of defense research money, is also using its talented research-oriented faculty and students to develop remote sensing and imaging systems that would "nullify the enemy's ability to hide inside complex mountain terrains and cityscapes."[159] Universities around the country are funded to do similar military-oriented research, producing everything from global positioning systems to undersea surveillance technologies.[160]

Military research is not limited to the applied sciences. Eyal Weizman has analyzed what has been called "an international 'shadow world' of military urban research institutes and training centers that have been established to rethink military operations in cities [and] could be understood as somewhat similar to the international matrix of élite architectural academies."[161] In analyzing this benighted world, Weizman provides an instructive example of how the Israeli Defense Force (IDF) critically appropriates the work of critical theory in order to legitimate and conduct particular types of militarized urban research. In this case, the IDF draws not only upon the work of Guy Debord, Gilles Deleuze, and Felix Guattari but also from fields such as cybernetics and postcolonial and poststructuralist thought. Theory in this instance becomes a kind of smart-weapon used to refigure space and reconceptualize the urban domain, according to the concepts of the Deleuzian "war machine." In military terms, this means rejecting traditional configurations of space as "straited" or "enclosed by fences, walls, ditches, road blocks, and so on."[162] Translated into a military strategy, the Israeli military moves through space in heavily populated areas in a polymorphous fashion, blowing up walls while ignoring traditional markers and creating their own polymorphic maps of movement. Space now becomes "smooth," amorphous, as if it had no borders. Weizman considers the consequences of applying this theory as a tool of war. He writes at length:

> To begin with, soldiers assemble behind the wall and then, using explosives, drills or hammers, they break a hole large enough to pass through. Stun grenades are then sometimes thrown, or a few random shots fired into what is usually a private living-room occupied by unsuspecting civilians. When the soldiers have passed through the wall, the occupants are locked inside one of the rooms, where they are made to remain—sometimes for several days—until the operation is concluded, often without water, toilet, food or medicine. Civilians in Palestine, as in Iraq, have experienced the unexpected penetration of war into the private domain of the home as the most profound form of trauma and humiliation. A Palestinian woman identified only as Aisha, interviewed by a journalist for the *Palestine Monitor*, described the experience: "Imagine it—you're sitting in your living-room, which you know so well; this is the room where the family watches television together after the evening meal, and suddenly that wall disappears with a deafening roar, the room fills with dust and debris, and through the wall pours one soldier after the other, screaming orders. You have no idea if they're after you, if they've come to take over your home, or if your house just lies on their route to somewhere else. The children are screaming, panicking. Is it possible to even begin to imagine the horror experienced by a five-year-old child as four, six, eight, 12 soldiers, their faces painted black, sub-machine-guns pointed everywhere, antennas protruding from their backpacks, making them look like giant alien bugs, blast their way through that wall?"[163]

The "hypermodern militarized knowledge factory" now uses critical theory as a tool for killing and lays to rest the as-

sumption that theory, even in its more abstract forms, is removed from the messy relations of power, ideology, politics,
and public life. As theory is militarized, it becomes another
version of "shock and awe" and suggests that intellectuals in
the academy, in order to prevent such theoretical work from
being misappropriated, need to challenge in every instance
both the militarization of knowledge and the militarization of
higher education itself. This can take many forms, from refusing to accept research money associated with militarized
research, to exposing such research where it takes place,
and to using direct collective action to mobilize students
and faculty in opposition to all connections between higher
education and military research. Military recruiters under
the new forms of militarization neither limit their appropriation of knowledge to particular disciplines nor recruit only
working-class youth to fight their wars. They now use the
academy to recruit middle- and upper-middle-class youth
to research, design, and produce the highly advanced tech-
nological weapons that constitute the face of the new war
machine, used by mostly youth recruited from the ranks
of the poor. Given the present state of affairs, those in the
academy must ask themselves uncomfortable questions:
What role do intellectuals play in the conditions that allow
theory and knowledge to be appropriated in such a manner, and what can they do politically to prevent theory,
knowledge, and information from being militarized in the
first place? How does such opposition connect to their work
and extend their sense of social and political responsibility
to the world outside of the academy?

Military research on campuses has dangerous implications for the academy and for the larger social order. It
produces lethal weapons, subverts the peaceful use of scientific knowledge, fuels an arms race, debases the talents
of faculty and students, promotes secrecy and prevents
full disclosure, and corrupts the ethical standards of the
university. Moreover, it expands and strengthens the connection between the military-industrial complex and academia and, in doing so, remakes "civilian institutions to suit
military desires as if this were but the natural way of the

world."[164] Of course, this is about more than how knowledge is obtained, shaped, and used by different elements of the military-industrial complex; it is also about the kind of pressure that can be brought to bear by the power of the Department of Defense and the war industries on colleges and universities to orient themselves toward a society in which nonmilitarized knowledge and values play a minor role, thus removing from higher education its fundamental purpose in educating students to be ethical citizens; learn how to take risks; connect knowledge to power in the interests of social responsibility and justice; and defend vital democratic ideals, values, and institutions. In this context, it would be worthwhile to heed the warning of Jay Reed:

> Universities are not only hotbeds of military activity, they are adversely affected by the ethical compromises and threats to academic freedom that accompany a Department of Defense presence. The dream of the University as a place of disinterested, pure learning and research is far from reality as scientists and administrators from across the country are paid directly by the military to sit on Department of Defense scientific advisory boards and perform other research. It is naive to think that an abundance of funding from the military does not affect the projects chosen to be worthy of scientific inquiry. University research is not the result of objective decisions made in the spirit of an enlightened quest for knowledge; rather, these scientists' agendas are determined by the bloodthirsty architects of military strategy.[165]

Demonized by neoconservatives and the popular press as hotbeds of radical left-wing and totalitarian thought, universities are increasingly becoming the handmaidens of war—hardly a socialist utopia. Another crucial element of the military-industrial-academic complex that contributes to the growing presence of military values and interests on campuses can be found in the increasing numbers of college degree programs that service military employees. Fueled by a desire for more students, more tuition money, and a larger share of the market for online and off-campus programs, many universities and colleges are altering their curricula and delivery services to attract part of the lucrative education market for military personnel. This newfound interest in providing educational benefits for the military is due partially to revised policies on the part of the military. As part of a new recruiting strategy, the military adjusted its policies so that its personnel can get benefits to pay for their education while they are in the service rather than after discharge. In addition, military spending for educational benefits has spiked in the last few years to more than "half a billion dollars a year in tuition assistance for the members of its active-duty force,"[166] thus opening up a lucrative market for profit and nonprofit educational institutions. Not only does the Army pay "about $4,000 per year for a student's college education," it also provides students with "veterans' benefits, which can also include money for college."[167] As an added bonus, military students can use these funds to apply to any accredited college of their choice. The military's increased interest in education has proven to be such a bonanza for recruiting and retaining soldiers that one Army officer claimed, "The military has turned the entire recruiting force into essentially admissions counselors."[168] Some branches such as the Navy are increasing the importance of education by requiring all sailors beginning in 2011 to have "an associate degree to qualify for promotion to senior enlisted ranks."[169]

The rush to cash in on such changes has been dramatic, particularly for all online, for-profit educational institution such as the University of Phoenix, which has high visibility on the Internet. Other colleges such as Grantham University and the American Military University use military-friendly messages distributed across cyberspace in order to reach this new market of students and potentially large profits. Creating virtual universities has been a boon for colleges willing to provide online courses, distance-education degrees, and programs that appeal to military personnel. In some cases, enrollment figures have skyrocketed as colleges tap this lucrative market. Dan Carnevale, a writer for the *Chronicle of Higher Education,* reports that at Touro University International in California "about 4,000 of its 6,000 students serve in the military. And more than half of the nearly 11,000 students at Grantham University are in the armed forces."[170] The importance of online education can be seen in the creation of *eArmyU,* which is a partnership between the Armed Forces and higher education that allows enlisted personnel to use tuition assistance money to take online courses through twenty-eight selected colleges. Those colleges that offer traditional classroom instruction rely heavily on setting up satellite campuses on or close to military bases in order to get a profitable share of the market. Some colleges such as Central Texas provide both online courses and on-base classroom instruction. At Central Texas, 74 percent of its 63,000 students are members of the active-duty military.

I should like to be very careful in describing how this expansion of educational benefits to military personnel contributes to the militarization of the academy. I certainly believe that people who serve in the armed services should be given ample educational opportunities, and that for me is not at issue. What I think is problematic is both the nature of these programs and the wider culture of privatization and militarization produced and legitimated by them. With respect to the former, the incursion of the military presence in higher education furthers and deepens the ongoing privatization of education and of knowledge itself. Most of the players in this market are for-profit institutions that are problematic not only for the quality of education they offer but also for their aggressive support of education less as a public good than as a private initiative, defined in this case through its service to the military in return for a considerable profit. And as this sector of higher education grows, it will become not only more privatized but also more instrumentalized, largely defined as a credentializing factory to serve the needs of the military, thus falling into the trap of confusing training with a broad-based education. This expanding sector of higher education is the ultimate representation of neoliberal logic with its faith in the two pillars of market fundamentalism: outsourcing information and globalization. The growth of this higher-education sector also contributes to the rise of militarized knowledge factories that normalize the ideas, values, and experiences of war, warrior culture, hyper-masculinity, violence, and a reckless abuse of executive authority. Catering to educational needs of the military makes it all the more difficult to offer educational programs that would challenge militarized notions of identity, knowledge, values, ideas, social relations, and visions. Questions about what it means to get a broad-based liberal arts education or to be well-versed in the best that the arts, humanities, social sciences, and natural sciences have to offer democratic public life are not a high priority in this model of education, which is much more committed to skills training than to asking critical questions.

The for-profit institutions catering to the military market also represent a threat to and are at odds with those institutional structures and policies that provide faculty with rights, decent wages, and labor unions. In the first place, being virtual is about more than appropriating new technologies as pedagogical tools; it is also about restructuring the university less as a democratic public sphere than as a globalized sweat shop. These are institutions that neither protect the welfare of their faculty nor care about empowering their students to live in and extend the meaning of a genuine democracy. Second, the increasing presence of the military on campuses in towns and cities already dominated by military bases has a kind of multiplier effect through its ability to affect laws, social relations, ideologies, and how people deal with authority and dissent.[171] Military institutions radiate power in their communities and often resemble updated versions of the old company towns of nineteenth-century America—hostile to critical inquiry, cultural differences, people who take risks, and any discourse that might question authority. Moreover, the sheer power of the military apparatus, further augmented by its corporate and political alliances and fueled by an enormous budget, provides the Pentagon with a powerful arm-twisting ability capable of bending higher education to its will, an ominous and largely ignored disaster in-the-making in the

United States. Finally, as the military increasingly controls the type of education offered to its personnel, it creates a cadre of young people who will have less and less tolerance for a critical education and will accept as commonsensical a connection between militarized knowledge and education that is both anti-democratic and dangerous. The increasing militarization of knowledge and research in the university raises serious questions about whether students are receiving the critical education necessary for them to recognize and resist the potential threat of a military takeover in the United States. Such threats cannot be dismissed as fictions spawned by left-wing conspiracy theorists. For instance, General Tommy Franks, former commanding general of the United States Central Command, who also led the 2003 invasion of Iraq and the overthrow of Saddam Hussein, has speculated that in the event of another terrorist attack "the Constitution will likely be discarded in favor of a military form of government," a position he appears to support.[172] The potential for such a coup has also been noted by such reputable scholars as Chalmers Johnson, Kevin Baker, Andrew Bacevich, and Noam Chomsky.[173]

The CIA and Higher Education

While the Cold War and Sovietology are gone from the scene, a parallel project is now under way: the launching of large-scale initiatives to create a cadre and set of institutions that penetrate our campuses and link them to national security, military, and intelligence agencies. The aim is nothing less, as Congressional hearings show, than to turn back opposition on our campuses to imperial war, and turn campuses into institutions that will, over the next generation, produce scholars and scholarship dedicated to the so-called war on terror. These programs are part of a broader effort to normalize a constant state of fear, based on the emotion of terror, while criminalizing anti-war and anti-imperial consciousness and action. As in the past, universities, colleges and schools have been targeted precisely because they are charged with both socializing youth and producing knowledge of peoples and cultures beyond the borders of Anglo-America.[174]

One of the more disturbing indications of academe's willingness to accommodate the growing presence and legitimating ideologies of the national security state can be found in the increasing presence of the CIA and other spy agencies on American campuses. Daniel Golden, writing for the *Wall Street Journal* in 2002, noted that in the aftermath of 9/11 an increasing number of faculty and universities—capitalizing on both a newfound sense of patriotism and a less politicized sense of self-interest—were turning to the sixteen intelligence agencies and offering them their services and new recruitment opportunities.[175] Moreover, as universities recognize that the intelligence agencies have deep pockets for funding opportunities, the CIA has benefited from this new receptivity and is reciprocating by "turning more to universities . . . to develop high-tech gadgets that track down terrorists and dictators."[176] In addition, it is developing more federal scholarship programs, grants, and other initiatives in order to attract students for career opportunities and to involve faculty in various roles that address "security and intelligence goals."[177] The CIA's cozy relationship with academics has also been reinforced by the agency's increased presence at annual meetings held by academic groups such as the International Studies Association and the American Anthropological Association.

While part of this receptivity by faculty can be attributed to the scramble for research funding, it is only one factor in the equation. At a time when college students are in desperate need of jobs in an increasingly fragile market, the CIA because of its political prominence in fighting the war on terrorism is expanding rather than shrinking its employment opportunities and is viewed by many students—who seem to be beating a path to the agency's employment officers—as a promising career choice. Equally significant is the upsurge in patriotic correctness following 9/11 coupled with the ongoing right-wing campaign to squelch "un-American" dissent in the university. Hence, amid the resurgence of political quietism and hyper-patriotism, and the growing job insecurities among college graduates, an unparalleled detente has emerged between academia and the CIA at the beginning of the new millennium. This detente is furthered in part by a new generation of academics more favorable to forging a connection with the CIA. A resurgent sense of patriotism has also energized an older generation of closeted pro-CIA faculty, who either formerly worked with the CIA but did so in secrecy or supported efforts for collaborative work between academia and the intelligence agencies but were hesitant to make their views public. These older-generation academics are now on the offensive, not only acknowledging to colleagues their own positive views of collaboration between the CIA and higher education but also publicly urging younger faculty to heed the government's call "to serve in the war against terrorism—especially by serving as consultants to the Agency."[178] These include Columbia University's Robert Jervis, recent president of the American Political Science Association, Yale's H. Bradford Westerfield, and Harvard's Joseph S. Nye—all of whom have admitted working for the CIA. Elizabeth Rindskopf Parker, dean of the McGeorge School of Law at the University of the Pacific and former legal counsel for the CIA and National Security Agency, announced in the *Chronicle of Higher Education* that "[i]t is time to close the 'cultural divide' between academe and the intelligence community, a divide that should be of concern to all Americans.... It should be obvious that to have an effective foreign policy, not to mention successfully wage a war on terrorism, the United States must have the commitment and cooperation of its scholars and its national-security experts. Such a truism should require no further discussion."[179] Given that a dismissive response toward potential critics should be cause for concern, what does it bode, after all, for American democracy when high-profile academics adopt a military-like rigidity and argue that controversial issues of public interest should warrant "no further discussion"?

Another well-known example of strong academic support for university-CIA collaboration is in the work of Felix Moos. Moos, a professor of anthropology at the University of Kansas, circulated a proposal among his colleagues after the September 11 attacks for a federally funded project that would bring scholars and intelligence analysts together in American universities as part of a program to train potential agents "in certain languages, cultures, and technical fields that U.S. intelligence agencies deem to be critically important."[180] Moos is a former instructor at the Naval War College, worked in various advisory positions for the military, and is "a longtime advocate of anthropological contacts with military and intelligence agencies."[181] He has unabashedly argued that the universities had a duty to work with the CIA, conduct classified research, and offer their services in an effort to help the U.S. government win the war on terrorism.[182] Moos made his position clear in a live interview with David Glenn, published by the *Chronicle of Higher Education:*

> The United States is at war, and thus, simply put, the existing cultural divide between the intelligence community, the U.S. military and academe has become a critical, dangerous, and very real detriment to our national security at home and abroad. The former global symmetry of inter-nation conflict has become the asymmetry of terrorism and insurgency. Long gone are the days where academic anthropology might occasionally be applied to tourism and gender studies but not to critical area and language studies with a direct, practical use to national defense. James Fallows in the April 2005 *Atlantic Monthly* puts it well: "Until the United States understands that the 'battle for hearts and minds' is more than a slogan, it will lose. To win, it needs to deal with Iraq on far more intimate terms than are possible from fighter bombers dropping munitions or from armored Humvees. It needs to learn the language, penetrate the culture, recruit spies and sympathizers—to do the slow and messy work of building support for its side."[183]

In light of the willingness of many academics to forget the unsavory history of the CIA in shaping foreign diplomacy as well as its relationship to academia, the CIA has made public outreach "a top priority and targets academia in particular."[184] What seems to be forgotten in the newfound collaboration between the CIA and the academy is the history of the CIA's secret funding of the activities of the National Student Association in the 1960s, its attempt to "destroy the career of University of California President Clark Kerr,"[185] its harassment of anti-war activists and of numerous students, faculty, and others critical of American domestic and foreign policy during the 1960s and 1970s, as well as its unsavory efforts to interfere in and overthrow foreign governments that were at odds with American policies—for instance, Allende's elected socialist government in Chile and the August 1953 coup against Iranian Premier Mohammad Mossadeq.[186] A number of scholars have argued that some disciplines in the social sciences such as political science work quite regularly with the CIA and that a number of fields such as international relations "are so interwoven with the federal government, particularly with military and intelligence agencies, that they cannot avoid aping the political ideology of those agencies."[187] In the 1970s, a Senate committee reported that "[t]he CIA is now using several hundred American academics located in more than 100 American colleges, universities and related institutes. In addition, there are several American academics abroad who serve operational purposes, primarily the collection of intelligence."[188] Given the resurgence of the popularity of government intelligence agencies, there is no reason to doubt that such connections have ended; in fact, there are plenty of reasons, given that the intelligence agencies are flush with money and power, to believe that this kind of involvement is going to increase far beyond anything in the past.[189]

One of the most controversial post-9/11 programs sponsored by the CIA, based on the urging of Professor Moos, is the Pat Roberts Intelligence Scholars Program (PRISP). The program is named after Senator Pat Roberts,[190] who was the head of the Senate Select Committee on Intelligence under the Bush administration until the takeover of the

Senate by Democrats in 2006. Moos and Roberts share a certain affinity in their admiration for intelligence agencies and, clearly, a similar ideology about the role such agencies should play both in shaping foreign policy and as a major presence on American campuses. There is a certain irony in recalling that Senator Roberts was well known for siding with the Bush administration on warrantless domestic spying programs, blocking a vote to investigate the program, consistently stonewalling an investigation into Bush's use of prewar intelligence to justify the war in Iraq, defending Guantanamo Bay Prison, and refusing to investigate the CIA's complicity in the abuse and torture of detainees. The *Los Angeles Times* claimed that "[i]n a world without Doublespeak, the panel, chaired by GOP Sen. Pat Roberts of Kansas, would be known by a more appropriate name—the Senate Coverup Committee."[191]

The Roberts Program began as a two-year pilot program scheduled to run until the end of 2006, although it is still up and running in 2007. It was designed to train 150 analysts in anthropology, each of whom would receive a $25,000 stipend per year, with a maximum of $50,000 over the two-year period. The program also provided tuition support, loan paybacks, and bonuses for immediate hiring of those candidates considered to have critical skills. In return, each participant in the program agreed to work for an intelligence agency for one-and-a-half times the period covered by the scholarship support. For example, two years of support would necessitate that an analyst work for a government intelligence agency for three years. Students who receive such funding cannot reveal their funding source, are not obligated to inform their professors or fellow students that they are being funded by and will work for an intelligence agency, and are required to attend military intelligence camps.[192]

Defense of both the Roberts Program and the more general issue of academics working with intelligence agencies is often grounded in the assumption that if academics participated in the process of intelligence-gathering, many of the problems and abuses that the agencies have committed could be corrected in the future. But such a position ignores the fact that the intelligence agencies are guided not by rationality and open inquiry but by politics, and often by a politics that is utterly indifferent both to the rights of citizens of other countries and to the democratic interests of the larger international community. Even when the intelligence communities have produced information that has challenged policies pursued by the Bush administration, such as its reasons for launching an invasion on Iraq, the information was largely ignored in favor of intelligence that supported such views.[193] Moreover, such agencies have on occasion used academic scholarship not to promote a spirit of understanding complex cultural differences, critical reflection, and self-critique but to expand their own methods of torture and abuse. One such example recently surfaced at the 2006 American Anthropological Association's annual meeting. Scholars attending the meeting were appalled to discover that the work of some of their colleagues in the field of cultural anthropology had been used by the U.S. Armed Services to develop certain interrogation tactics at Abu Ghraib Prison as well as other locations. Professor Roberto J. Gonzales, an anthropologist who opposes the use of social science knowledge to further the "science of suffering," has pointed to the emergence of what he calls the "anthropology of insurgency."[194] Included in this category are the numerous intelligence agencies such as the CIA, the Defense Department, and new government offices such as the Cultural Operations Research Human Terrain that now actively recruit social scientists, including anthropologists, or simply expropriate their work in the interests of purely military functions.[195] This type of knowledge appropriation is particularly indicative of the increasing militarization of the field of anthropology and the emergence of anthropological counterinsurgents such as Dr. David Kilcullen, an Australian anthropologist and lieutenant colonel, who unabashedly works (on loan) with the U.S. State Department's counterterrorism office and refers, with no apologies, to counterinsurgency as "armed social work."[196] Under such circumstances, as Gonzales points out, "[a]nthropology . . . appears as just another weapon to be used on the battlefield—not as a tool for building bridges between peoples, much less as a mirror that we might use to reflect upon the nature of our own society."[197] In opposition to this developing biopolitics of academic militarization, Gonzales has also played a prominent role in convincing the American Anthropological Association to unanimously condemn "the use of anthropological knowledge as an element of physical and psychological torture."[198]

Nevertheless, criticisms of the Roberts Program, the Human Terrain Project, and other attempts to recruit academics in the service of military wars and intelligence-gathering have emerged among a few prominent academics, including Dave Price, David Gibbs, Mary Louise Pratt, and William Martin. Price, an associate professor of anthropology at St. Martin's College in Olympia, Washington, argues that the Roberts Program not only permits the "CIA to return to its historical practice of operating within universities"[199] but also allows it to revert to its old habit of collecting information on teachers, dissenting students, and what goes on in general in the classroom.[200] Price's overall condemnation of the Roberts Program is worth repeating:

> Healthy academic environments need openness because they (unlike the CIA) are nourished by the self-corrective features of open disagreement, dissent, and synthetic-reformulation. The presence of the PRISP's secret sharers brings hidden agendas that sabotage these fundamental processes of academia. The Pat Roberts Intelligence Scholars Program infects all of academia with a germ of dishonesty and distrust as participant scholars cloak their intentions and their ties to the cloaked masters they serve.[201]

Professor Price also believes that such programs give authoritarian regimes "an excuse to forbid all American social scientists to conduct research in those countries on the grounds that they are spies."[202] Phil Baty, writing in the *Times Higher Education Supplement,* furthers this argument by insisting that such a program places the lives of all anthropologists in the field at risk of physical danger because they might be suspected of being spies and a danger to the people whom they study. Gibbs, an associate professor of history and political science at the University of Arizona in Tucson, argues that any close relationship between the intelligence services and higher education compromises the ability of academia to make power accountable by undermining the possibility of academics to criticize the policies and practices of intelligence agencies. He argues that the secrecy imposed on scholars working for the CIA is antithetical to the notion of the university as a democratic sphere that fosters critique, open dialogue, and engaged debate. He also insists that the CIA practices of engaging in disinformation and propaganda tactics along with its vast and sordid history of destabilizing democratic governments, committing human rights abuses, engaging in acts of abduction and torture, and undermining popular democratic movements put it at odds with any viable notion of what higher education should represent.[203] At the very least, the research that is supported in many universities under the funding of the intelligence agencies raises serious questions about the kind of relationship being established between these agencies and academia, and whether such a relationship is capable of producing the ends for which it is purportedly espoused in the first place. For instance, Mary Louise Pratt, past president of the Modern Language Association of America, describes the Bush government's war-oriented National Security language program initiatives, designed to create translators who can facilitate espionage, interrogation, and other military activities, as "reactive" and inherently incapable of producing the security that is stipulated as their principle goal: "There is a fundamental contradiction between the social and communicative nature of language and the rupture of human relations that is warfare. We cannot build a national language policy on that contradiction. The real role language has to play in national security is that of developing and sustaining the vast spectra of personal, institutional, commercial, diplomatic, and intellectual relations that prevent conflicts from turning into national security crises in the first place."[204]

Perhaps of even greater concern are the tactics deployed by the CIA to keep the public ignorant of its growing influence on academe. CIA analyst Karl Speilmann "calls for concerted scholarly inquiry into methods of denial and deception."[205] And at the Rochester Institute of Technology, John Philips, a CIA scientist, urged students to develop a technology to "make him invisible" and "to figure out how to identify a terrorist in disguise based on bone structure, and how to bend light rays to keep a spy in the shadows."[206] Of course, there is also the massive research under way in developing new kinds of sensors, making objects disappear, and generating new weapons of destruction. Perhaps the most stinging criticism of such research agendas comes from William Martin, whose comments are aimed not merely at the CIA but at all Homeland Security Programs working in conjunction with higher education. He writes:

> What these programs signal is thus not simply an attack on academic freedom or even the diversion of education funding into secret intelligence projects. For students and scholars alike these new programs threaten to solidify dangerous institutional changes. Secret military and intelligence agencies will increasingly dictate which languages, religions, and peoples—both beyond and within our borders—will be studied and by whom. New networked centers and programs, created by and tied to federal security funding, will form an academic homeland security complex destined to implement the fear of "un-American others," all in pursuit of an increasingly profitable and increasingly illusory "war on terror." Meanwhile, hidden behind these facades, marches the development of security and intelligence student trainees who report to security agencies and move back and forth, unknown and unobserved, from our classrooms to security agencies. The forgotten exposes of the 1970s demonstrate what these kinds of programs produce: an academy not simply compromised and at risk, but riddled with secret military and intelligence projects, slowly spreading all over the world in service of misguided imperial ambitions.[207]

Martin's argument appears to be lost on a majority of academics. What is overlooked in the growing, enthusiastic collaboration between the military-industrial complex and academe within the context of developing a powerful post-9/11 national security state is that the increasing militarization of higher education is itself a problem that may be even more insidious, damaging, and dangerous to the fate of democracy than that posed by terrorists who "hate our freedoms." Heretofore, the university has been one of the few remaining sites where genuine criticism, critical scholarship, spirited debate, and organized resistance to the abuse of government power could take place.

Conclusion

The militarization of American society suggests more than a crisis in politics. It is also representative of a fundamental crisis in democracy and the critical educational foundation upon which it rests. As education is increasingly divorced from its prior role in producing critical citizens committed to the public good, now reduced to the obligations of consumerism or other utterly privatized conceptions of agency, it becomes more difficult for the public to understand how militarization is normalized and how it is connected to an authoritarian politics, the globalization of arms trading, and the spread of catastrophic violence. Andrew Bacevich is right in suggesting that more is at stake here than rethinking "the fundamentals of U.S. military policy."[208] What is needed first is "a change of consciousness, seeing war and America's relationship to it in a fundamentally different way."[209] Such a challenge requires taking seriously how knowledge production—our chief export—is still militarized in an "information age," what democratic institutions are under attack as a result, and what steps can be taken to resist the drift toward "perpetual war for perpetual peace."[210] As militarization spreads throughout the various pedagogical sites and circuits of power that animate the educational force of the culture, whether newspapers, talk radio, television, the Internet, public schools, or higher education, it becomes all the more crucial to prevent militarization from becoming further normalized, from allowing war, violence, and hyper-masculine aggression to become so embedded in what and how we learn that the ideology and practices of militarization become a matter of common sense, and thus invisible, unquestionable and much more dangerous.

Higher education should play a particularly important role in opposing not only its own transformation into a "hypermodern militarized knowledge factory"[211] but also the growing impact of militarization in the larger society. One crucial step in this process is to reclaim higher education as a democratic public sphere, one that provides the pedagogical conditions for students to become critical agents who connect learning to expanding and deepening the conditions for the struggle for genuine democratization. Students should be versed in the importance of the social contract, provided classroom opportunities to become informed citizens, and given the resources to understand politics in both historical and contextual terms as part of the broader discourse of civic engagement. Educators have a responsibility to provide rationales for defending higher education as a public sphere while putting into place long-term strategies and policies that resist the ongoing militarization (and corporatization and political homogeneity) of the university. This means refusing to instrumentalize the curriculum; giving the humanities a larger role in educating all undergraduate students; putting into place curricula, programs, and courses that stress a critical education over job training; and enabling students to learn how to read the political and pedagogical forces that shape their lives not as consumers but as critically engaged citizens. As Jorge Mariscal points out, "Militarization and open democratic societies . . . do not make a good match, the former producing pathologies at both the individual and collective levels. The face of militarization on the ground is perhaps most disturbing insofar as it reveals a disconnected hardening of individuals to human suffering."[212] Large numbers of students pass through the hallowed halls of academe, and it is crucial that they be educated in ways that enable them to recognize creeping militarization and its effects throughout society, particularly in terms of how these effects threaten "democratic government at home just as they menace the independence and sovereignty of other countries."[213] But students must also recognize how such anti-democratic forces work in attempting to dismantle the university itself as a place to learn how to think critically and engage in public debate and civic engagement, an issue I discuss throughout this book.[214] In part, this means giving them the tools to fight for the demilitarization of knowledge on college campuses—to resist complicity with the production of knowledge, information, and technologies in classrooms and research labs that contribute to militarized goals and purposes, which is, to quote Michael Geyer again, "the process by which civil society organizes itself for the production of violence."[215]

Even so, there is more at stake than simply educating students to be alert to the dangers of militarization and the way in which it is redefining the very mission of higher education. Chalmers Johnson, in his continuing critique of the threat the politics of empire presents to democracy at home and abroad, argues that if the United States is not to degenerate into a military dictatorship, a grass-roots movement will have to occupy center stage in opposing militarization and reclaiming the basic principles of the republic—though he is far from optimistic. He writes:

> The evidence strongly suggests that the legislative and judicial branches of our government have become so servile in the presence of the imperial Presidency that they have largely lost the ability to respond in a principled and independent manner.... So the question becomes, if not Congress, could the people themselves restore Constitutional government? A grass-roots movement to abolish secret government, to bring the CIA and other illegal spying operations and private armies out of the closet of imperial power and into the light, to break the hold of the military-industrial complex, and to establish genuine public financing of elections may be at least theoretically conceivable. But given the conglomerate control of our mass media and the difficulties of mobilizing our large and diverse population, such an opting for popu-

lar democracy, as we remember it from our past, seems unlikely.[216]

Such a task may seem daunting, but if the American people are to choose democracy over empire, as Johnson puts it, then there is also the crucial need for faculty, students, administrators, and concerned citizens to develop alliances and for long-term organizations to resist the growing ties among government agencies, corporations, and higher education that engage in reproducing militarized knowledge, which might require severing all relationships between the university and intelligence agencies and war industries. It also means keeping military recruiters out of public and higher education. One such example can be found in People Against Militarization (PAMO) of the Ontario Institute for Studies in Education (OISE), which brought faculty, students, and community activists together to protest a partnership between OISE and the Atlantis Systems Corporation, a company that provides knowledge, training, and simulation equipment for the militaries of a number of countries, including the United States and Saudi Arabia. PAMO provides a valuable model, proving that such protests can be used to make visible the ongoing militarization of higher education, while also providing strategies indicating how faculty, students, and others can organize to oppose it.[217]

Opposing militarization as part of a broader pedagogical strategy in and out of the classroom also raises the question of what kinds of competencies, skills, and knowledge might be crucial to such a task. One possibility is to develop a kind of praxis that addresses what I call an "oppositional pedagogy of cultural production," one that defines the pedagogical space of learning not only through the critical consumption of knowledge but also through its production for peaceful and socially just ends. What is at stake here is the crucial need for students to learn how to do more than critically engage and interpret print, visual, and media texts, as significant as such a task might be as part of their learning experience. That is, while the importance of learning how to read different forms of media critically should not be underestimated, it does not go far enough in the critical education of our students. What also matters is that the discourse of critique be connected to issues of intervention with a focus on forms of cultural production that can be appropriated in the struggle to demilitarize knowledge, social relations, and values, as well as the sites of public pedagogy that produce them. As the forces of militarization increasingly monopolize the dominant media, students, activists, and educators must imagine ways to expand the limits of humanities education in ways that enable the university to shape coming generations of cultural producers capable of not only negotiating the old media forms, such as broadcasting and reporting, but also generating new electronic media, which have come to play a crucial role in bypassing those forms of media concentrated in the hands of corporate and military interests. The current monopolization of the media suggests that students will have to be educated in ways that allow them to develop alternative public spheres where they can produce their own films, videos, music, radio talk shows, newspapers, magazines, and other modes of public pedagogy. The militarization of everyday life, from the production of videogames to the uncritical analysis of war and violence in the nightly news, must be challenged through alternative media. Examples of this type of public pedagogy can be seen in the wide range of individuals and groups who make cultural politics and public pedagogy central to their opposition of a number of anti-democratic forces such as militarization and neoliberalism. Examples extend from the incredible work of the Media Education Foundation, which produces a range of documentaries, many of which address topics such as war games and videos for youth and other topics related to the militarization of the culture,[218] to the Global Network Against Weapons and Nuclear Power in Space, which consists of songwriters and singers who produce music protesting the militarization of space.[219] The central issue here is how the university and the liberal arts in particular can be reimagined in the interests of producing critical discourses, practices, knowledges, and counterpublics committed to enabling students to expand their capacities and skills as engaged citizens committed to the realization of a genuine democracy.

What PAMO and other university protests make clear is that any viable biopolitics of demilitarization must reject utterly the collapse of a democratic culture of politics into the culture of violence and disposability and work vigorously to connect theory and practice to collective struggles with long-term goals for global sustainability waged from multiple sites. Militarized knowledge and values touch everyone in American society, and the process of militarization must be exposed and resisted at every place in which it appears. Too much is at stake, especially for the next generation, to allow such a process to continue unchecked. Indeed, Jorge Mariscal is right once again in pointing out that " militarization must be systematically exposed and resisted at every site where it appears in the culture.... Perhaps yet another march and demonstration will prove less productive than focusing our energy on devising strategies to slow down a process that threatens both the future of our children and the soul of the nation."[220]

In the fight against the biopolitics of militarization, educators need a language of critique, but they also need a language that embraces a sense of hope and collective struggle. This means elaborating the meaning of politics through a language of critique *and* possibility, on the one hand, and a concerted effort to expand the space of politics by reclaiming "the public character of spaces, relations, and institutions regarded as private," on the other.[221] Such a task suggests a struggle for the very preconditions of political engagement, one in which thinking about knowledge, agency, values, and the relationship of the self to the other opens directly onto the social terrain, relations of power, and "the intertwined fates of individual agency and democratic politics."[222] Borrowing from Nick Couldry, I want to argue that a revitalized democratic politics must develop shared sites of collective struggle, overcome "the divisions that block off the sites of possible politics from the rest of life," and sustain practices of public connection in which "people's fragmented, uncertain, incomplete narratives of agency are valued, preserved, and made available for exchange, while being related, analytically, to wider contexts of power."[223]

While it has become fashionable in the academy to talk about biopolitics through the language of "bare life," "state of exception," and "state of emergency," this discourse often represents a very limited conception of agency, politics, and sovereignty—one that misrepresents both the complexity of power and the multifaceted nature of resistance. We need a more capacious understanding of biopolitics, one in which power is not reduced exclusively to domination and the citizen can achieve more than the limited role of consumer or soldier. We live at a time when matters of life and death are central to political sovereignty. While registering the shift in power toward the large-scale production of death, disposability, and exclusion, a new biopolitics must also point to notions of agency, power, and responsibility that operate in the service of life, democratic struggles, and the expansion of human rights. Such struggles must be made visible, and can be found among AIDS workers in Africa, organized labor in Latin America, and Palestinians acting as human shields against Israeli tanks in the West Bank and Gaza. We can also see a biopolitics of resistance and hope at work in a long tradition of anti-militarist struggles in the United States, which have taken place not only in the wider public sphere but also in the military itself.[224] Efforts to end violence, speak out against war, and criticize acts of torture and abuse extend from the founding of the nation to the anti-war movements of the 1960s and the new millennium, including the emergence of groups fighting against global sweat shops, the arms race, global racism, wage slavery, child poverty, the rise of an imperial presidency, and the ongoing wars in Iraq, Afghanistan, and the Middle East. Catherine Lutz illuminates this tradition as follows: "In the United States, an antimilitarist tradition has been a vigorous force at many points from the framing of the Constitution through the anti-ROTC movement of the World War I period to the antiwar novels and films of the 1930s and the 1960s to the current mass movement to combat the democratic losses and intensified militarization of this more recent period."[225]

In addressing the militarization of the academy and everyday life, it is also crucial for educators to recognize that power works in myriad ways in the interest of both domination and struggle. In contemporary times, this suggests that educators should pay more attention to how different modes of domination inform each other so that strategies for resistance can be layered, complex, and yet held together by more generalized notions of hope and freedom. As Timothy Brennan and Keya Ganguly have argued, progressives need a more adequate theory of power and, as I have argued, a more profound sense of history and a more complicated notion of politics.[226] For example, any redemptive biopolitics of demilitarization would have to be understood in relation to an equally powerful biopolitics of capital, raising fundamental questions about how capital in its neoliberal incarnation and militarization in its various forms connect and inform each other on the level of the local, national, and global. We might, for instance, raise the question of how neoliberalism, with its fragmenting of democratic solidarities, privatized notions of agency, and eviscerated conception of politics, paves the way for the production of militarized subjects, as well as the normalization of military mentalities and moralities, and how these practices affect generations of young people.

The threat that the military-industrial-academic complex poses to higher education, a meaningful politics, and a substantive democracy has a long history and will not go away once the Bush-Cheney-neoconservative crowd is pushed out of office. Rooted in political, economic, ideological, and social relations that engulf various layers of power and daily life—including jobs for workers—the military-industrial-academic complex is a huge systemic behemoth that must be engaged by numerous groups from multiple sites of intervention. Such a struggle is by necessity not only pedagogical and political but also historical in its need to connect historical understanding with the task of exposing and debunking the reverence that the military now enjoys in the United States. The biopolitics-of-militarization claim to safeguarding peace must be addressed against the 201 overseas military interventions that the U.S. government has waged since 1941.[227] The militarized state's endless invocation of democracy must be understood in terms of its military and financial support of some of the world's most ruthless dictatorships and its role as the major arms supplier in the world. The military-industrial-academic complex's reputed invocation of honor must be measured against the thousands of people killed because of its high-tech weaponry and the support services it provides for covert and overt military and political interventions.[228] Chalmers Johnson, I believe, is right in suggesting that the citizenry and its intellectuals need to do some memory-work in figuring out how the American people were persuaded to allow the Constitution to be dismantled by the Bush-Cheney crowd, how they were seduced into accepting the notion that capitalism and democracy are synonymous, how they were sold the concept of endless war as a protocol of legitimate policy, and how they allowed the social state to be dismantled so that public money could flow to the war industries greedy for massive profits at the public expense, permitting the United States to become infamous for its remote-control killing and its willingness to kidnap, maim, and torture—all in the name of either safeguarding or promoting democracy. As Johnson points out:

> I believe that George W. Bush and Dick Cheney have led the country into the perilous cul-de-sac, but they did not do it alone and removing them from office will not necessarily solve the problem. The crisis of government in the United States has been building at least since World War II. The emergence of the imperial presidency and the atrophying of the legislative and judicial branches have deep roots in the postwar military-industrial complex, in the way broad sectors of the public have accepted the military as our most effective public institution, and in aberrations in our electoral system. The interesting issue is not the damage done by Bush, Cheney and their followers but how they were able to get away with it, given the barriers that exist in the

Constitution to prevent just the sorts of misuses of power for which they have become notorious.[229]

Finally, if higher education is to come to grips with the multilayered pathologies produced by militarization, it will have to rethink not merely the space of the university as a democratic public sphere but also the global space in which intellectuals, academics, students, artists, labor unions, and other social movements can form transnational alliances both to address the ongoing effects of militarization on the world—which include war, pollution, massive poverty, the arms trade, growth of privatized armies, civil conflict, and child slavery—and to develop global organizations that can be mobilized in the effort to resist a culture of war with a culture of peace, whose elemental principles are grounded in the relations of economic, political, cultural, and social democracy. As Andrew Bacevich has argued, we can no longer afford to live in a world in which soldiers are elevated to the status of national icons, military violence is mystified in a shroud of aesthetic respectability, force becomes the privileged mechanism for mediating conflicts, and military spending exceeds spending for schools, health, and other social provisions combined.[230] Since militarization operates simultaneously on symbolic, material, and institutional levels, strategies must be developed and waged that address all of the terrains on which it is operational. Militarization poses a serious threat to higher education, but, more important, it poses a danger to the promise of democracy at home and abroad, and to the very meaning of democratic politics and the sustainability of human life. Surely it is time for educators to take a stand and oppose the death-dealing ideology of militarization and its distorting effects on higher education and everything else it touches outside of the university.

Notes

1. Dwight D. Eisenhower, "Military-Industrial Complex Speech, Dwight D. Eisenhower, 1961—The Avalon Project at

Yale Law School," *The Avalon Project (1961),* available online at
http://www.yale.edu/lawweb/avalon/presiden/speeches/eisen-
hower001.htm.

2. More recently, the military-industrial complex has been
defined through a conglomeration of social forces known as the
"Iron Triangle," and as James M. Cypher points out, it includes
the following interest groups: "One side of the triangle includes
the 'civilian' agencies that shape U.S. military policy—the Office
of the President, the National Security Council, the Senate and
House Armed Services Committees, and civilian intelligence agencies like the CIA and NSA. A second side includes the military
institutions—the Joint Chiefs of Staff; the top brass of the Air
Force, Army, Marines, and Navy; the powerful 'proconsul' regional
commands (known as 'CINCs'); and, in a supporting role, veterans'
organizations like the American Legion and the Veterans of Foreign
Wars. At the base of the triangle are the 88,000 private firms that
profit from the military contracting system, and that use their
sway over millions of defense workers to push for ever-higher
military budgets." See James M. Cypher, "The Iron Triangle: The
New Military Buildup," *Dollars and Sense Magazine* (January/Feb-
ruary 2002), available online at http://www.thirdworldtraveler.
com/Militarization_America/Iron_Triangle.html.

3. The concept of "armed democracies" is taken from Ulrich
Beck, *The Reinvention of Politics: Rethinking Modernity in the Global
Social Order* (London: Polity, 1999), p. 78.

4. Eisenhower, "Military-Industrial Complex Speech."

5. See the thoughtful documentary film *Why We Fight*
(2006), directed by the talented Eugene Jarecki, which makes
Dwight Eisenhower its central figure. Documenting the rise of
the military-industrial complex in America, the film begins with
Eisenhower's warning about the profound danger posed by a war/
business apparatus in which corporations and greedy politicians
enter into collusion with the military in order to reap billions in
power and profits, regardless of the consequences in human suffering, misery, and death.

6. See Anatol Lieven, "We Do Not Deserve These People,"
London Review of Books 27:20 (October 20, 2005), available online
at http://www.lrb.co.uk/v27/n20/print/liev01_.html.

7. Eisenhower, "Military-Industrial Complex Speech."

8. Of course, at the time, the National Defense Educational
Act had been passed as part of the post-Sputnik legislation that
linked national defense with federal investment in higher educa-

tion. As Sophia McClennen points out in a brilliant essay in *College Literature,* the Soviet launching of Sputnik created a sense of vulnerability and opened the door for dynamics that further fueled the rise of the military-industrial-academic complex. See Sophia McClennen, "The Geopolitical War on U.S. Higher Education," *College Literature* 33:4 (Fall 2006), pp. 43–75.

9. Cited in Kathryn Albrecht, "'Camp Justice': A Sign of How We Cherish Our Freedoms," *Mountain Mail Newspaper* (February 9, 2006), available online at http://www.mymountainmail.com/stories/opikkathrynalbrecht02-09-0620060306.php. The full speech can be found in William J. Fulbright, "The War and Its Effects: The Military-Industrial-Academic Complex," *Super-State: Readings in the Military-Industrial Complex,* ed. Herbert I. Schiller (Urbana: University of Illinois, 1970).

10. Clark Kerr, *The Uses of the University* (Cambridge, MA: Harvard University Press, 1963).

11. Rebecca S. Lowen, *Creating the Cold War University: The Transformation of Stanford* (Berkeley: University of California Press, 1997), p. 2.

12. Ibid., p. 3.

13. Charles DeBenedetti and Charles Chatfield, *An American Ordeal: The Antiwar Movement of the Vietnam Era* (Syracuse, NY: Syracuse University Press, 1990); Terry Anderson, *The Movement and the Sixties: Protest in America from Greensboro to Wounded Knee* (New York: Oxford University Press, 1995); Alexander Bloom and Wini Breines, eds., *"Takin' It to the Streets": A Sixties Reader,* 2nd ed. (New York: Oxford University Press, 2003).

14. There were dozens of plots by the U.S. government to kill Castro, as reported in William Blum, *Killing Hope* (Monroe, ME: Common Courage Press, 1995), p. 189. See also *The Church Committee Report on Cuba,* available online at http://history-matters.com/archive/church/reports/ir/html/ChurchIR_0043a.htm.

15. There is a distinguished body of literature written about the emerging historical relationship among the government, the military, and higher education. See, for example, Roger L. Geiger, *To Advance Knowledge: The Growth of American Research Universities, 1900–1940* (New York: Oxford University Press, 1986); Everett Mendelsohn, Merritt Roe Smith, and Peter Weingart, *Science, Technology, and the Military* (Dordrecht, The Netherlands, 1988); Clyde W. Barrow, *Universities and the Capitalist State: Corporate Liberalism and the Reconstruction of American Higher Education, 1894–1928* (Madison: University of Wisconsin Press, 1990); Sigmund Diamond,

Compromised Campus: The Collaboration of Universities with the Intelligence Community, 1945–1955 (New York: Oxford University Press, 1992); Stuart W. Leslie, *The Cold War and American Science: The Military-Industrial-Academic Complex at MIT and Stanford* (New York: Columbia University Press, 1993); G. Pascal Zachary, *Endless Frontier: Vannevar Bush, Engineer of the American Century* (New York: The Free Press, 1997); Christopher Simpson, ed., *Universities and Empire: Money and Politics in the Social Sciences During the Cold War* (New York: The New Press, 1998).

16. Andrew J. Bacevich, *The New American Militarism* (New York: Oxford University Press, 2005), p. 14.

17. Beck, *The Reinvention of Politics,* p. 78.

18. It would be difficult to look at the rise of militarism in American life without reading the seminal work of Noam Chomsky, Chalmers Johnson, Howard Zinn, and Gore Vidal. Following is a partial listing of their brave and crucial writings: Noam Chomsky, *Failed States: The Abuse of Power and the Assault on Democracy* (New York: Metropolitan Books, 2006); Noam Chomsky, *Towards a New Cold War* (New York: The New Press, 2003); Noam Chomsky, *Hegemony or Survival: America's Quest for Global Dominance* (New York: Metropolitan Books, 2003); Noam Chomsky, *Rogue States* (Boston: South End Press, 2000); Howard Zinn, *A Power Governments Cannot Suppress* (San Francisco: City Lights, 2007); Howard Zinn, *Terrorism and War* (New York: Seven Stories Press, 2002); Howard Zinn, *On War* (New York: Seven Stories Press, 1997); Gore Vidal, *Imperial America: Reflections on the United States of Amnesia* (New York: Nation Books, 2004); and Gore Vidal, *Perpetual War for Perpetual Peace* (New York: Nation Books, 2002). Other important work includes Chalmers Johnson, *The Sorrows of Empire: Militarism, Secrecy, and the End of the Republic* (New York: Metropolitan Books, 2004); Bacevich, *The New American Militarism*; and Carl Boggs, *Imperial Delusions: American Militarism and Endless War* (Boulder, CO: Paradigm Publishers, 2005). One of the best books on American militarism and empire building is Chalmers Johnson, *Nemesis: The Last Days of the American Republic* (New York: Metropolitan Books, 2006).

19. Chomsky, *Failed States*, p. 3.

20. John Armitage, "Beyond Hypermodern Militarized Knowledge Factories," *Review of Education, Pedagogy, and Cultural Studies* 27 (2005), p. 221.

21. While there are some excellent older analyses of the military-academic complex, more recent critiques are marginal to the literature on the military-industrial complex. Some recent analyses

include: Sigmund Diamond, *Compromised Campus: The Collaboration of Universities With the Intelligence Community, 1945–1955* (New York: Oxford University Press, 1992); Stuart W. Leslie, *The Cold War and American Science: The Military-Industrial-Academic Complex at MIT and Stanford* (New York: Columbia University Press, 1993); G. Pascal Zachary, *Endless Frontier: Vannevar Bush, Engineer of the American Century* (New York: The Free Press, 1997); Rebecca S. Lowen, *Creating the Cold War University: The Transformation of Stanford* (Berkeley: University of California Press, 1997); Noam Chomsky et al., *The Cold War and the University: Toward an Intellectual History of the Postwar Years* (New York: The New Press, 1998); Christopher Simpson, ed., *Universities and Empire: Money and Politics in the Social Sciences During the Cold War* (New York: The New Press, 1998); Cary Nelson, "The National Security State," *Cultural Studies* 4:3 (2004), pp. 357–361; John Armitage, "Beyond Hypermodern Militarized Knowledge Factories," *Review of Education, Pedagogy, and Cultural Studies* 27 (2005), pp. 219–239; Michael Perelman, "The Role of Higher Education in a Security State," *Thought & Action* (Fall 2005), pp. 179–186; and Greg McColm and Sherman Dorn, "A University's Dilemma in the Age of National Security," *Thought & Action* (Fall 2005), pp. 163–177.

22. Nicholas Turse, "The Military-Academic Complex," *TomDispatch.com* (April 29, 2004), available online at http://www.countercurrents.org/us-turse290404.htm.

23. These figures are taken from ibid. See also Johnson, *The Sorrows of Empire*, especially pp. 97–130.

24. Association of American Universities, *National Defense Education and Innovation Initiative: Meeting America's Economic and Security Challenges in the 21st Century* (January 2006), available online at http://www.aau.edu/reports/NDEII.pdf.

25. Ibid.

26. Nelson, "The National Security State," p. 359.

27. Dave H. Price, "The CIA's Campus Spies," *Counterpunch* (March12/13, 2005), available online at www.counterpunch.org/price03122005.html.

28. This figure was recently provided by National Intelligence Director John Negroponte in a 2006 speech at the National Press Club. See "Spy Chief Discloses Total Number of U.S. Intelligence Personnel," *USA Today* (April 20, 2006), available online at www.usatoday.com/news/washington/2006-04-20-intelligencepersonnel_x.htm?csp=34.

29. Daniel Golden, "After Sept. 11 CIA Becomes a Growing

Force on Campus," *Wall Street Journal* (October 4, 2002), available online at http://www.mindfully.org/Reform/2002/CIA-Growing-On-Campus4oct02.htm.

30. Chris Mooney, "Good Company," *The American Prospect* (November 18, 2002), available online at http://www.prospect.org/print/V13/21/mooney-c.html.

31. Marissa Carl, "Spanier to Head New FBI Board," *The Daily Collegian* (September 19, 2005), available online at http://www.collegian.psu.edu/archive/2005/09/09-19-05tdc/09-19-05dnews-05.asp.

32. Ibid.

33. Press Release, "FBI Appoints National Security Higher Education Advisory Board," Federal Bureau of Investigation (September 15, 2005), available online at http://www.fbi.gov/pressrel/pressrel05/highed091505.htm.

34. William G. Martin, "Manufacturing the Homeland Security Campus and Cadre," *ACAS Bulletin* 70 (Spring 2005), pp. 1–7.

35. Stephen John Hartnett and Laura Ann Stengrim, "War Rhetorics: *The National Security Strategy of the United States* and President Bush's Globalization-Through-Benevolent-Empire," *South Atlantic Quarterly* 105:1 (Winter 2006), p. 176. Gore Vidal dates the rise of the national security state to 1947 with passage of the National Security Act. See Gore Vidal *Imperial America* (New York: National Books, 2004, p. 97).

36. Nikhil Singh, "The Afterlife of Fascism," *South Atlantic Quarterly* 105:1 (Winter 2006), p. 85.

37. Michael Perelman, "The Role of Higher Education in a Security State," *Thought & Action* (Fall 2005), p. 179.

38. I have taken up this question of an emerging authoritarianism in the United States in two books. See Henry A. Giroux, *Against the New Authoritarianism: Politics After Abu Ghraib* (Winnipeg: Arbeiter Ring Publisher, 2005); and Henry A. Giroux, *America on the Edge: Henry Giroux on Politics, Culture, and Education* (New York: Palgrave, 2006).

39. Jean Comaroff, "Beyond the Politics of Bare Life: AIDS and the Neoliberal Order," unpublished manuscript (October 6, 2005), p. 3.

40. Michel Foucault, *Society Must Be Defended: Lectures at the College de France, 1975–1976* (New York: Picador, 1997), p. 249.

41. Michael Hardt and Antonio Negri, *Multitude: War and Democracy in the Age of Empire* (New York: Penguin Press, 2004), p. 334.

42. Giorgio Agamben, *Homo Sacer: Sovereign Power and Bare*

Life, trans. Daniel Heller-Roazen (Stanford: Stanford University Press, 1998); Giorgio Agamben, *Remnants of Auschwitz: The Witness and the Archive,* trans. Daniel Heller-Roazen (Cambridge: Zone Books, 2002); Giorgio Agamben, *State of Exception,* trans. Kevin Attell (Chicago: University of Chicago, 2003); Foucault, *Society Must Be Defended.*

43. Giorgio Agamben, "On Security and Terror," trans. Soenke Zehle, *Frankfurter Allegemeine Zeitung* (September 20, 2001), available online at http://www.egs.edu/faculty/agamben/agamben-on-security-and-terror.html.

44. Comaroff, "Beyond the Politics of Bare Life," pp. 17–18.

45. Some of the most important analyses of disposability can be found in the work of Zygmunt Bauman, *Wasted Lives* (London: Polity Press, 2004).

46. Zygmunt Bauman, *Liquid Fear* (London: Polity, 2006), pp. 4.

47. Bauman, *Wasted Lives,* p. 6.

48. Achille Mbembe, "Necropolitics," trans. Libby Meintjes, *Public Culture* 15:1 (2003), p. 11.

49. Jane Mayer, "A Deadly Interrogation," *New Yorker* (November 14, 2005), available online at http://www.newyorker.com/fact/content/articles/051114fa_fact; and Seymour Hersh, *Chain of Command: The Road from 9/11 to Abu Ghraib* (New York: Harper Collins, 2005).

50. Neil Smith, "Global Executioner," *South Atlantic Quarterly* 105:1 (Winter 2006), p. 61.

51. Irene Kahn, *Amnesty International Report 2005* (May 25, 2005), available online at http://web.amnesty.org/library/Index/ENGPOL100142005. See also Editorial, "Torture in the U.S. Gulag," *The Nation* (June 20, 2005), p. 3.

52. Joshua Holland, "The Mystery of the Marine Massacre in Iraq," *AlterNet* (June 1, 2006), available online at http://www.alternet.org/story/36752.

53. Stephen Gray, *Ghost Plane: The True Story of the CIA Torture Program* (New York: St. Martin's Press, 2006). For a personal narrative about the abuse and torture inflicted on an innocent Canadian citizen at the hands of the U.S. government's extraordinary rendition program, see Maher Arar, "The Horrors of 'Extraordinary Rendition,'" *Foreign Policy in Focus* (October 18, 2006), available online at http://www.fpif.org/fpiftxt/3636. And for an excellent analysis of the role of academics in working with the CIA in developing physically brutal torture methods, see Alfred

W. McCoy, *A Question of Torture: CIA Interrogation—From the Cold War to the War on Terror* (New York: Owl Books, 2006).

54. A Canadian public inquiry completely cleared Arar of any terrorist activities. See www.ararcommission.ca/eng/AR_English.pdf.

55. Dana Priest, "Wrongful Imprisonment: Anatomy of a CIA Mistake," *Washington Post* (December 5, 2005), pp. 12–18.

56. See Dana Priest, "CIA Holds Terror Suspects in Secret Prisons," *Washington Post* (November 2, 2005), p. A01.

57. On the FBI's Counter Intelligence Program, see Nelson Blackstock, *Cointelpro: The FBI's Secret War on Political Freedom* (New York: Pathfinder Press, 1999); Ward Churchill and Jim Vander Wall, eds., *The Cointelpro Papers: Documents from the FBI's Secret Wars Against Dissent in the United States,* 2nd ed. (Boston: South End Press, 2002); and David Cunningham, *There's Something Happening Here: The New Left, the Klan, and FBI Counterintelligence* (Berkeley: University of California Press, 2004).

58. Anup Shah, "US Military Commissions Act 2006—Unchecked Powers?" *Z Magazine* (October 2, 2006), available online at http://www.zmag.org/content/print_article.cfm?itemID=11095&sectionID=1.

59. I take up the issue of the Bush administration's response to Hurricane Katrina as symptomatic of a new biopolitics of disposability in Henry A. Giroux, *Stormy Weather: Katrina and the Politics of Disposability* (Boulder, CO: Paradigm Publishers, 2006).

60. Bauman, *Liquid Fear,* p. 41.

61. Hardt and Negri, *Multitude,* p. 334.

62. Ibid.

63. See Agamben, *State of Exception*; and Agamben, *Homo Sacer: Sovereign Power and Bare Life.*

64. Jacques Ranciere, "Who Is the Subject of the Human Rights of Man?" *South Atlantic Quarterly* 102:2/3 (Spring/Summer 2004), pp. 301–302.

65. George Monbiot, "States of War: Appeasing the Armed Forces Has Become a Political Necessity for the American President," *The Guardian/UK* (October 14, 2003), available online at http://www.commondreams.org/views03/1014-09.htm.

66. Mbembe, "Necropolitics," p. 12. For an interesting historical analysis of the militarization of the social body in the United States, see Jeffrey Montez De Oca, "'As Our Muscles Get Softer, Missile Race Becomes Harder': Cultural Citizenship and

the 'Muscle Gap,'" *Journal of Historical Sociology* 18 (September 2005), pp. 145–172.

67. John R. Gillis, "Introduction," in *The Militarization of the Western World*, ed. John R. Gillis (New York: Rutgers University Press, 1989), p. 1.

68. Michael Geyer, "The Militarization of Europe, 1914–1945," in *The Militarization of the Western World*, ed. John R. Gillis (New York: Rutgers University Press, 1989), p. 79.

69. Catherine Lutz, "Making War at Home in the United States: Militarization and the Current Crisis," *American Anthropologist* 104:3 (September 2002), p. 723.

70. Tony Judt, "The New World Order," *New York Review of Books* 11:12 (July 14, 2005), p. 16.

71. John R. Gillis, ed., *The Militarization of the Western World*. On the militarization of urban space, see Mike Davis, *City of Quartz* (New York; Vintage, 1992); and Kenneth Saltman and David Gabbard, eds., *Education as Enforcement: The Militarization and Corporatization of Schools* (New York: Routledge, 2003). On the current neoconservative influence on militarizing American foreign policy, see Donald Kagan and Gary Schmidt, *Rebuilding America's Defenses*, which is one of many reports outlining such an issue developed under the auspices of the Project for the New American Century; it is available online at http://www.newamericancentury.org.

72. Bacevich, *The New American Militarism*, p. 3.

73. Etienne Balibar, *We, the People of Europe: Reflections on Transnational Citizenship* (Princeton: Princeton University Press, 2004), p. 125.

74. Gillis, "Introduction," in *The Militarization of the Western World*, p. 9.

75. The militarization of the war against the urban poor, for example, is discussed in Daryl Meeks, "Police Militarization in Urban Areas: The Obscure War Against the Underclass," *The Black Scholar* 35:4 (Winter 2006), pp. 33–41.

76. Peter B. Kraska, "The Military-Criminal Justice Blur: An Introduction," in *Militarizing the American Criminal Justice System,* ed. Peter B. Kraska (Boston: Northeastern University Press, 2001), p. 3.

77. Ibid., p. 10.

78. Nikhil Singh, "The Afterlife of Fascism," *South Atlantic Quarterly* 105:1 (Winter 2006), p. 85.

79. Hardt and Negri, *Multitude*, p. 17.

80. I have borrowed this idea from the criticisms made of the Israeli Defense Force by the writer Yitzhak Laor. See Laor, "You Are Terrorists, We Are Virtuous," *London Review of Books* 28:16 (August 17, 2006), available online at http://www.lrb.co.uk/v28/n16/print/laor01_.html.

81. Michael Geyer, "The Militarization of Europe, 1914–1945," in John R. Gillis, ed., *The Militarization of the Western World* (New York: Rutgers University Press, 1989), p. 68.

82. I want to thank Sophia McClennen for this insight.

83. Agamben, "On Security and Terror."

84. This issue is brilliantly explored in Richard J. Bernstein, *The Abuse of Evil: The Corruption of Politics and Religion Since 9/11* (London: Polity Press, 2005).

85. C. Wright Mills, *The Power Elite* (New York: Oxford University Press, 1993, originally published in 1956), p. 191.

86. Kevin Baker, "We're in the Army Now: The G.O.P.'s Plan to Militarize Our Culture," *Harper's Magazine* (October 2003), p. 37.

87. Ruth Rosen, "Politics of Fear," *San Francisco Chronicle* (December 30, 2003), available online at http://www.commondreams.org/views02/1230-02,htm.

88. Ibid.

89. Chris Hedges, *War Is a Force That Gives Us Meaning* (New York: Anchor Books, 2003), p. 16.

90. I take up this issue in Henry A. Giroux, *Breaking into the Movies* (Malden, MA: Basil Blackwell, 2002). See also C. Kay Weaver and Cynthia Carter, eds., *Critical Readings: Violence and the Media* (New York: Open University Press, 2006).

91. Jonathan Rutherford, "At War," *Cultural Studies* 19:5 (September 2005), p. 622.

92. Bacevich, *The New American Militarism,* pp. 1, 5.

93. How this affects domestic and foreign policy in the United States can be seen in Chomsky, *Hegemony or Survival.*

94. Christopher Hellman, "The Runaway Military Budget: An Analysis," *FCNL Washington Newsletter* (March 2006), available online at http://www.fcnl.org/now/pdf/2006/mar06.pdf.

95. Ibid.

96. Anap Shah, "High Military Expenditures in Some Places," *Global Issues* (November 9, 2006), available online at http://www.globalissues.org/Geopolitics/ArmsTrade/Spending.asp?p=1.

97. William Sonnenberg, *Federal Support for Education: FY 1980 to FY 2003* (Washington, DC: National Center for Educa-

tion Statistics, 2004), available online at http://nces.ed.gov/pubs2004/2004026.pdf.

98. Richard Falk, "Will the Empire Be Fascist?" available online at http://www.transnational.org/forum/meet/2003/Falk_FascistEmpire.html.

99. James Sterngold, "After 9/11 U.S. Policy Built on World Bases," *San Francisco Chronicle* (March 21, 2004), available online at http://www.sfgate.com/cgi-bin/article.cgi?file=/c/a/2004/03/21/MNGJ65OS4J1.DTL&type=printable.

100. Francis Fukuyama, "The Neocons Have Learned Nothing from Five Years of Catastrophe," *The Guardian/UK* (January 31, 2007), available online at www.commondreams.org/views07/0131-26.htm.

101. Jim Wolf, "US Predicts Bumper Year in Arms Sales," *Reuters* (December 4, 2006), available online at http://news.yahoo.com/s/nm/20061204/pl_nm/aero_arms_summit_arms_sales_usa_dc

102. Leslie Wayne, "Heady Days for Makers of Weapons," *New York Times* (December 26, 2006), p. 7.

103. Chalmers Johnson, "Republic or Empire: A Nation's Intelligence Estimate on the United States," *Harper's Magazine* (January 2007), p. 63.

104. Julian Borger and David Teather, "So Much for the Peace Dividend," *The Guardian/UK* (May 22, 2003), available online at http://www.commondreams.org/cgi-bin/print.cgi?file=/headlines03/0522-01.htm.

105. James Glanz, "The Reach of War; U.S. Is Said to Fail in Tracking Arms Shipped to Iraq," *New York Times* (October 30, 2006), available online at http://select.nytimes.com/search/restricted/article?res=F30B1FFC395B0C738FDDA90994DE404482. On the sloppiness in weapons oversight, see Heather Wokusch, "Bush's Permanent War Economy Must Crash (Before it Endangers You and Your Bank Account Even More)," *Dissident Voice* (November 2, 2006), available online at http://www.dissidentvoice.org/Nov06/Wokusch02.htm.

106. Bryan Bender, "Iraqi Audit Can't Find Billions," *Boston Globe* (October 16, 2004), available online at www.boston.com/news/nation/articles/2004/10/16/iraqi_audit_can't_find_billions/.

107. James Surowiecki, "Unsafe at Any Price," *New Yorker* (August 7 and 14, 2006),p. 32.

108. George Monbiot, "States of War," *The Guardian/UK*

(October 14, 2003), available online at http://www.commondreams .org/views03/1014-09.htm.

109. David Leonhardt, "What $1.2 Trillion Can Buy," *New York Times* (January 17, 2007), p. C1.

110. William Greider, "Under the Banner of the 'War' on Terror," *The Nation* (June 21, 2004), p. 14.

111. Judt, "The New World Order," p. 18. See also Chris Hedges, *American Fascists: The Christian Right and the War on America* (New York: The Free Press, 2007).

112. Paul Gilroy, *Against Race: Imagining Political Culture Beyond the Color Line* (Cambridge, MA: Harvard University Press, 2000), p. 148.

113. Andrew J. Bacevich, "The Normalization of War," *Mother Jones* (April 2005), available online at http://www.motherjones. com/news/dailymojo/2005/04/bacevich.html

114. Slavoj Zizek, "The Depraved Heroes of 24 Are the Himmlers of Hollywood," *The Guardian* (January 10, 2006), available online at http://www.guardian.co.uk/print/0,,5370717-103677,00. html.

115. Raymond Williams, *Communications* (New York: Barnes and Noble, 1967), p. 15.

116. Bob Herbert, "Truth in Recruiting," *New York Times* (August 27, 2005), p. A17. See also Jim Ryan, "Army's War Game Recruits Kids," *San Francisco Chronicle* (September 23, 2004), available online at http://www.commondreams.org/ views04/0923-11.htm.

117. Nick Turse, "The Pentagon Invades Your Xbox," *Dissident Voice* (December 15, 2003), available online at http://www. dissidentvoice.org/Articles9/Turse_Pentagon-Video-Games.htm. See also Clive Thompson, "The Making of an X Box Warrior," *New York Times Magazine* (August 22, 2004), pp. 33–37.

118. Max Schmookler, "Iraq War Impacts Military Recruitment Practices," *Miscellany News* (November 10, 2005), available online at http://misc.vassar.edu/archives/2005/11/iraq_war_impact. html.

119. Whitney Joiner, "The Army Be Thuggin It," *Slate* (October 17, 2003), available online at www.salon.com/mwt/feature/2003/10/17/army/print.html.

120. Bob Herbert, "Truth in Recruiting," p. A17.

121. Cited in Ruth Conniff, "Walter Reed Shows Administration Priorities," *The Progressive* (March 7, 2007), available online at http://www.commondreams.org/views07/0307-20.htm.

122. Dana Priest and Anne Hull, "Soldiers Face Neglect, Frustration at Army's Top Medical Facility," *Washington Post* (February 18, 2007), p. A01.
123. Dana Priest and Anne Hull, "Swift Action Promised at Walter Reed," *Washington Post* (February 21, 2007), p. A08.
124. Bob Herbert, "Lift the Curtain," *New York Times* (March 8, 2007), p. A23.
125. Nicholas Turse, "The Pentagon Crawls into MySpace," *TomDispatch.com* (October 3, 2006), available online at http://www.alternet.org/module/printversion/42434.
126. See "Background on the Pentagon's Illegal Database," *Leave My Child Alone* (July 3, 2005), available online at http://www.leavemychildalone.org/index.cm?event=showContent&contentid=38.
127. Charlie Savage, "Military Recruiters Target Schools Strategically," *Boston Globe* (November 29, 2004), available online at http://www.boston.com/news/nation/articles/2004/11/29/military_recruiters_pursue_target_schools_carefully?mode=PF.
128. Cited on CBS News, "Sexual Abuse by Military Recruiters," April 20, 2006, available online at http://www.cbsnews.com/stories/2006/08/19/national/printable1913849.shtml.
129. Cited in Karen Houppert, "Military Recruiters Are Now Targeting Sixth Graders: Who's Next?" *The Nation* (September 12, 2005), p. 17.
130. The underlying racial dynamics at work in JROTC has been analyzed by Christopher Robbins and is worth repeating at length. He writes: "A corrosive racial subtext is operative with JROTC. Not only were urban and poor rural schools originally targeted by the JROTC, but they also continue to open their doors to (or be bribed into supporting) the JROTC program. In 1992, the Department of Defense's (DOD) expenditures on the JROTC were $76 million. By 2002, the DOD's total spending on JROTC reached $243 million, doubling the number of operating programs from 1500 to 3000 (the current cap) in the same period. These expenditures contribute to the increasing numbers of youth of color who later join the military. Lutz and Bartlett note that as of 1995, '45% of cadets completing JROTC enter[ed] some branch of the service, a rate much higher than the general student population,' whereas more than 50% of JROTC cadets were observed to join the military post–high school graduation after 2000. The Combined Arms Center reported that as of 2001, JROTC cadets were more than 5 times as likely as the general student population to later

join the military, a disproportionate number of whom were African American or Latino. (Approximately 8% of high school graduates from the general school population enlist upon graduation.) For instance, in Chicago alone, Claire Schaeffer-Duffy reports that not only are Chicago Public Schools 91% nonwhite and 85% poor, but also '[f]orty-four of the city's 93 high schools have the JROTC program,' and the JROTC wishes to increase the cadets' later enlisting rate from 37% to 55% in coming years in Chicago Public Schools. This racial dynamic is visible in all urban public schools that are attended by disproportionate numbers of poor students of color. Twenty-two of Detroit public's 39 high schools have JROTC programs; nearby middle- to-upper-middle-class predominantly white schools systems, like Bloomfield Hills or Novi, have zero JROTC programs. Ten of the school districts of Philadelphia's 45 high schools provide JROTC programs; very nearby and very wealthy and white Haverford, Ardmore, and Wynnewood schools systems have zero JROTC programs. These racial dynamics help explain, in part, why 50% of JROTC cadets are African American or Latino on a national level, though their combined representation in the national population is approximately 27%." See Christopher Robbins, *Expelling Hope: Zero Tolerance and the Attack on Youth, Schooling, and Democracy* (Albany: SUNY Press, in press), pp. 125–126.

131. Jennifer Wedekind, "The Children's Crusade," *In These Times* (June 20, 2005), p. 6.

132. Houppert, "Military Recruiters Are Now Targeting Sixth Graders," p. 15.

133. For an excellent analysis of this issue, see Frank Rich, *The Greatest Story Ever Told: The Decline and Fall of Truth from 9/11 to Katrina* (New York: The Penguin Press, 2006).

134. David Barstow and Robin Stein, "Under Bush, a New Age of Prepackaged TV News," *New York Times* (March 13, 2005), available online at http://www.nytimes.com/2005/03/13/politics/13covert.html?ei=5088%22&en=2e1b834f0ba8a53c&ex=1268456400&pagewanted=print&position=.

135. I want to thank Max Haiven for bringing this to my attention. See David Robb, *Operation Hollywood* (Amherst: Prometheus, 2004); Carl Boggs, "Pentagon Strategy, Hollywood and Technowar," *New Politics* 11:1 (Summer 2006), available online at www.wpunj.edu/newpol/issue41/Boggs41.htm; and Lewis Lapham, "Terror Alerts," *Harper's* (March 2007), pp. 9–11.

136. See Eric Alterman, "Is Koppel a Commie?" *The Nation*

(May 24, 2004), p. 10. Of course, beyond censorship, there is the outright intimidation of the media by the Bush administration. See, for example, Eric Alterman, "Bush's War on the Press," *The Nation* (May 9, 2005), pp. 11–20; and John Nichols and Robert W. McChesney, "Bush's War on the Press," *The Nation* (December 2, 2005), pp. 8–9.

137. See, for example, Lewis H. Lapham, "Tentacles of Rage—The Republican Propaganda Mill, A Brief History," *Harper's Magazine* (September 2004), pp. 31–41.

138. Donald Kagan, Gary Schmitt, and Thomas Donnelly, *Rebuilding America's Defenses: Strategy, Forces and Resources for a New Century* (Washington, DC: A Report of the Project for the New American Century, 2000), p. iv.

139. Maureen Dowd, "Pouring Chardonnay Diplomacy," *New York Times* (November 15, 2006), p. A27.

140. These citations are from Bacevich, *The New American Militarism*, p. 85.

141. Cited in Jim Lobe, "Neo-Con Favorite Declares World War III," *CommonDreams.org* (September 13, 2006), available online at http://www.commongroundcommonsense.org/forums/index.php?showtopic=63109&pid=612652&st=0&.

142. Jerry Falwell, "God Is Pro-War," *WorldNet Daily* (January 31, 2004), available online at http://worldnetdaily.com/news/article.asp?ARTICLE_ID=36859.

143. For an interesting critical commentary on the contemporary mixture of conservative politics and religion, see Esther Kaplan, *With God on Their Side* (New York: The New Press, 2004); Chris Hedges, *American Fascists: The Christian Right and the War on America* (New York: Free Press, 2006); Kevin Phillips, *American Theocracy* (New York: Viking, 2006);, Michelle Goldberg, *Kingdom Coming: The Rise of Christian Nationalism* (New York: Norton, 2006). See also Garry Wills, "A Country Ruled by Faith," *New York Review of Books* 53:18 (November 16, 2005), available online at http://www.nybooks.com/articles19590.

144. Immanuel Wallerstein, *European Universalism: The Rhetoric of Power* (New York: The Free Press, 2006), p. 26.

145. Cynthia Enloe, "Sneak Attack," *Ms. Magazine* 12:1 (December 2001/January 2002), p. 15.

146. On the interrelationship between fashion and militarization, see the various examples on display in the November 2006 issue of *Marie Clare* magazine. For a commentary on this issue, see Lucinda Marshall, "War Chic," *Dissident Voice* (December 1,

2006), available online at http://www.dissidentvoice.org/Dec06/
Marshall01.htm.

147. Ford Motor Company, "Ford SYNUS," North American
International Auto Show 2005, available online at http://www.
fordvehicles.com/autoshow/concept/synus/. See also Dale Wick-
ell, "Ford SynUS Concept Introduced at 2005 NAIAS in Detroit,"
About: Trucks (September 2005), available online at http://trucks.
about.com/od/conceptcars/ss/05_fordconcepts.htm.

148. Carl Boggs, *Imperial Delusions: American Militarism and
Endless War* (Boulder, CO: Paradigm Publishers, 2005), p. 143.

149. See Joan Roelofs, "Military Contractor Philanthropy: Why
Some Stay Silent," *CounterPunch.org* (January 25, 2006), available
online at http://www.counterpunch.org/roelofs01252006.html.

150. Armitage, "Beyond Hypermodern Militarized Knowledge
Factories," p. 221.

151. Turse, "The Military-Academic Complex."

152. Ibid.

153. Ibid.

154. Jay Reed, "Towards a 21st Century Peace Movement: The
University of Texas Connection," *UTWatch.org,* (September 12, 2001),
available online at http://www.utwatch.org/war/ut_military.html.

155. See, for example, Steve Featherstone, "The Coming Robot Army," *Harper's Magazine* (February 2007), pp. 43–52; David
Hambling, "Military Builds Robotic Insects," *Wired Magazine*
(January 24, 2007), available online at www.commondreams.org/
headlines07/0124-03.htm; and CNN Technology, "Ray Gun Makes
Targets Feel As If They Are on Fire," *CNN.com* (January 25, 2007),
available online at http://www.cnn.com/2007/TECH/01/24/ray.
gun.ap/index.html.

156. William Cole, "Gladiator Robot Looks to Join Marine
Corps," *HonoluluAdvertiser.com* (July 7, 2003), available online
at http://the.honoluluadvertiser.com/article/2003/Jul/07/mn/
mn01a.html.

157. Corilyn Shropshire, "The Gladiator Robot's First Public
Appearance," *Pittsburgh Post-Gazette* (August 5, 2005), available
online at http://www.primidi.com/2005/08/08.html.

158. Reed, "Towards a 21st Century Peace Movement."

159. John Edwards, "Military R&D 101," *ElectronicDesign.com*
(September 1, 2006), available online at http://www.elecdesign.
com/Articles/Index.cfm?AD=1&ArticleID=13281.

160. On the types of future combat systems being developed
by the armed services, see Frida Berrigan, "Raptors, Robots,

and Rods from God: The Nightmare Weaponry of Our Future," *TomDispatch.com* (January 10, 2007), available online at www. commondreams.org/views07/0110-22.htm.

161. Eyal Weizman, "The Art of War," *Frieze.com* (August 1, 2006), available online at http://slash.autonomedia.org/print. pl?sid=06/08/01/2112203. Gen. David H. Petraeus, the new military commander in Iraq, assembled a "small band of warrior-intellectuals ... to reverse the downward trend in the Iraqui war." Petraeus is providing a much expanded role for academics in the war, thus redefining the value of theory and academic knowledge as a tool of warfare. See Thomas E. Ricks, "Officers with PhDs Advising War Effort," *Washington Post* (February 5, 2007), p. A01.

162. Ibid.

163. All of the ideas in this section as well as the quotation are taken from ibid.

164. Turse, "The Military-Academic Complex."

165. Reed, "Towards a 21st Century Peace Movement."

166. Goldie Blumenstyk, "The Military Market," *Chronicle of Higher Education* 52:44 (July 7, 2006), p. A25.

167. Dan Carnevale, "Military Recruiters Play Role of College Counselors," *Chronicle of Higher Education* 52:44 (July 7, 2006), p. A33.

168. Ibid.

169. Blumenstyk, "The Military Market," p. A26.

170. Carnevale, "Military Recruiters Play Role of College Counselors," p. A33.

171. Joan Roelofs, "Military Contractor Philanthropy: Why Some Stay Silent," *CounterPunch.org* (January 25, 2006), available online at http://www.counterpunch.org/roelofs01252006. html. As I mentioned earlier, for a detailed analysis of a military town and the way in which it intersects with industry, politics, power, and ideology, see Lutz, *Homefront: A Military City and the American Twentieth Century.* For a list of cities near military bases, see http://www.militarytowns.com/Cities.asp?Branch=usa.

172. Newsmax, "Tommy Franks: Martial Law Will Replace Constitution After Next Terror Attack" (November 21, 2003), available online at http://www.propagandamatrix.com/211103martiallaw.html.

173. See Chalmers Johnson, *Nemesis* (New York: Metropolitan Books, 2006); Andrew J. Bacevich, *The New American Militarism* (New York: Oxford University Press, 2005); Kevin Baker, "We're in the Army Now," *Harper's Magazine* (October 2003), p. 46; and Chomsky, *Failed States.*

174. Martin, "Manufacturing the Homeland Security Campus and Cadre," p. 1.

175. Golden, "After Sept. 11 CIA Becomes a Growing Force on Campus."

176. Kirsten Searer, "ASU's Crow Partners with CIA on Research Projects," *The Tribune* (March 30, 2003), available online at http://license.icopyright.net/user/viewFreeUse. act?fuid=MTU5NTM5.

177. Mark Clayton, "Higher Espionage," *Christian Science Monitor* (April 29, 2003), available online at http://www.csmonitor.com/2003/0429/p13s01-lehl.html.

178. David N. Gibbs, "The CIA Is Back on Campus," *Times Higher Education Supplement* (April 7, 2003), available online at http://www.counterpunch.org/gibbs04072003.html.

179. Elizabeth Rindskopf Parker, "Academe Must Work with the Intelligence Community," *Chronicle of Higher Education Review* 50:33 (April 23, 2004), p. B24.

180. David Glenn, "Cloak and Classroom," *Chronicle of Higher Education* (March 25, 2005), available online at http://chronicle. com/free/v51/i29/29a01401.htm.

181. Dave H. Price, "The CIA's Campus Spies," *Counterpunch* (March12/13, 2005), available online at www.counterpunch.org/price03122005.html.

182. For background material on Professor Moos's ties to the military and intelligence agencies, see ibid.

183. David Glenn, "Cloak and Classroom—Interview with Felix Moos," *Chronicle of Higher Education* (March 23, 2005), available online at http://chronicle.com/colloquy/2005/03/spies/.

184. David N. Gibbs, "Academics and Spies: The Silence That Roars," *Los Angeles Times* (January 28, 2001), available online at http://www.fas.org/irp/news/2001/01/lat012801.html. For a recent commentary on the unsavory workings of the CIA with its propensity for torture, abduction, and secret prisons, see James Risen, *State of War: The Secret History of the CIA and the Bush Administration* (New York: The Free Press, 2006).

185. Seth Rosenfeld, "Secret FBI Files Reveal Covert Activities at UC Bureau's Campus Operations Involved Reagan, CIA," *The Tribune* (March 30, 2003), available online at http://archives.econ.utah.edu/archives/marxism/2004w22/msg00213.htm.

186. See, for instance, John Prados, *Safe for Democracy: The Secret Wars of the CIA* (Chicago: Ivan Dee Publishers, 2006).

187. This claim was reported by Peter Monaghan in 1999, but I think it is fair to argue that the trend accelerated after September 11, 2001. See Monaghan, "Does International-Relations Scholarship Reflect a Bias Toward the U.S.?" *Chronicle of Higher Education* (September 24, 1999), available online at http://chronicle.com/free/v46/i05/05a02001.htm. See also the more recent commentary in Gibbs, "The CIA Is Back on Campus." For a history of such relations, see Christopher Stimpson, ed., *Universities and Empire: Money, Politics, and Social Sciences During the Cold War* (New York: The New Press, 1980).

188. Cited in Chris Bunting, "I Spy with My Science Eye," *Times Higher Education Supplement* (April 12, 2002), available online at http://homepages.stmartin.edu/fac_staff/dprice/i-spy.html.

189. In fact, the power of the CIA and FBI in domestic intelligence gathering is expanding, as was reported in a 2007 issue of the *New York Times*. Both agencies are now using their power to obtain the banking and credit records of Americans and others who have been accused of terrorism and other crimes in the United States. See Eric Lichtblau and Mark Mazzetti, "Military Expands Intelligence Role in U.S.," *New York Times* (January 14, 2007), p. 1.

190. For an extensive analysis of Senator Roberts's role as chairman of the Senate Select Committee on Intelligence, see "Sen. Pat Roberts (R-KS): Chairman of the Senate Cover-Up Committee," *Think Progress* (March 8, 2006), available online at http://thinkprogress.org/roberts-coverup/.

191. Editorial, "Advice and Assent," *Los Angeles Times* (February 19, 2006), available online at http://www.truthout.org/cgi-bin/artman/exec/view.cgi/48/17831.

192. A description of this program can be found at the government website: www.intelligence.gov/0-prisp.shtml.

193. See, for instance, Seymour M. Hersh, "Last Stand: The Military's Problem with the President's Iran Policy," *New Yorker* (July 7, 2006), available online at www.newyorker.com/printables/fat/060710fa_fact. On Dick Cheney and Donald Rumsfeld's disdain for any intelligence that questioned their absolutist view of the world, see Joan Didion, "Cheney: The Fatal Touch," *New Yorker* (October 5, 2006), available online at http://www.nybooks.com/articles/19376. Of course, there is also the damning evidence revealed in the Downing Street Memo about the Bush administration having already made up its mind to go to war with Iraq despite intelligence that disproved its arguments for doing

so. See Walter Pincus, "British Intelligence Warned of Iraq War," *Washington Post* (May 13, 2005), p. A18.

194. Roberto J. Gonzales, "We Must Fight the Militarization of Anthropology," *Chronicle of Higher Education*, 53:22 (February 2, 2007), p. B20.

195. George Packer, "Knowing the Enemy: Can Social Scientists Redefine the 'War on Terror?'" *New Yorker* (December 11, 2006), available online at http://www.newyorker.com/printables/fact/061218fa_fact2.

196. Ibid.

197. Gonzales, "We Must Fight the Militarization of Anthropology," p. B20.

198. Scott Jaschik, "Torture and Social Scientists," *Inside Higher Ed* (November 22, 2006), available online at http://insidehighered.com/news/2006/11/22/anthro.

199. Cited in David Glenn, "Cloak and Classroom," *Chronicle of Higher Education* (March 25, 2005).

200. See David H. Price, *Threatening Anthropology: McCarthyism and the FBI's Surveillance of Activist Anthropologists* (Durham, NC: Duke University Press, 2004).

201. Price, "The CIA's Campus Spies."

202. Both this quote and the previous one are cited in Glenn, "Cloak and Classroom" (March 25, 2005).

203. See Gibbs, "The CIA Is Back on Campus."

204. Mary Louise Pratt, "Language and National Security: Making a New Public Commitment," *Modern Language Journal* 88:2 (June 2004), p. 291. See also the NSEP/Boren awards created in 1991 to facilitate language study for the purposes of national security, available online at www.iie.org/programs/nsep/graduate/default.htm. For more information on the Bush administration's language initiatives, see Rob Capriccioso and David Epstein, "Bush Push on 'Critical' Foreign Languages," *InsideHigherEd.com* (January 6, 2006), available online at http://www.insidehighered.com/news/2006/01/06/foreign.

205. Cited in Chris Mooney, "For Your Eyes Only: The CIA Will Let You See Classified Documents—But at What Price?" *Lingua Franca* (November 2000), p. 35.

206. Cited in Golden, "After Sept. 11 CIA Becomes a Growing Force on Campus."

207. Martin, "Manufacturing the Homeland Security Campus and Cadre," p. 4.

208. Bacevich, *The New American Militarism*, p. 208.

209. Ibid.

210. Vidal, *Perpetual War for Perpetual Peace*.

211. Armitage, "Beyond Hypermodern Militarized Knowledge Factories."

212. Jorge Mariscal, "Lethal and Compassionate: The Militarization of US Culture," *CounterPunch* (May 3, 2003), available online at http://www.counterpunch.org/mariscal05052003.html.

213. Johnson, *The Sorrows of Empire*, p. 291.

214. See Nelson, "The National Security State," pp. 357–361.

215. Geyer, "The Militarization of Europe, 1914–1945," p. 79.

216. Chalmers Johnson, "Empire v. Democracy," *TomDispatch. com* (January 31, 2007), available online at http://www.commondreams.org/cgi-bin/print.cgi?file=/views07/0131-27.htm.

217. For information on the PAMO and its efforts to resist the militarization of OISE, see http://www.homesnotbombs.ca/oiseprotest.htm.

218. The work of the Media Education Foundation can be found online at http://www.mediaed.org/about.

219. See "No Space Wars: Songs for Peace in Space," available online at http://www.spinspace.com/cd/artists.html.

220. Mariscal, "Lethal and Compassionate."

221. Jacques Ranciere, "Democracy, Republic, Representation," *Constellations* 13:3 (2006), p. 299.

222. Nick Couldry, "In the Place of a Common Culture, What?" *Review of Education, Pedagogy, and Cultural Studies* 26 (2004), p. 11.

223. Ibid., p. 12.

224. See, for example, the very powerful film *Sir, No Sir!* at http://www.sirnosir.com/.

225. Lutz, "Making War at Home in the United States," p. 731.

226. Timothy Brennan and Keya Ganguly, "Crude Wars," *South Atlantic Quarterly* 105:1 (Winter 2006), pp. 28–29.

227. Gore Vidal, *Perpetual War for Perpetual Peace: How We Got to Be So Hated* (New York: Nation Books, 2002), pp. 22–40.

228. See William Blum, *Killing Hope: US Military and CIA Interventions Since World War II* (Monroe, ME: Common Courage Press, 1995); Clara Nieto, *Masters of War: Latin America and U.S. Aggression* (New York: Seven Stories Press, 2003); and Chomsky, *Hegemony or Survival.*

229. See Johnson, *Nemesis*, p. 15.

230. Andrew J. Bacevich, "The Normalization of War," *Mother Jones* (April 2005), available online at http://www.motherjones. com/news/dailymojo/2005/04/bacevich.html.

◇

2

Marketing the University

Corporate Power and the Academic Factory

> Democracy expresses itself in a continuous and re-
> lentless critique of institutions; democracy is an an-
> archic, disruptive element inside the political system;
> essentially, a force of *dissent* and change. One can
> best recognize a democratic society by its constant
> complaints that it is not democratic enough.
>
> —*Zygmunt Bauman*

In a United States that seems increasingly intent on corporatizing the public sphere and shifting wealth from the
working poor and middle class to the rich, too little attention
has been given by the American public to the way in which
higher education is being divorced from its traditionally
vaunted role as a crucial pedagogical site for educating
students as engaged and critical citizens.[1] Similarly, considered primarily as an elite class due to their educational
status and the practice of tenure, professors working for
universities have largely been ignored.[2] Moreover, questions
regarding whether the university should serve the public
rather than private interests no longer carry the weight of
forceful criticism as they did when raised by Thorstein Veblen, C. Wright Mills, and Robert Lynd in the first half of the
twentieth century.[3] However, given the university's key role
in public life as the protector and promoter of democratic

102

values, it is worthwhile to take a look at how public policy is changing American higher education.

Under the governance of the Bush administration, right-wing forces have attempted to exert more control over higher education, and there is little in their vision of the university that imagines young people as anything other than a market for corporate exploitation or an appendage of the Department of Homeland Security. In a country where corporations such as Halliburton and Bechtel rapaciously profit from the war in Iraq, the Food and Drug Administration appears more concerned about the financial well-being of the pharmaceutical industry than the health of the general public, and the federal government extends massive tax cuts to the rich amid increasing poverty, hunger, and job losses, the university seems to offer no escape and little resistance. Instead, the humanistic knowledge and values of the university are being excised as higher education becomes increasingly corporatized. The corporate university, according to Richard Ohmann,

> acts like a profit-making business rather than a public or philanthropic trust. Thus, we hear of universities applying productivity and performance measures to teaching (Illinois); of plans to put departments in competition with one another for resources (Florida); of cutting faculty costs not only by replacing full-timers with part-timers and temps and by subcontracting for everything from food services to the total management of physical plants, but also by substituting various schemes of computerized instruction; and so on.[4]

Such corporatization affects not only the culture of the campus but also the very content delivered by the university, as academic labor is increasingly based on corporate needs rather than on the demands of research for the public good or on education designed to improve public life.[5] In the corporate university, academics are now expected to be "academic entrepreneurs," valuable only for the money and prestige they bring, and not for the education they can offer. Sacrificed in this transformation is any notion of higher education as a crucial public sphere in which critical citizens and democratic agents are formed and become capable of addressing the anti-democratic forces that threaten democracy in the United States.

The appeal to excellence by university CEOs now functions like a corporate logo, hyping efficiency while denuding critical thought and scholarship of any intellectual and political substance. The language of market fundamentalism and the emerging corporate university radically alter the vocabulary available for appraising the meaning of citizenship, agency, and civic virtue. Within this discourse everything is for sale, and what is not has no value as a public good or practice. The traditional academic imperative to "publish or perish" is now supplemented with the neoliberal mantra "privatize or perish" as everyone in the university is transformed into an entrepreneur, customer, or client, and every relationship is ultimately judged in bottom-line, cost-effective terms. As the university is annexed by defense, corporate, and national security interests, critical scholarship is replaced by research for either weapons technology or commercial profits, just as the private intellectual now replaces the public intellectual, and the public relations intellectual supplants the engaged intellectual in the wider culture.

While the university should equip people to enter the workplace, it should also educate them to contest workplace inequalities, imagine democratically organized forms of work, and identify and challenge those injustices that contradict and undercut the most fundamental principles of freedom, equality, and respect for all people who constitute the global public sphere. Higher education is about more than job preparation and consciousness-raising; it is also about imagining different futures and politics as a form of intervention into public life. In contrast to the cynicism and political withdrawal fostered by media culture, education demands that citizens be able to negotiate the interface of private considerations and public issues, be able to recognize those undemocratic forces that deny social, economic, and political justice, and be willing to give some thought to the nature and meaning of their experiences in struggling for a better world.

The University as Brand-Name Corporation

Anyone who spends any time on a college campus in the United States these days cannot miss how higher education is changing. Strapped for money and increasingly defined through the language of corporate culture, many universities seem less interested in higher learning than in becoming licensed storefronts for brand-name corporations—selling off space, buildings, and endowed chairs to rich corporate donors. University bookstores are now managed by big corporate conglomerates such as Barnes & Noble, while companies such as Sodexho-Marriott (also a large investor in the U.S. private prison industry) run a large percentage of college dining halls, and McDonald's and Starbucks occupy prominent locations on the student commons. Student IDs are now adorned with MasterCard and Visa logos, providing students who may have few assets with an instant line of credit and an identity as full-time consumers.

In addition, housing, alumni relations, health care, and a vast array of other services are now being leased out to private interests to manage and run. One consequence is that spaces on university campuses once marked as public and noncommodified—places for quiet study or student gatherings—now have the appearance of a shopping mall. Commercial logos, billboards, and advertisements plaster the walls of student centers, dining halls, cafeterias, and bookstores. Administrators at York University in Toronto solicited a number of corporations to place their logos on university-sponsored online courses "for ten thousand dollars per course."[6] Everywhere students turn outside of the university classroom, they are confronted with vendors and commercial sponsors who are hawking credit cards, athletic goods, soft drinks, and other commodities that one associates with the local shopping mall. Universities and

colleges compound this marriage of commercial and educational values by signing exclusive contracts with Pepsi,
Nike, and other contractors, further blurring the distinction
between student and consumer. The message to students
is clear: Customer satisfaction is offered as a surrogate for
learning; "to be a citizen is to be a consumer, and nothing
more. Freedom means freedom to purchase."[7]

Why should we care? Colleges and universities do not
simply produce knowledge and new perspectives for students; they also play an influential role in shaping their
identities, values, and sense of what it means to become
citizens of the world. If colleges and universities are to define themselves as centers of teaching and learning vital
to the democratic life of the nation and globe, they must
acknowledge the real danger of becoming mere adjuncts to
big business, or corporate entities in themselves. As Robert
Zemsky warns, "When the market interests totally dominate colleges and universities, their role as public agencies
significantly diminishes—as does their capacity to provide
venues for the testing of new ideas and the agendas for
public action."[8]

And the threat is real. Commercial deals are no longer
just a way for universities to make money. Corporate brand-
ing drives the administrative structure of the university.
College presidents are now called CEOs and are known
less for their intellectual leadership than for their role as
fundraisers and their ability to bridge the world of academe
and business. Gone are the days when university presidents
were hired for their intellectual status and public roles. One
example can be found in the hiring of Michael Crow as the
president of Arizona State University (ASU) in 2002. Crow,
a former vice-provost at Columbia University and head of
In-Q-Tel Inc., a nonprofit venture capital arm of the CIA,
has attempted with a vengeance to organize ASU along corporate lines. G. A. Clark, a faculty member at ASU, sums
up Crow's approach to corporatizing the university:

> His strategy: stripping the university of any form of faculty
> governance (he threatened the leaders of our notoriously

invertebrate Academic Senate), firing anyone who didn't agree with his "vision" regardless of their qualifications and service records, using existing units and programs as "cover" for on-campus classified research, ordering faculty appointments for government and industry biochemists with no academic experience, over the objections of unit heads (who were then sacked from their administrative posts), increasing our debt load to [more than] $850M (so much so that it has threatened our bonding authority), agreeing to increase our enrollments to 100,000 students by 2020 (ASU is already the largest university in the country), and creating a 2-tier faculty consisting of a minority who will have what I regard as a "normal" university experience, and condemning the rest to community college status (understandably, anyone who can do so is leaving).[9]

With entrepreneurial types such as Crow now filling the ranks of university presidents, it is not surprising that venture capitalists scour colleges and universities in search of big profits to be made through licensing agreements, the control of intellectual property rights, and investing in university spinoff companies. Deans are likewise often hired from the ranks of the business community and, increasingly, the intelligence agencies, and are evaluated on the basis of their ability to attract external funding and impose business models of leadership and accountability. As Stanley Aronowitz points out, "Today . . . leaders of higher education wear the badge of corporate servants proudly."[10] And why not, when the notion of market-driven education has the full support of the Bush-type Republicans and their corporate allies? Scholarship is increasingly measured not by the search for truth, rigor, or its social contributions. On the contrary, it is all too willingly defined in support of market needs, just as funding for university programs is related to the commodification of ideas and the accumulation of profits. The dean at my former university, Penn State, not only viewed education as a depoliticized discourse, he also completely collapsed the distinction between scholarship and grant-getting by handing out distinguished professorships to academics who secured large grants but did very little in the way of either making important theoretical contributions or publishing widely recognized scholarly work. Needless to say, his contempt for rigorous and engaged scholarship was reinforced by his utter lack of vision and leadership regarding the role the college of education and university might assume outside a narrow and instrumentalized corporate logic. What is missing from the space of the corporate university is any perspective suggesting that, at the very least, university administrators, academics, students, and others exercise the political, civic, and ethical courage needed to refuse the commercial rewards that would reduce them to becoming simply another brand name, corporate logo, or adjunct to corporate interests.

Public Policy and Corporate Education

The Bush administration has willingly supported the corporatization of higher education through both overt statements and reinforcing the conditions that make such corporatization possible. Reductions in grants for students, pressure on students to use their education as job-training, and the replacement of government grants with corporate-sponsored loans have facilitated the process. As the Bush administration cut student aid, plundered public services, and pushed states to the brink of financial disaster, higher education increasingly became a privilege rather than a right. Many middle- and working-class students have either found it financially impossible to enter college or, because of increased costs, have had to drop out. As the *Chronicle of Higher Education* reported, young people from poor and disadvantaged families face even more difficult hurdles in trying to attain a college education because the Bush administration decided to cut Pell Grants, the nation's largest federal student aid program. In addition, because Congress changed the federal needs-analysis formula, more than 90,000 disadvantaged students were disqualified in 2005 from receiving not only Pell Grants but also state financial aid.[11]

As all levels of government reduce their funding to higher education, not only will tuition increase but student loans will gradually replace grants and scholarships. Lacking adequate financial aid, students, especially poor students, will have to finance the high costs of their education through private corporations such as Citibank, Chase Manhattan, Marine Midland, and other lenders. According to The Project on Student Debt, nearly two-thirds of both undergraduate and graduate students at four-year colleges and public universities have student loans.[12] While it makes sense to focus on such issues as the impact of corporate interests on research, the shift in governance from faculty to business-oriented administrators, and the massive increase in adjuncts and casual labor, little has been said about the corporate structuring of student debt and its impact on a sizeable number of people attending higher education. Rather than work their way through college, students now borrow their way to graduation and, in doing so, have been collectively labeled a "generation of debt."[13] As Jeff Williams points out, the average student now graduates with debts that are staggering:

> The average undergraduate student loan debt in 2002 was $18,900. It more than doubled from 1992, when it was $9,200. Added to this is charge card debt, which averaged $3,000 in 2002, boosting the average total debt to about $22,000. One can reasonably expect, given still accelerating costs, that it is over $30,000 now. Bear in mind that this does not include other private loans or the debt that parents take on to send their children to college. (Neither does it account for "'post-baccalaureate loans,'" which more than doubled in seven years from $18,572 in 1992–1993 to $38,000 in1999–2000, and have likely doubled again).[14]

Saddled with enormous debts, many students find that their career choices are severely limited to jobs in the corporate workforce that offer them entry-level salaries that make it possible to pay off their loans. Indentured for decades in order to pay off such loans, these students find it difficult to consider public service jobs or jobs that offer rewards other than high salaries. One recent survey reported that "two-thirds of law graduates say that debt is a primary factor in keeping them from considering a career in public interest law. . . . Other surveys have found that about half of the students who begin law school with stated public interest law commitments go into private practice law upon graduation in large part because of their debt burden."[15]

For many young people caught in the margins of poverty, low-paying jobs, recession, and "jobless recovery," the potential costs of higher education, regardless of its status or availability, will dissuade them from even thinking about attending college. Unfortunately, as state and federal agencies and university systems direct more and more of their resources (such as state tax credits and scholarship programs) toward middle- and upper-income students and away from need-based aid, the growing gap in college enrollments between high-income students (95 percent enrollment rate) and low-income students (75 percent enrollment rate) with comparable academic abilities will widen even further.[16] In fact, a report by a federal advisory committee claimed that nearly 48 percent of qualified students from low-income families would not be attending college in the fall of 2002 because of rising tuition charges and a shortfall in federal and state grants. The report specifically noted that "[n]early 170,000 of the top high-school graduates from low- and moderate-income families are not enrolling in college this year because they cannot afford to do so."[17] A 2006 government report titled "Mortgaging Our Future: How Financial Barriers to College Undercut America's Global Competitiveness" stated that "1.4 million to 2.4 million bachelor's degrees will be lost this decade as financial concerns prevent academically qualified students from the lowest income bracket from attending college." And the report suggested that these figures are conservative.[18]

When universities can no longer balance their budget through tuition increases or federal grants, they turn to corporate money and self-branding to balance their finances. Students become "customers," both of the university's own brand and of corporations that sell to them directly through university deals. It gets worse. As Michael Yates points out,

> management tells us that our students are consumers of a product, no different in principle than the fact that they are consumers of CD players and sneakers. We must be concerned only with the quality of our product, but the clear implication is that education must be on par with CD players if education's quality is to be measured in the same way as that of the CD player. Measurable competencies are taking the place of all-around education, something which (by its very nature) cannot be measured or quality-controlled. And as students pick up on this notion of themselves as consumers of a measurable product, they come to treat education as a purchase.[19]

Although higher education has never been free of the market, there is a new intimacy between higher education and corporate culture, characterized by what Larry Hanley has called a "new, quickened symbiosis."[20] The result is "not a fundamental or abrupt change perhaps, but still an unmistakable radical reduction of [higher education's] public and critical role."[21] What was once the hidden curriculum of many universities—the subordination of higher education to capital—has now become an open and much celebrated policy of both public and private higher education. Increasingly, references to higher education as a valuable commodity or for-profit business have become all too common.[22] For example, the former president of American University, Milton Greenberg, argues that it is an utterly romanticized assumption to suggest education is *not* a business, and that such romanticism is reinforced by another myth attributed to the romantic age of higher education: namely, "that the substance of teaching, research and learning—protected by academic freedom and professional standards—is not ordinarily subject to profit-and-loss analysis."[23] For Greenberg, education and training for employment appear to be the same thing and, as such, reinforce the charge that the liberal arts have become useless since they do not translate directly into jobs. Greenberg is utterly indifferent to the increasing commodification of knowledge, the secrecy imposed on academics on corporate payrolls, the dismantling of democratic forms of governance, and the increased use of higher education to produce products that can be sold in the market. Not unlike the market fundamentalists or super-patriots who want to either privatize higher education or turn it into a bastion of the national security state, Greenberg is blind to the assumption that such forces might pose a grave threat to academic freedom and the function of the university as a democratic public sphere.

But Greenberg is more than indifferent; he also believes that investments in the public good are a burden on taxpayers, which explains his view that there is no need for faculty to meet students in classrooms when both parties can communicate over email, thus cutting back on large investments (subsidized partly by tax dollars) in buildings and infrastructures. And, finally, there is the tenure system, which Greenberg suggests has nothing to do with academic freedom and is at odds with the managerial principles that work so well in the world of business—that is, outsourcing, downsizing, privatization, increasing casual labor, rule by the few, and deadening forms of accountability. I have focused on Greenberg because he is all too representative of what Stanley Aronowitz calls a powerful and growing "administrative class whose economic and ideological interests are tied to the corporate order and an increasingly intrusive state in everyday academic affairs, especially abrogating faculty's control over hiring, tenure, and promotion, curricular matters, and its own production of knowledge."[24]

As the line between for-profit and not-for-profit institutions of higher education blurs, the distinctions between democratic values and market interests, between education and job training, collapse. If right-wing reforms in higher education continue unchallenged, the consequence will be a highly undemocratic, bifurcated civic body. In other words, we will have a society in which a highly trained, largely white elite will be allowed to command the techno-information revolution while a low-skilled majority of poor and minority workers will be relegated to filling the McJobs proliferating in the service sector.

An even closer symbiosis of corporate and university culture takes place among faculty who traditionally have sought outside support for research. As government grant money dries up, such researchers must turn for support to corporate funders (for example, as I mention elsewhere in this book, funding from the agencies that make up the national security state). Higher education's need for new sources of funding neatly dovetails with the inexhaustible need on the part of corporations for new products. Within this symbiotic relationship, knowledge is directly linked to its application in the market, resulting in a collapse of the distinction between knowledge and commodity. At the same time, as universities increasingly begin to pattern themselves after multinational businesses, they are more willing to allow corporations that sponsor research to influence the outcome of or place questionable restrictions on what can be published. Knowledge, especially scientific knowledge, has become privatized and commodified, and collaborative relationships among faculty suffer as some firms insist that the results of corporate-sponsored research be kept secret. In a similar manner, researchers funded by corporations have been prohibited from speaking about their research at conferences, talking on the phone with colleagues, or making their labs available to faculty and students not directly involved in the research. Derek Bok reports that "[n]early one in five life-science professors admitted that they had delayed publication by more than six months for commercial reasons."[25] Equally disturbing are both the growing number of academics who either hold company stocks or have financial connections to the company sponsoring their research and the refusals on the part of many universities to institute disclosure policies that would reveal such conflicts of interest.[26] Not only have corporate-sponsored protocols regarding disclosure had "a chilling effect on the tradition of scientific transparency, shared knowledge, and open debate about scientific discoveries," but, in other cases, "as corporate partners demand that researchers keep ahead of the competition, the erosion of the ethic of honesty has led to frequent instances of fraud in reporting evidence."[27] As the boundaries between public and commercial values become blurred, many academics appear less as disinterested truth seekers than as apologists for corporate profiteering.

The disintegration of academic integrity and openness is particularly startling with respect to corporate-funded medical research. The *New England Journal of Medicine* reported in 2002 that "medical schools that conduct research sponsored by drug companies routinely disregard guidelines intended to ensure that the studies are unbiased and that the results are shared with the public."[28] And the *Journal of the American Medical Association* reported in 2003 that "one fourth of biomedical scientists have financial affiliations with industry ... and that research financed by industry is more likely to draw commercially favourable conclusions."[29] Corporate power and influence also shape the outcome of the research and design of clinical trials. Hence, it is not surprising to find, as the latter journal stated, that "studies reported by the tobacco industry reported pro-industry results [and that] studies on pharmaceuticals were affected by their source of funds as well."[30] In some instances, corporations place pressure on universities to suppress the publication of those studies whose data question the effectiveness of the wares, threatening not only academic integrity but also public health and safety. For example, Canada's largest pharmaceutical company, Apotex, attempted to suppress the findings of a University of Toronto researcher, Dr. Nancy Olivieri, when she argued that the "drug the company was manufacturing was ineffective, and could even be toxic."[31] The University of Toronto not only refused to provide support for Dr. Olivieri, it also suspended her from her administrative role as program director and warned her and her staff not to talk publicly about the case. It was later disclosed that "the university and Apotex had been for some years in discussions about a multimillion-dollar gift to the university and its teaching hospitals."[32] There is also the troubling case of Professor

Ignacio H. Chapela, an assistant professor of ecology at the University of California at Berkeley and an outspoken critic of what he calls the university's "dangerous liaisons with the biotechnology industry."[33] In denying him tenure, the university overruled his department and an outside ad hoc committee of specialists, appointed by a committee of the academic senate. One member of the ad hoc committee, Professor Wayne Getz, expressed shock at the refusal of the university to give Chapela tenure. Getz stated that "I've been here 24 years, and my understanding is that if the department and the ad hoc committee recommend for tenure, you get tenure."[34] Many people believe that Professor Chapela did not get tenure because he had been a resolute critic of a 1998 multimillion-dollar research grant deal between UC-Berkeley and Novartis, a Swiss biotechnology company. In an article coauthored with David Quist, a graduate student, published in *Nature* in November 2001, he further antagonized the biotech industries by criticizing the development of genetically modified crops. In what was viewed as a highly controversial paper, Chapela and Quist argued that "native corn in Mexico had been contaminated by material from genetically modified corn,"[35] a charge that disputed the claim of many agricultural companies that genetically modified materials do not travel from one field to another. Mexico took this claim seriously and banned the planting of bioengineered corn for fear that it might damage the country's native varieties; the Environment Ministry of the Mexican Government later verified Chapela and Quist's findings. Their paper came under attack from a number of scientists, especially on biotech-related websites, many of whom wrote letters to *Nature* calling the science in the paper faulty. Researchers determined that "two of the most vocal critics denouncing the paper online were 'Mary Murphy' and 'Andura Smetacek,' names that were later revealed to be fabricated. It was discovered that one of the electronic personas came from a Washington, DC–based public relations company that worked for Monsanto, a leading biotechnology company."[36] The pressure put on *Nature* prevailed, and for the first time in its history it published a disclaimer indicating that the research findings did not justify the paper's conclusions. Chapela claims that "the journal had been pressured by scientists working with the biotechnology industry."[37]

Some universities such as Yale, the University of Pennsylvania, and Stanford have instituted new regulatory controls to eliminate some of the more blatant conflicts of interest and corrupting industry influences that characterize the increasingly cozy relationship between higher education and corporations. For example, Stanford University Medical Center "prohibits physicians from accepting any gifts from industry representatives while the physicians are working on the medical-center campus or at off-campus clinical sites. It also bans industry representatives from patient-care areas and the medical school, including research areas, unless they have appointments to train health-care workers to use their companies' equipment."[38]

Turning higher education into the handmaiden of corporate culture works against the critical social imperative of educating citizens who can sustain and develop inclusive democratic public spheres. Lost in the merging of corporate culture and higher education is a historic and honorable democratic tradition that extends from John Adams to W.E.B. DuBois to John Dewey and that extols the importance of education as essential for a vibrant democracy.[39] Education within this democratic tradition integrated individual autonomy with the principles of social responsibility. Moreover, it cast a critical eye on the worst temptations of profit-making and market-driven values. For example, Sheila Slaughter has argued persuasively that at the close of the nineteenth century, "professors made it clear that they did not want to be part of a cutthroat capitalism.... Instead, they tried to create a space between capital and labor where [they] could support a common intellectual project directed toward the public good."[40] Amherst College President Alexander Meiklejohn echoed this sentiment in 1916 when he suggested:

> Insofar as a society is dominated by the attitudes of competitive business enterprise, freedom in its proper American

meaning cannot be known, and hence, cannot be taught. That is the basic reason why the schools and colleges, which are presumably commissioned to study and promote the ways of freedom, are so weak, so confused, so ineffectual.[41]

As university leaders increasingly appeal to the corporate world for funding, engage in money-making ventures as a measure of excellence, and ignore that the line between for-profit and not-for-profit institutions of higher education is collapsing, many schools, as educator John Palattela observes, will simply "serve as personnel offices for corporations"[42] and quickly dispense with the historically burdened though important promise of creating democratic mandates for higher education.

Of all groups, university and college educators should be the most vocal and militant in challenging the corporatization of education by making clear that at the heart of any form of inclusive democracy is the assumption that learning should be used to expand the public good, create a culture of questioning, and promote democratic social change. Individual and social agency becomes meaningful as part of the willingness to imagine otherwise, "in order to help us find our way to a more human future."[43] Under such circumstances, knowledge can be used for amplifying human freedom and promoting social justice, and not simply for creating profits.

The Academic Entrepreneur

As corporate culture and values shape university life, academic labor is increasingly being transformed into the image of a multinational conglomerate workforce. While corporate values such as efficiency and downsizing in higher education appear to have caught the public's imagination at the moment, this belies the fact that such "reorganization" has been going on for some time. What is new is that the ever growing and "steady corporatization of American higher education has threatened to relegate faculty governance to the historical archive."[44] The modern university was once governed, however weakly, by faculty, with the faculty senate naming the university president. That era of faculty control is long gone, with presidents now being named by boards of trustees, and governing through hand-picked (and well-paid) bureaucrats rather than through faculty committees. John Silber, the former president of Boston University from 1971 to 1996, best exemplifies this trend. As a number of notable academics and public figures have pointed out, Silber often used his administrative power to weaken faculty governance, "punish his critics—sometimes by denial of tenure (against faculty recommendation), sometimes by refusing merit raises and leaves, sometimes by personal abuse (including a false charge of arson, later withdrawn, against a member of the faculty)," by engaging in "repeated violations of civil liberties," and by promoting educational theories that by any progressive standard would have to be judged as reactionary.[45] Faculty power once rested in the fact that most faculty were full-time and a large percentage of them had tenure, so they could confront administrators without fear of losing their jobs. One of the first steps taken by the newly corporatized university in the 1980s was to limit faculty power by hiring fewer full-time faculty, promoting fewer faculty to tenure, and instituting "post-tenure" reviews that threaten to take tenure away.

When full-time academic labor is outsourced to temporary or contract labor, the intellectual culture of the university declines as overworked graduate students and part-time faculty assume the role of undergraduate teaching with little or no portion of their time and pay allotted for research. Moreover, these contingent faculty are granted no role in the university governance process, are detached from the intellectual life of the university, rarely have time to engage in sustained scholarship, and appear largely as interchangeable instructors acting more like temporary visitors. In short, the hiring of part-time faculty to minimize costs maximizes managerial control not just over faculty but over the educational process itself. Power now resides in the hands of a new cadre of corporate-oriented trustees and administrators who proudly define themselves as entrepreneurs rather than as educational leaders. As democratic decision-making in the university dwindles, questions regarding the social responsibility of higher education disappear from public view and both the democratization of the university and "the democratization of society" are undermined.[46]

One possibility of what the future holds for the corporatizing of higher education can be seen in the example of Rio Salado College in Tempe, Arizona. The college is the second largest in the Maricopa County Community College District and has a total of 13,314 students.[47] And yet it has "only 33 permanent faculty members, 27 of whom are full-time."[48] Its classes are almost entirely virtual, and it hires close to 1,000 part-time instructors scattered across the state. The part-time faculty carry the bulk of the teaching and are paid about $2,200 a course. Teaching eight courses, four each semester, calculates to slightly less than $18,000 a year, which amounts to poverty-level wages. The few, privileged full-time faculty earn between $40,000 and $88,000 a year.[49] The academic labor force at Rio Salado College in this instance has been, for the most part, entirely casualized with almost no possibility that any of its 1,000 members will land a full-time position. Linda Thor, the president of Rio Salado College, who proudly defines herself as a model of corporate leadership, often quotes from best-selling business books and "embraces the idea of students as customers."[50] Moreover, consistent with Thor's embrace of corporate principles and an efficiency-minded management style, the day-to-day duties of instructors at the college are "simplified by RioLearn, a course-management system designed specifically for the college through a partnership with Dell Inc. and the Microsoft Corporation."[51] Most important, this utterly privatized, fragmented, exploitative, and commercialized vision of higher education should not be dismissed as a quirky approach to university administration. In this view, power, time, and decision-making are completely controlled by administrators who view faculty subordination to corporate control "a thing of nature, and, more to the point, the royal road to academic and financial reward."[52] The latter is obvious in terms of the ways in which nonprofit institutions are emulating this model. For instance, the University of Illinois, which has three land-grant nonprofit campuses, plans to launch a whole new college, which would be completely online, operate as a for-profit entity, and consist almost entirely of part-time faculty, with no tenured faculty at all. Issues central to university culture such as tenure, academic freedom, and intellectual integrity are dispensed with as faculty governance is now put largely into the hands of administrators, and faculty are reduced to outsourced, casual labor—all in the name of official realpolitik. Allegedly, the rationale for this utterly corporatized approach to education is to make the University of Illinois more competitive, while providing "access to high-quality education first and foremost to the people of Illinois."[53] In my view, this educational model with its stripped-down version of teaching, its cost-efficiency model of management, and its view of students as customers and of faculty as a source of cheap labor is exactly what informs the current corporate understanding of the future of higher education. Representing the face of higher education in the age of global capital and market fundamentalism, it is less about education than about training, less about educating students to be informed and responsible citizens of the world than about short-term returns on revenue, all the time providing a pseudo-academic warrant to reduce education to an extension of the corporate world. Clearly, this is a view that needs to be resisted if higher education is to retain any democratic value and sense of social responsibility.

The American Council of Education reported in 2002 that "[t]he number of part-time faculty members increased by 79 percent from 1981 to 1999, to more than 400,000 out of a total of one million instructors overall," and that the "biggest growth spurt occurred between 1987 and 1993, when 82 percent of the 120,000 new faculty members hired during that period were for part-time positions."[54]

In fact, more professors are working part-time and at two-year community colleges now than at any other time in the country's recent history. The American Association of University Professors reported in 2004 that "44.5 percent of all faculty are part-time, and non-tenure-track positions of all types account for more than 60 percent of all faculty appointments in American higher education."[55] Creating a permanent underclass of part-time professional workers in higher education is not only demoralizing and exploitative for the many faculty who have such jobs but also deskills both part- and full-time faculty by increasing the amount of work they have to do. With less time to prepare, larger class loads, almost no time for research, and excessive grading demands, many adjuncts run the risk of becoming demoralized and ineffective. Any analysis concerning the deskilling and disempowering of faculty points to a politics of temporality, and how time is controlled and for whom at all levels of higher education. Time is crucial to how a university structures its public mission, shapes governance with faculty, controls the use of space, and limits or expands student access, as well as how it is organized in the legitimation and organization of particular forms of knowledge, research, and pedagogy. For the past twenty years, time as a value and the value of time have been redefined through the dictates of neoliberal economics, which have largely undermined any notion of public time guided by the noncommodified values central to a political and social democracy. In higher education, corporate time maps faculty relationships through self-promoting market agendas and narrow definitions of self-interest. Caught on the treadmill of getting more grants, teaching larger classes, and producing revenue for the university, faculty become another casualty of a business ideology that attempts to "extract labor from campus workers at the lowest possible cost, one willing to sacrifice research independence and integrity for profit."[56] Time in this context is less about providing opportunities for faculty dialogue, shared responsibilities, class preparation, and rigorous scholarship than it is about a notion of *corporate time*, which is sped up, accelerated, and compressed. Time in its corporate versions becomes a deprivation rather than a resource, a temporality designed to excise any notion of self-development, an expansive sense of agency, and critical thought itself. Grounded in the culture of hierarchical power relations, post-Fordist managerial principles, competitiveness, and bottom-line interests, corporate time reworks faculty loyalties, transforming educators into dispensable labor with little or no power over the basic decisions that structure academic work.[57] Faculty interaction is structured less around collective solidarities built upon practices that offer a productive relationship to public life than around corporate-imposed rituals of competition and production that conform to the "narrowly focused idea of the university as a support to the economy."[58] But more is reproduced than structural dislocations among faculty: There is also an alarming preponderance of crippling fear, insecurity, and resentment that makes it difficult for faculty to take risks, forge bonds of solidarity, engage in social criticism, and perform as public intellectuals rather than as technicians in the service of corporate largesse. These structural and ideological factors threaten to undermine the collective power that faculty need to challenge the increasingly corporate-based, top-down administrative structures that are becoming commonplace in many colleges and universities. Powerlessness breeds resentment and anger among part-time faculty, and fear and despair among full-time faculty, who feel their tenure is no longer secure. The ease with which tenured faculty can now be replaced has been demonstrated in recent years by major universities such as Penn State, which fired feminist, drama professor Nona Gerard for writing "derogatory" email messages in which she complained about the lack of resources for her program, criticized the performance of some of her colleagues, and staged a play that a right-wing donor found offensive because of its partial nudity and sexually explicit language.[59]

Such academic downsizing has been legitimized through a particularly debased notion of professionalism that bears little resemblance to its once-stated emphasis on quality teaching, creative research, and public service. The new corporate professionalism now positions and rewards educators as narrow specialists, unencumbered by matters of ethics, power, and ideology. No longer concerned with important social issues, democratic values, or the crucial task of educating students about important historical, cultural, social, and theoretical traditions, corporate-inspired notions of professionalism now shift the emphasis from the quality of academic work to a crude emphasis on quantity, from creativity and critical dialogue in the classroom to standardization and narrow assessment schemes, from supporting full-time tenured positions to constructing an increasing army of contract workers, and from rigorous scholarship and engagement with public issues to the push for grant writing and external funding.

The turn toward downsizing and deskilling faculty is also exacerbated by the attempts on the part of many universities to expand into the profitable market of "distance education," whose online courses reach thousands of students. David Noble has written extensively on the restructuring of higher education under the imperatives of the new digital technologies and the move into distance education. If he is correct, the news is not good. Distance education fuels the rise in the use of part-time faculty, who will be "perfectly suited to the investor-imagined university of the future."[60] According to Noble, online learning largely functions through pedagogical models and methods of delivery that not only rely on standardized, prepackaged curricula and methodological efficiency but also reinforce the commercial penchant toward training students and further deskilling the professoriate. The former president of Teachers College at Columbia University, Arthur Levine, has predicted that the new information technology may soon make the traditional college and university obsolete, and he is not alone in this view.[61] More than half of the nation's colleges and universities deliver courses online or over the Internet.[62] Mass-marketed degrees and courses are not only being offered by prestigious universities such as Seton Hall,

Stanford, Harvard, the New School, and the University of Chicago; they are also giving rise to cyber-backed colleges such as the Western Governors University and for-profit, stand-alone, publicly traded institutions such as the University of Phoenix. The marriage of corporate culture, higher education, and the new high-speed technologies also offers universities big opportunities to cut back on maintenance expenses, eliminate entire buildings such as libraries and classroom facilities, and trim labor costs.[63]

This is not to say that technologies such as email, on-line discussion groups, and the Internet cannot improve classroom instruction by ameliorating existing modes of communication, or by simply making academic work more interesting. The real issue is whether such technology in its various pedagogical uses in higher education is governed by a technocratic rationality that undermines human freedom and democratic values. As Herbert Marcuse has argued, when the rationality that drives technology is instrumentalized and "transformed into standardized efficiency ... liberty is confined to the selection of the most adequate means for reaching a goal which [the individual] did not set."[64] The consequence of the substitution of technology for pedagogy is that instrumental goals replace ethical and political considerations, diminishing classroom control by teachers while offering a dehumanizing pedagogy for students.

Increasingly, academics find themselves pressured to teach more service-oriented and market-based courses. The processes of vocationalization—fueled by corporate values that mimic "flexibility," "competition," or "lean production," and rationalized through the application of accounting principles—threaten to gut many academic departments and programs that cannot translate their subject matter into commercial gains. As Michael Peters observes, entire disciplines and bodies of knowledge are now either valued or devalued on the basis of their "ability to attract global capital and ... potential for serving transnational corporations. Knowledge is valued for its strict utility rather than as an end in itself or for its emancipatory effects."[65] Good value for students means taking courses labeled as "relevant" in market terms, which are often counterposed to courses in the social sciences, humanities, and the fine arts that are concerned with forms of learning that do not readily translate into either private gain or commercial value. Similarly, many universities are finding that their remedial programs, affirmative action programs, and other crucial pedagogical resources are under massive assault, often by conservative trustees who want to eliminate from the university any attempt to address the deep inequities in society, while simultaneously denying a decent education to minorities of color and class. For example, City University of New York, as a result of a decision made by its board of trustees, decided to end "its commitment to provide remedial courses for unprepared students, many of whom are immigrants requiring language training before or concurrent with entering the ordinary academic discipline.... Consequently ... a growing number of prospective college students are forced on an already overburdened job market."[66] Both professors and students increasingly bear the burden of overcrowded classes, limited resources, and hostile legislators.

At the same time, while compassion and concern for students and teachers wane, universities are eagerly courting big business: "In recent years academic institutions and a growing number of Internet companies have been racing to tap into the booming market in virtual learning."[67] As colleges and corporations collaborate over the content of degree programs, particularly with regard to online graduate degree programs, college curricula run the risk of being narrowly tailored to the needs of specific businesses. For example, Babson College developed a master's degree program in business administration specifically for Intel workers. Similarly, the University of Texas at Austin developed an online Masters of Science degree in science, technology, and commercialization that caters only to students who work at IBM. Moreover, the program will orient its knowledge, skills, and research to focus exclusively on IBM projects.[68] Not only do such courses come dangerously close to becoming company training workshops; they also open up higher education to powerful corporate interests that have little regard for the more time-honored educational mandate to cultivate an informed, critical citizenry.

Online courses also raise an important question about intellectual property: Who owns the rights for course materials developed for online use? Because of the market potential of online lectures and course materials, various universities have attempted to lay ownership claims to such knowledge. For example, at the University of California at Los Angeles, an agreement was signed in 1994 that allowed an outside vender, OnlineLearning.net, to create and copyright online versions of UCLA courses. The agreement was eventually "amended in 1999 to allow professors' rights to the basic content of their courses ... [but] under the amended contract, OnlineLearning retain[ed] their right to market and distribute those courses online, which is the crux of the copyright dispute."[69] As universities make more and more claims on owning the content of faculty notes, lectures, books, computer files, and media for classroom use, the first casualty is, as UCLA Professor Ed Condren points out, "the legal protection that enables faculty to freely express their views without fear of censorship or appropriation of their ideas."[70] At the same time, by selling course property rights for a fee, universities infringe on the ownership rights of faculty members by taking from them any control over how their courses might be used in the public domain.

Corporate interests are also exerting their influence over major aspects of university decision-making in and out of the classroom in a number of other ways. No longer content to make their presence felt on college campuses through the funding of endowed chairs, academic centers, or research about business issues that eventually is used as case studies, companies such as BMW and IBM are taking their involvement with higher education to a new level. When the German automaker BMW contributed $10 million to Clemson University in 2002 to help develop a $1.5 billion automotive and research center, Clemson gave BMW an extraordinary amount of control over curriculum and hiring procedures. Not only did BMW play a role in developing the curriculum for the automotive graduate engineering school, but it also "drew up profiles of its ideal students; [provided] a list of professors and specialists to interview, and even had approval rights over the school's architectural look."[71] In addition, BMW gave Clemson's president a BMW X5 to drive. In spite of Clemson's claims that it retains its independence as a public university despite its close ties with BMW, candidates for the endowed chairs were interviewed by BMW executives and "a network council composed of BMW managers meets monthly to advise Clemson on the curriculum."[72] Thomas Kurfess, the first person hired to fill a BMW-endowed professorship, has no reservations about the growing corporatization of higher education, stating that "[t]his is a different model. It is nice to be able to show that it's not just the name beyond the chair ... [and have] real ties to industry."[73] A lawsuit contesting the contract between BMW and Clemson made public a letter written by a BMW official who stated that "BMW is going to drive the entire campus."[74] At least BMW is honest about its intentions and the role it wants to play in shaping Clemson's relationship with industry.

Another indication of the growing symbiosis between higher education and the corporate world is exemplified in IBM's relationship with North Carolina State University. In return for a number of grants, IBM created a new academic discipline called "Service Sciences, Management and Engineering," along with a curriculum whose aim is to produce "graduates better prepared to work for IBM." In effect, IBM has created a specific program that is designed to serve its labor needs and is "tailored for potential employers." According to IBM, "the curriculum offers an academic way of understanding interaction between client and provider ... using a mix of scientific and business concepts to focus on areas that might not be core in either a Masters of Business Administration or computer-science program."[75] As should be clear, a number of universities are now working with IBM, along with an increasing number of faculty. At UC-Berkeley, one professor teaching at the School of Information met with "IBM executives at the company's Silicon Valley research center to seek their advice on his syllabus."[76] The result is that his students are now required to read "selections from the IBM Systems Journal."[77] Such partnerships violate the academic integrity of the university and bode badly for the future of higher education in that they subordinate democratic values to corporate values and undercut the power of faculty and administration to define the meaning and purpose of the university and its relationship to the larger society. Largely defined in a corporate environment, the meaning and function of the university are radically redefined in market terms, weakening, if not jettisoning altogether, the claim of the university as a democratic public sphere, the academic freedom essential to safeguarding a socially responsible faculty, and those democratic values so crucial to creating critical citizens capable of questioning received truths and constituted powers.

While the cult of professionalism inspires fear and insecurity in academics terrified about maintaining tenure, getting it, or for that matter simply securing a part-time position, university educators also face the harsh lessons of financial deprivation, overburdened workloads, and the loss of power in shaping the governance process. They devote less time to their role either as well-informed public intellectuals or as "cosmopolitan intellectuals situated in the public sphere."[78] Many faculty live under the constant threat of being downsized, punished, or fired and are less concerned about quality research and teaching than about accepting the new rules of corporate-based professionalism in order to simply survive in the new corporatized academy. Against the current drive to corporatize higher education, commodify curricula, treat students as customers and trainees, and relegate faculty to the status of contract employees, higher education needs to be defended as a public good. Central to such a task is the challenge to resist the university's development into what literary theorist Bill Readings has called a consumer-oriented corporation more concerned about accounting than accountability, and whose mission, defined largely through an appeal to excellence, is comprehended almost exclusively in terms of instrumental efficiency.[79] David Harvey is more specific and argues that the "academy is being subjected to neoliberal apparatuses of various kinds [while] also becoming a place where neoliberal ideas are being spread," and that democratically minded academics have an obligation to resist this onslaught within the academy.[80]

Writing about totalitarianism, the philosopher Cornelius Castoriadis insisted that one mark of such a regime is the disappearance of informed citizens who give substantive content to public space, wage ongoing struggles to preserve and expand the public spheres capable of educating the totality of citizens to participate in and shape a democratic society, and comprehend that civic education is an "essential dimension of justice."[81] What Castoriadis recognized was that matters of agency, critical thought, and politics itself were impossible under conditions in which education maintained a passive attitude toward power, democracy, and the future. This is especially relevant at a time, under the regime of neoliberalism, when the crucial imperatives of vision and hope have been stripped from any understanding of the future, mortgaged to a demoralized and corrupty "democracy of money and military power."[82] Corporate power, relations, and values lack any viable vision of the relationship between democracy and its future just as they also lack a language for recognizing the power of anti-democratic forces to prepare the ground for an authoritarian regime.

Finding our way to a more humane future demands a new politics, set of democratic values, and sense of the fragile nature of democracy. Against the regime of market fundamentalism, it means educating a new generation of scholars who not only defend higher education as a democratic public sphere but also frame their own agency as scholars willing to connect their research, teaching, knowledge, and service with broader democratic concerns over equality, justice, and an alternative vision of what the university might be and what society might become. Under the present circumstances, it is time to remind ourselves that academe may be one of the few public spheres available, though hardly breathing, where we can provide the educational conditions for students to embrace pedagogy as a space of dialogue and unmitigated questioning, imagine different futures, become border-crossers establishing a range of new connections and global relations, and embrace a language of critique and possibility that makes visible the urgency of a politics necessary to reclaim democratic values, identities, relations, and practices. The struggle for reclaiming the university must be connected to the best that democracy can offer, which as Bill Moyers points out, means putting into place the material and symbolic resources that constitute "the means of dignifying people so they can become fully free to claim their moral and political agency."[83]

Notes

1. A number of books take up the relationship between schooling and democracy. Some of the more important critical contributions are John Dewey, *Democracy and Education* (New York: Dover Publishing, 2005, originally published in 1919); Amy Gutmann, *Democratic Education* (Princeton: Princeton University Press, 1999); Howard Zinn and Donaldo Macedo, *Howard Zinn on Democratic Education* (Boulder, CO: Paradigm Publishers, 2005); and Henry A. Giroux, *Schooling and the Struggle for Public Life* (Boulder, CO: Paradigm Publishers, 2006).

2. Recent books that do address this issue include Russell J. Jacoby, *The Last Intellectuals: American Culture in the Age of Academe* (New York: Basic Books, 1987); Henry A. Giroux and Stanley Aronowitz, *Education Still Under Siege,* 2nd ed. (Westport, CT: Bergin and Garvey, 1993); John Michael, *Anxious Intellectuals: Academic Professionals, Public Intellectuals* (Durham, NC: Duke University Press, 2000); Stanley Aronowitz, *The Knowledge Factory: Dismantling the Corporate University and Creating True Higher Learning* (Boston: Beacon Press, 2004); Jeffrey R. Di Leo and Walter R. Jacobs, eds., *If Classrooms Matter: Progressive Visions of Educational Environments* (New York: Routledge, 2004); Henry A. Giroux and Susan Searls Giroux, *Take Back Higher Education* (New York: Palgrave, 2006); Michael Berube, *What's Liberal About the Liberal Arts?* (New York: Basic Books, 2006); and Timothy Brennan, *Wars of Position* (New York: Columbia University Press, 2006).

3. Thorstein Veblen, *The Higher Learning in America* (Chicago: Cosimo, 2005, originally published in 1918); Robert Lynd, *Knowledge for What: The Place of Social Science in American Culture* (Princeton: Princeton University Press, 1939); C. Wright Mills, *The Power Elite* (New York: Oxford University Press, 2000, originally published in 1956).

4. Richard Ohmann, "Citizenship and Literacy Work: Thoughts Without a Conclusion," *Workplace* (November 25, 2002),

available online at http://www.louisville.edu/journal/workplace/
issue7/ohmann.html.

5. Critical educators have provided a rich history of how both
public and higher education have been shaped by the politics, ideologies, and images of industry. See, for example, Samuel Bowles
and Herbert Gintis, *Schooling in Capitalist America* (New York: Basic
Books, 1976); Michael Apple, *Ideology and Curriculum* (New York:
Routledge, 1977); Martin Carnoy and Henry Levin, *Schooling and
Work in the Democratic State* (Stanford: Stanford University Press,
1985); and Stanley Aronowitz and Henry A. Giroux, *Education Still
Under Siege* (Westport, CT: Bergin and Garvey, 1993). Some impor-
tant and recent books on the corporatization of the university are
Stanley Aronowitz and William DiFazio, *The Jobless Future* (Minne-
apolis: University of Minnesota Press, 1994); Cary Nelson, ed., *Will
Teach for Food: Academic Labor in Crisis* (Minneapolis: University
of Minnesota Press, 1997); Sheila Slaughter and Larry L. Leslie,
*Academic Capitalism: Politics, Policies, and the Entrepreneurial Uni-
versity* (Baltimore: Johns Hopkins University Press, 1997); D. W.
Livingstone, *The Education-Jobs Gap* (Boulder, CO: Westview, 1998);
Bill Readings, *The University in Ruins* (Cambridge, MA: Harvard
University Press, 1996); Geoffrey D. White with Flannery C. Hauck,
eds., *Campus Inc.: Corporate Power in the Ivory Tower* (New York:
Prometheus Books, 2000); Stanley Aronowitz, *The Knowledge Fac-
tory: Dismantling the Corporate University and Creating True Higher
Learning* (Boston: Beacon Press, 2000); Eric Gould, *The University
in a Corporate Culture* (New Haven: Yale University Press, 2003);
Derek Bok, *Universities in the Marketplace* (Princeton: Princeton
University Press, 2003); David Kirp, *Shakespeare, Einstein, and the
Bottom Line: The Marketing of Higher Education* (Cambridge, MA:
Harvard University Press, 2005); Jennifer Washburn, *University
Inc.: The Corporate Corruption of American Higher Education* (New
York: Basic Books, 2005); and Henry A. Giroux and Susan Searls
Giroux, *Take Back Higher Education* (New York: Palgrave, 2006). An
important work on the corporatization of higher education in Canada
is Neil Tudiver, *Universities for Sale* (Toronto: Lorimer, 1999).

6. Michael Yates, "Us Versus Them: Laboring in the Academic Factory," *Monthly Review* 51:8 (January 2000), available
online at http://www.monthlyreview.org/100yates.htm.

7. Jennifer L. Croissant, "Can This Campus Be Bought?"
Academe (September–October 2001), available online at http://
www.aaup.org/publications/Academe01SO/so01cro.html.

8. Robert Zemsky, "Have We Lost the 'Public' in Higher

Education?" *Chronicle of Higher Education* (May 30, 2003), pp. B7–B9.

9. G. A. Clark, "Corporatism at Arizona State University," *Anthropology News* 47:6 (September 2006), p. 39.

10. Stanley Aronowitz, "The New Corporate University," *Dollars and Sense* (March/April 1998), p. 32.

11. Stephen Burd, "Change in Federal Formula Means Thousands May Lose Student Aid," *Chronicle of Higher Education* (January 7, 2005), available online at http://chronicle.com/free/v51/i18/18a00101.htm.

12. "Quick Facts About Student Debt," *The Project on Student Debt* (April 4, 2006), available online at http://projectonstudentdebt.org/files/File/Debt_Facts_and_Sources_4_4_06.pdf.

13. Anya Kamenetz, *Generation of Debt* (New York: Riverside Books, 2006).

14. Jeffrey J. Williams, "Debt Education: Bad for the Young, Bad for America," *Dissent* (Summer 2006), p. 53.

15. Stuart Tannock, "Higher Education, Inequality, and the Public Good," *Dissent* (Spring 2006), p. 49.

16. This information is taken from Editorial, "Pricing the Poor Out of College," *New York Times* (March 27, 2002), p. A27.

17. Stephen Burd, "Lack of Aid Will Keep 170,000 Qualified, Needy Students Out of College This Year, Report Warns," *Chronicle of Higher Education* (June 27, 2002), p. 1, available online at http://chronicle.com/daily/2002/06/2002062701n.html.

18. Cited in Jane R. Porter, "Financial Strains Keep Millions Out of College, Panel Says," *Chronicle of Higher Education* (September 22, 2006), p. A25.

19. Michael Yates, "Us Versus Them: Laboring in the Academy," *Monthly Review* (January 2000), available online at www.monthlyreview.org/100yates.htm

20. Larry Hanley, "Conference Roundtable," *Found Object* 10 (Spring 2001), p. 103.

21. Masao Miyoshi, "'Globalization,' Culture, and the University," in *The Cultures of Globalization*, ed. Fredric Jameson and Masao Miyoshi (Durham: Duke University Press, 1998), p. 263.

22. Steven Pearlstein, "The Lesson Colleges Need to Learn," *Washington Post* (December 17, 2003).

23. Milton Greenberg, "A University is Not a Business (and Other Fantasies)," *Educause* (March–April 2004), p. 11.

24. Stanley Aronowitz, "Higher Education in Everyday Life," in *Deconstructing Derrida: Tasks for a New Humanities*, ed. Peter Trifonas (New York: Palgrave, 2006), p. 115.

25. Derek Bok, *Universities in the Marketplace* (Princeton: Princeton University Press, 2003), p. 65.

26. Ibid., pp. 200–201.

27. Ibid., p. 107.

28. Cited in Katherine S. Mangan, "Medical Schools Routinely Ignore Guidelines on Company-Sponsored Research, Study Finds," *Chronicle of Higher Education* (October 25, 2002), available online at http://chronicle.com/daily/2002/10/200210250ln.htm.

29. Cited in Lila Guterman, "Conflict of Interest Is Widespread in Biomedical Research, Study Finds," *Chronicle of Higher Education* (January 22, 2003), available online at http://chronicle.com/daily/2003/01/2003012202n.htm.

30. Ibid.

31. Cited in Mangan, "Medical Schools Routinely Ignore Guidelines."

32. Bok, *Universities in the Marketplace*, p. 75.

33. See Ignacio Chapela, Berkeley, California, June 26, 2003, available online at http://www.cust.educ.ubc.ca/workplace/issue5p2/chapela626.html.

34. Sharon Walsh, "Berkeley Denies Tenure to Ecologist Who Criticized University's Ties to the Biotechnology Industry," *Chronicle of Higher Education* 50:18 (January 9, 2004), p. A10.

35. Ibid.

36. Cited in "Seeds of Conflict," *NOW with Bill Moyers* (October 4, 2002), available online at http://www.pbs.org/now/science/genenature.html.

37. Aronowitz, "Higher Education in Everyday Life," p. 109.

38. Katherine Mangan, "Stanford Cracks Down on Gifts to Physicians," *Chronicle of Higher Education* (September 22, 2006), p. A24.

39. For a defense of this tradition, see Anne Colby, Thomas Ehrlick, Elizabeth Baumont, and Jason Stephens, *Educating Citizens* (San Francisco: Jossey-Bass, 2003).

40. Sheila Slaughter, "Professional Values and the Allure of the Market," *Academe* (September–October 2001), p. 1.

41. Cited in Beth Huber, "Homogenizing the Curriculum: Manufacturing the Standardized Student," available online at http://www.louisville.edu/journal/workplace/huber.html.

42. John Palattela, "Ivory Towers in the Marketplace," *Dissent* (Summer 2001), p. 73.

43. Noam Chomsky, "Paths Taken, Tasks Ahead," *Profession* (2000), p. 34.

44. Stanley Aronowitz, "Should Academic Unions Get Involved in Governance?" *Liberal Education* (Fall 2006), available online at http://www.aacu.org/liberaleducation/le-fa06/le-fa06_feature3.cfm.

45. These quotations are taken from Frances Fox Piven, Freda Rebelsky, Helen Vendler, Howard Zinn, S. M. Miller, and Shane Hunt, "Letter—Academic Freedom at B.U.," *New York Review of Books* (June 12, 1980), available online at http://www.nybooks.com/articles/7376. For a devastating critique of Silber's presidency at Boston University, see "A Report on Academic Freedom at Boston University," *Boston University Faculty Bulletin* (February 1996), pp. 1–50. For some insightful criticisms of Silber, see Daniel Gross, "Under the Volcano: Boston University in the Silber Age," *Lingua Franca* (November/December 1995), pp. 44–53; and Howard Zinn, *You Can't Be Neutral on a Moving Train* (New York: Fitzhenry and Whiteside, 1995). On my particular tenure case, see Russell Jacoby, *The Last Intellectuals* (New York: Basic Books, 2000).

46. Ian Angus, "Academic Freedom and the Corporate University," in *Utopian Pedagogy*, ed. Mark Coté, Richard Day, and Greg de Peuter (Toronto: University of Toronto Press, 2007), p. 73.

47. Elyse Ashburn, "The Few, the Proud, the Professors," *Chronicle of Higher Education* (October 6, 2006), p. A12.

48. Ibid., p. A10.

49. Ibid., p. A11.

50. Ibid., p. A12.

51. Ibid.

52. Aronowitz, "Higher Education in Everyday Life," p. 117.

53. Scott Jachik, "The New State U," *Inside Higher Ed* (August 31, 2006), available online at http://insidehighered.com/news/2006/08/31/illinois.

54. Sharon Walsh, "Study Finds Significant Increase in Number of Part-Time and Non-Tenure-Track Professors," *Chronicle of Higher Education* (October 29, 2002), available online at http://chronicle.com/daily/2002/10/2002102904n.htm. The full text of the American Council of Education study can be found on the council's website.

55. American Association of University Professors, "Contin-

gent Faculty Appointments," *AAUP Bulletin* (September 29, 2004), available online at http://www.aaup.org/Issues/part-time/.

56. Cary Nelson, "Between Anonymity and Celebrity: The Zero Degrees of Professional Identity," *College English* 64:6 (July 2002), p. 717.

57. Evan Watkins, *Throwaways: Work Culture and Consumer Education* (Stanford: Stanford University Press, 1993).

58. Geoff Sharp, "The Idea of the Intellectual and After," in *Scholars and Entrepreneurs: The University in Crisis,* ed. Simon Cooper, John Hinkson, and Geoff Sharp (Melbourne, Australia: Arena Publications, 2002), p. 280.

59. Paula Reed Ward, "PSU Fires Tenured Theater Professor," *Post-Gazette.Com* (March 2, 2004), available online at http://www. post-gazette.com/[g/04062/279825.

60. David F. Noble, "The Future of the Digital Diploma Mill," *Academe* 87:5 (September–October 2001), p. 31. These arguments are developed further in David F. Noble, *Digital Diploma Mills: The Automation of Higher Education* (New York: Monthly Review Press, 2002).

61. Cited in Eyal Press and Jennifer Washburn, "Digital Diplomas," *Mother Jones* (January/February 2001), p. 2, available online at http://www.motherjones.com.

62. Ibid., p. 2.

63. Jennifer Washburn, *University Inc.: The Corporate Corruption of American Higher Education* (New York: Basic Books, 2005).

64. Herbert Marcuse, "Some Social Implications of Modern Technology," in *Technology, War, and Fascism,* ed. Douglas Kellner (New York: Routledge, 1998), p. 45.

65. Michael Peters, "The University in the Knowledge Economy," in *Scholars and Entrepreneurs: The University in Crisis,* ed. Simon Cooper, John Hinkson, and Geoff Sharp (Melbourne, Australia: Arena Publications, 2002), p. 148.

66. Aronowitz, *The Knowledge Factory,* pp. 63, 109–110.

67. Press and Washburn, "Digital Diplomas," p. 2.

68. For more details on the creation of online degrees for corporations, see Dan Carnevale, "Colleges Tailor Online Degrees for Individual Companies," *Chronicle of Higher Education* (January 28, 2002), p. 1, available online at http://chronicle.com/cgi2-bin/printable.cgi.

69. Press and Washburn, "Digital Diplomas," p. 8.

70. Cited in ibid., p. 8.

71. Lynnley Browning, "BMW's Custom-Made University," *New York Times* (August 29, 2006), p. C1.

72. Ibid., p. C6.

73. Scott Jaschik, "BMW Professors," *Inside Higher Ed* (August 25, 2006), available online at http://insidehighered. com/news/2006/08/25/clemson.

74. Browning, "BMW's Custom-Made University," p. C6.

75. Anne Marie Chaker, "Majoring in IBM," *Wall Street Journal* (September 12, 2006), p. D1.

76. Ibid.

77. Ibid. Concerned about corporate influence on academic freedom and research policies, faculty members at the University of California at Berkeley are protesting a planned "$500-million-research institute to be financed by energy giant BP." See Goldie Blumenstyk, "Faculty Skeptics Seek a Voice in Berkeley's Controversial Energy-Research Deal with BP," *Chronicle of Higher Education* (April 5, 2007), p. 15.

78. Aronowitz, "The New Corporate University," p. 444.

79. Bill Readings, *The University in Ruins* (Cambridge, MA: Harvard University Press, 1996).

80. Stephen Pender, "An Interview with David Harvey," *Studies in Social Justice* 1:1(2007), p. 14.

81. Cornelius Castoriadis, "The Nature and Value of Equity," *Philosophy, Politics, Autonomy: Essays in Political Philosophy* (New York: Oxford University Press, 1991), p. 140.

82. Harvey in Pender, ibid., p. 16.

83. Bill Moyers, "A Time for Anger, A Call to Action," *Common Dreams* (February 7, 2007), available online at http://www. commondreams.org/views07/0322-24.htm.

◇

3

The New Right-Wing Assault on Higher Education

Academic Unfreedom in America

> This [modern] university claims and ought to be granted in principle, besides what is called academic freedom, an *unconditional* freedom to question and to assert, or even their right to say publicly all that is required by research, knowledge, and thought concerning the *truth*.
>
> —*Jacques Derrida*

Higher education in the United States appears to be caught in a strange contradiction. By all objective measures, the American academic system is regarded as one of the finest educational systems in the world. A recent study conducted at Shanghai Jiao Tong University, for instance, evaluated five hundred of the world's top universities and concluded that "The United States has 80 percent of the world's twenty most distinguished research universities and about 70 percent of the top fifty. We lead the world in the production of new knowledge and its transmission to undergraduate, doctoral and postdoctoral students. Since the 1930s, the United States has dominated the receipt of Nobel Prizes, capturing roughly 60 percent of these awards."[1] But the American system of higher education is unique not only for the quality of its research universities and its role in preparing students for emerging industries that drive the new global economy; it is also renowned, in spite of its limitations, as a democratic public sphere that gathers its "force and relevance by its democratic, secular, and open character."[2] Offering faculty a substantial measure of academic freedom and students the opportunity to learn within a culture of questioning and critical engagement, American higher education strongly affirms, at least in principle, the knowledge, values, skills, and social relations required for producing individual and social agents capable of addressing the political, economic, and social injustices that diminish the reality and promise of a substantive democracy at home and abroad. While the American university faces a growing number of problems that range from the increasing loss of federal and state funding, the incursion of corporate power, a galloping commercialization, and the growing influence of the national security state, it nevertheless remains, as Edward Said has insisted, "the one public space available to real alternative intellectual practices: no other institution like it on such a scale exists anywhere else in the world today."[3]

In spite of its broad-based, even global, recognition, higher education in the United States is currently being targeted by a diverse number of right-wing forces that have hijacked political power and waged a focused campaign against the principles of academic freedom, sacrificing critical pedagogical practice in the name of patriotic correctness and dismantling the university as a bastion of autonomy, independent thought, and uncorrupted inquiry. Ironically, it is through the vocabulary of individual rights, academic freedom, balance, and tolerance that these forces are attempting to slander, even vilify, liberal and left-oriented professors, to cut already meager federal funding for higher education, to eliminate tenure, and to place control of what is taught and said in classrooms under legislative oversight.[4] There is more at work in the current attack than the rampant anti-intellectualism and paranoid style of American politics outlined in Richard Hofstadter's *Anti-Intellectualism in American Life*, written over forty years ago.[5] There is also the collective power of radical right-wing organizations, which in their powerful influence on all levels of government (in spite of the Democratic Party–controlled Congress) and most social institutions feel compelled to dismantle the open, questioning cultures of the academy. Viewed as a particularly potent threat and social irritant to several right-wing radicals, the academy, as Ellen Willis has pointed out, "not only allows liberals and leftists to express their views, but provides them with the opportunity to make a living, get tenure, publish books, and influence students. Indeed, the academy is inherently a liberal institution, in the sense that it is grounded in the credo of the Enlightenment: the free pursuit and dissemination of knowledge for its own sake."[6]

Underlying recent attacks on the university is an attempt not merely to counter dissent but to destroy it and, in doing so, to eliminate all of those remaining public spaces, spheres, and institutions that nourish and sustain a democratic civil society.[7] Jonathan Cole, former provost at Columbia University, echoes this view in claiming that

> [t]oday, a half century after the 1954 House of Un-American Activities Committee held congressional hearings on communists in American universities, faculty members are witnessing once again a rising tide of anti-intellectualism and threats to academic freedom. They are increasingly apprehensive about the influence of external politics on university decision making. The attacks on professors like Joseph Massad, Thomas Butler, Rashid Khalidi, Ward Churchill, and Edward Said, coupled with other actions taken by the federal government in the name of national security, suggest that we may well be headed for another era of intolerance and repression.[8]

Criticisms of the university as a bastion of dissent have a long and inglorious history in the United States, extending from attacks in the nineteenth century by religious fundamentalists to anti-communist witch-hunts conducted in the 1920s, 1930s, and again in the 1950s, during the infamous era of McCarthyism. The 1951 publication of

God and Man at Yale, in which ultra-conservative William F. Buckley railed against secularism at Yale University and called for the firing of socialist professors, was but a precursor to the present era of politicized and paranoid academic assaults. Several of these efforts shared a commitment to the notion that the university and its dissenting intellectuals posed a threat to government power and to its entry into World War I, contributed to acts of treason by sympathizing with the Russian Revolution, and exhibited a vile form of anti-Americanism in their criticism of unbridled corporate power and capitalism more generally. These attacks, often launched by government committees, cast a dark cloud over the exercise of academic freedom and were largely aimed at specific individuals who were condemned either for their alleged communist fervor and left-wing affiliations or for their political activities outside of the classroom. One of the most notorious of these attacks occurred during the 1950s when Senator Joe McCarthy of Wisconsin spearheaded a government witch-hunt that resulted in the blacklisting and firing of many dissident intellectuals both in and out of the university.[9] During that period, not only were many faculty members fired, but untold others, especially nontenured junior faculty, "censored themselves and eschewed political dissent."[10] Harkening back to the infamous McCarthy era, a newly reinvigorated war is currently being waged by Christian nationalists, reactionary neoconservatives, and corporate fundamentalists against the autonomy and integrity of all those independent institutions that foster social responsibility, critical thought, and critical citizenship. While the attack is being waged on numerous fronts, the universities are where the major skirmishes are taking place.

Former University of Colorado President Elizabeth Hoffman warned her faculty audience in March 2005 that higher education was facing a grave danger from a "new McCarthyism that may be emerging in the United States."[11] Hoffman's comments have been echoed by a range of distinguished intellectuals such as renowned historian Joan W. Scott, writer Lewis Lapham, and prominent academics such as Stanley Aronowitz. One of the most noted historians of the McCarthy era, Ellen Schrecker, both furthers and qualifies this position by arguing that "today's assault on the academy is more serious" because "[u]nlike that of the McCarthy era, it reaches directly into the classroom."[12] Put differently, the assault being waged against higher education is not simply against dissenting professors and academic freedom but also over who controls the hiring process, the organization of curricula, and the nature of pedagogy itself.

What is crucial to recognize is that the rise of the "new McCarthyism" cannot simply be attributed to the radical curtailment of civil liberties that was initiated by the George W. Bush administration after the cataclysmic events of September 11, 2001, though it must be recognized that "[a]cademic freedom suffered serious setbacks ... [with] the hasty passage of the bill with the Orwellian name, the Patriot Act, [which] has compromised privacy protections, eroded civil liberties and chilled dissent."[13] Nor can it be entirely reduced to the logic of a newly energized post-9/11 patriotic correctness movement, most clearly exemplified by actions of the right-wing American Council of Trustees and Alumni (ACTA), which issued a report shortly after the attacks accusing an unpatriotic academy of being the "weak link in America's response to the attack."[14] Although a growing culture of fear and jingoistic patriotism emboldened religious, neoliberal, and right-wing activists who viewed the university as one of the last strongholds of liberal dissent and secular inquiry, the right-wing strategy to wage a political and pedagogical battle to strongly influence, if not control, those institutions that had a powerful educational influence on American life—such as the media and higher education—gained importance as a tactical strategy among conservatives long before 9/11.

To understand the current attack on academe, it is necessary to comprehend the power that conservatives attributed to the political nature of education and the significance this view had in shaping the long-term strategy they put into place in the 1960s and 1970s to win an ideological war against liberal intellectuals, who argued for holding government and corporate power accountable as a precondition for extending and expanding the promise of an inclusive democracy. The current concerted assault on academia represents the high point of a fifty-year strategy that was first put into place by conservative ideologues such as Frank Chodorov, the founder of the Intercollegiate Studies Institute; publisher and author William F. Buckley; former Nixon Treasury Secretary William Simon; and Michael Joyce, the former head of both the Olin Foundation and the Lynde and Harry Bradley Foundation. The most succinct statement, if not the founding document, for establishing a theoretical framework and political blueprint for the current assault on the academy has become rather infamously known as the Powell Memo, released on August 23, 1971, and authored by Lewis F. Powell, who would later be appointed as a member of the Supreme Court of the United States.

Powell identified the American college campus "as the single most dynamic source" for producing and housing intellectuals "who are unsympathetic to the [free] enterprise system."[15] He was particularly concerned about the lack of conservatives on social sciences faculties and urged his supporters to use an appeal to academic freedom as an opportunity to argue for "political balance" on university campuses. Powell recognized that one crucial strategy in changing the political composition of higher education was to convince university administrators and boards of trustees that the most fundamental problem facing universities was "the imbalance of many faculties."[16] Powell insisted that "the basic concepts of balance, fairness and truth are difficult to resist, if properly presented to boards of trustees, by writing and speaking, and by appeals to alumni associations and groups."[17] The Powell Memo was designed to develop a broad-based strategy not only to counter dissent but also to develop a material and ideological infrastructure with the capability to transform the American public consciousness through a conservative pedagogical commitment to reproduce the knowledge, values, ideology, and social relations of the corporate state. For Powell, the war against liberalism and a substantive democracy was primarily a pedagogical *and* political struggle designed both to win the hearts and minds of the general public and to build a power base capable of eliminating those public spaces, spheres, and institutions that nourish and sustain what Samuel Huntington would later call (in a 1975 study on the "governability of democracies" by the Trilateral Commission) an "excess of democracy."[18] Central to such efforts was Powell's insistence that conservatives nourish a new generation of scholars who would inhabit the university and function as public intellectuals actively shaping the direction of policy issues. He also advocated the creation of a conservative speakers bureau, staffed by scholars capable of evaluating "textbooks, especially in economics, political science and sociology."[19] In addition, he advocated organizing a corps of conservative public intellectuals who would monitor the dominant media; publish their own scholarly journals, books, and pamphlets; and invest in advertising campaigns to enlighten the American people on conservative issues and policies. The Powell Memo, while not the only influence, played an important role in convincing a "cadre of ultraconservative and self-mythologising millionaires bent on rescuing the country from the hideous grasp of Satanic liberalism"[20] to match their ideological fervor with their pocketbooks by "disbursing the collective sum of roughly $3 billion over a period of thirty years in order to build a network of public intellectuals, think tanks, advocacy groups, foundations, media outlets, and powerful lobbying interests."[21] As Dave Johnson points out, the initial effort was slow but effective:

> In 1973, in response to the Powell memo, Joseph Coors and Christian-right leader Paul Weyrich founded the Heritage Foundation. Coors told Lee Edwards, historian of the Heritage Foundation, that the Powell memo persuaded him that American business was "ignoring a crisis." In response, Coors decided to help provide the seed funding for the creation of what was to become the Heritage Foundation, giving $250,000. Subsequently, the Olin Foundation, under the

direction of its president, former Treasury Secretary William Simon (author of the influential 1979 book *A Time for Truth*), began funding similar organizations in concert with "the Four Sisters"—Richard Mellon Scaife's various foundations, the Lynde and Harry Bradley Foundation, the Olin Foundation and the Smith Richardson Foundation—along with Coors's foundations, foundations associated with the Koch oil family, and a group of large corporations.[22]

The most powerful members of this group were Joseph Coors in Denver, Richard Mellon Scaife in Pittsburgh, John Olin in New York City, David and Charles Koch in Wichita, the Smith Richardson family in North Carolina, and Harry Bradley in Milwaukee—all of whom agreed to finance a number of right-wing think tanks, which over the past thirty years have come to include the Lynde and Harry Bradley Foundation, the Koch Foundation, the Castle Rock Foundation, and the Sarah Scaife Foundation. This formidable alliance of far-right-wing foundations deployed their resources in building and strategically linking "an impressive array of almost 500 think tanks, centers, institutes and concerned citizens groups both within and outside of the academy.... A small sampling of these entities includes the Cato Institute, the Heritage Foundation, the American Enterprise Institute, the Manhattan Institute, the Hoover Institution, the Claremont Institute, the American Council of Trustees and Alumni, [the] Middle East Forum, Accuracy in Media, and the National Association of Scholars, as well as [David] Horowitz's Center for the Study of Popular Culture."[23] For several decades, right-wing extremists have labored to put into place an ultra-conservative re-education machine—an apparatus for producing and disseminating a public pedagogy in which everything tainted with the stamp of liberal origin and the word "public" would be contested and destroyed. Commenting on the rise of this vast right-wing propaganda machine organized to promote the idea that democracy needs less critical thought and more citizens whose only role is to consume, well-known author Lewis Lapham writes:

The quickening construction of Santa's workshops outside the walls of government and the academy resulted in the increased production of pamphlets, histories, monographs, and background briefings intended to bring about the ruin of the liberal idea in all its institutionalized forms—the demonization of the liberal press, the disparagement of liberal sentiment, the destruction of liberal education—and by the time Ronald Reagan arrived in triumph at the White House in 1980 the assembly lines were operating at full capacity.[24]

Higher Education and Post-9/11 McCarthyism

The events of September 11, 2001, strengthened many of the conservative forces already in place in American society and provided a new dynamism for the right-wing attack machine and pedagogical infrastructure. Individuals and groups who opposed George W. Bush's foreign and domestic policies were put on the defensive—some overtly harassed—as right-wing pundits, groups, and foundations repeatedly labeled them as traitors and un-American. In some cases, conservative accusations that seemed disturbing, if not disturbed, before the events of 9/11 now appeared perfectly acceptable, especially to the dominant media, when aligned with a culture of fear and insecurity (im)mobilized by the call for patriotism and national security. For instance, prior to September 11, 2001, there was a growing concern that the university was too removed from public life, too secular in its concerns, and too markedly elitist in its embrace of cosmopolitan modernity. After the events of 9/11, the nature of conservative acrimony was marked by a new language, but the goal was largely the same: to remove from the university all vestiges of dissent and to reconstruct it as an increasingly privatized sphere for reproducing the interests of corporations and the national security state while also assuming a front-line position in the war against terror. In short, criticisms of Israeli government policy were labeled as anti-Semitic; universities were castigated as hotbeds of left-wing radicalism; conservative students alleged that they were being humiliated and discriminated against in college and university classrooms all across the country; Ward Churchill became the poster boy standing in for all faculty to the left of Bill O'Reilly; and McCarthy-like blacklists were posted on the Internet by right-wing groups such as Campus Watch, ACTA, Target of Opportunity,[25] and *DiscovertheNetworks.org* attempting to both out and politically shame allegedly radical professors who were giving aid and comfort to the enemy because of their refusal to provide unqualified support of the Bush administration. Traditional right-wing complaints were now coded as part of the discourse calling for academic freedom, balance, and individual rights. Professors were no longer elitist; they were now accused of being both too liberal and un-American. Universities were accused of not giving equal weight to conservative concerns such as the teaching of a consensus-based view of American history, the celebration of Western civilization, and a notion of science mediated less through the presentation of argument, logic, and evidence than through an appeal to a religious and ideological grid of conservative moral values. Academic balance was now invoked as a way to promote a form of affirmative action for hiring conservative faculty, while academic freedom was redefined through the prism of student rights and as a legitimating referent for dismantling professional academic standards and imposing outside political oversight of the classroom. But if the strategy and project of conservative ideologues became more bold and persistent after 9/11, it is also fair to say that right-wing efforts and demands to reform higher education took a dangerous turn that far exceeded the threat posed by the previous "cultural wars."

What was new about the condemnation of the university was that a right-wing ideological coalition of Christian evangelicals, militant nationalists, market fundamentalists, and neoconservatives, among others, controlled the legislative, executive, and judicial branches of government, the top civilian ranks of the Pentagon, and most of the intelligence services. In the midst of such power, the coalition had ample political, cultural, and economic resources to attempt to exercise total control over all aspects of public life and to implement a political agenda consistent with the goals of maintaining uncontested U.S. military and economic dominance globally. Beshara Doumani argues that it is crucial to understand the "campaign to discipline the academy unleashed after 9/11 as part of a sustained effort to shift public discourse in favor of four major agendas in foreign and domestic policies: dominating the globe through the doctrine of preemptive military intervention with special focus on the Middle East, dismantling the New Deal society, reversing the gains of the various civil-rights and environmental movements, and blurring the line between the church and state."[26] Central to implementing this project was the desperate attempt by right-wing forces "to neutralize two institutions where there is some minimal commitment to free and open inquiry—the media and the university system."[27] Right-wing efforts to roll back the gains of the welfare state and dismantle all institutions that serve the public good attested to the exercise of a logic of total control that was not only characteristic of all political movements with a totalitarian bent but also symptomatic of a growing authoritarianism in the United States.[28]

Furthering this authoritarian agenda, the Bush administration made it difficult for scientists, because of extraordinary laboratory constraints, to conduct important research unrelated to the war on terrorism. At the same time, scientists who resisted the ban on stem-cell research as well as the official government position on global warming, HIV transmission, and sex education were intimidated by congressional committees, which audited their work or threatened "to withdraw federal grant support for projects whose content they find substantively offensive."[29] The attempt to selectively restrict the free flow of independent or critical knowledge and ideas was also evident in the government's efforts to obstruct foreign students, scholars, and citizens critical of American policies from obtaining visas to teach, work, study, lecture, or travel in the United States, thereby "disrupting the flow of the best talent to American universities."[30]

Using the "war on terrorism" as a pretext for labeling all noncitizens as potential "enemy combatants" who might threaten national security, the Bush administration revoked the visas of a number of foreign intellectuals who were critical of U.S. foreign policy or who allegedly posed a risk to the country according to the Department of Homeland Security. For example, a group of Cuban intellectuals and scholars who were invited to attend a national meeting of the Latin American Studies Association had all of their visas denied by the Bush administration. One of the more outlandish government abuses concerned the internationally recognized scholar Tariq Ramadan, a Swiss citizen and Islamic scholar, who has published over twenty books. In 2003, he was offered the prestigious Henry B. Luce Professorship of Religion, Conflict and Peace at the University of Notre Dame. Ramadan accepted the job, resigned his position in Switzerland, and obtained a work visa early in 2004. Nine days before he was to fly to the United States, the Department of Homeland Security revoked his work visa, thus preventing him from assuming his teaching position at Notre Dame. While not offering a specific explanation for revoking his visa, the government suggested, without any substantial proof, that Professor Ramadan "endorsed or espoused" terrorist activities. Not only was Professor Ramadan an outspoken critic of terrorism in all of its forms, he was a strong advocate of reconciling the democratic principles of both Islam and Western modernity. Professor Ramadan's advocacy in the name of peace and against global violence later earned him the distinction of being named by Prime Minister Tony Blair "to serve on a British commission to combat terrorism."[31] In 2005, a federal court, rejecting the government's claim that Ramadan had anything to do with terrorism, ordered the Bush administration either to provide a visa or to offer detailed arguments as to why it would not do so. In the end, the government rejected his visa application, offering up a new and specious argument in which it claimed that Professor Ramadan had contributed to charities that supported Hamas, named by the United States as a terrorist organization. In fact, the two humanitarian organizations to which Professor Ramadan contributed and which provided relief for welfare of the Palestinian people were not blacklisted by the U.S. government until 2003, a year after Professor Ramadan contributed to them. Ultimately, Professor Ramadan was prevented from obtaining a U.S. visa because he was critical of Bush's Middle East policies and a moderate who refused the violence of all fundamentalisms. Writing in response to the government's refusal to issue him a visa, Ramadan eloquently stated that at the heart of this abuse of power were the underlying principles of democracy, justice, and freedom. He wrote, "I fear that the United States has grown fearful of ideas. I have learned firsthand that the Bush administration reacts to its critics not by engaging them, but by stigmatizing and excluding them. Will foreign scholars be permitted to enter the United States only if they promise to mute their criticisms of U.S. policy? It saddens me to think of the effect this will have on the free exchange of ideas, on political debate within America, and on our ability to bridge differences across cultures."[32] What must be added to this statement is that Ramadan's case was exemplary of the growing authoritarianism that characterized the Bush administration and increasingly posed a threat to democracy at home and throughout the rest of the world.

A third instructive instance pertains to the historian Waskar Ari, a Bolivian scholar who earned all of his graduate degrees in the United States. Prior to being offered a job at the University of Nebraska at Lincoln, Ari was an assistant professor of history at Western Michigan University. Subsequent to taking his position at Nebraska, he learned that all of his existing visas had been canceled and that he would not be allowed to assume the appointment. According to the Department of Homeland Security, Ari was denied a visa "because his name appears on a list of individuals considered security risks," a position completely at odds with Ari's academic work and his long-standing experience in the United States.[33] In 2007, the University of Nebraska took the unprecedented action of suing the U.S. government to try to force it to issue Professor Ari a visa and "counter what critics say is a growing number of cases in which the government has kept out foreign scholars for ideological reasons."[34] U.S. government officials have neither acted on the university's petition nor responded publicly to the lawsuit. The *Chronicle of Higher Education* reported that the government's refusal to issue Mr. Ari a visa may be "connected with Mr. Ari's ethnic identity. He is a member of the Aymara ethnic group—one of Bolivia's two main indigenous groups and the same one as its president, Evo Morales. Mr. Morales is a supporter of the Venezuelan president, Hugo Chavez, and a critic of the Bush administration's policies toward Bolivia."[35] As implausible as this suggestion appears, it has some credibility given the Bush administration's long record of punishing people it considers at odds with its own ideological beliefs.

Similarly, John Milios, a faculty member at the National Technical University of Athens and twice a candidate for the Greek parliament, was detained on his arrival at John F. Kennedy International Airport, questioned about his political beliefs for eight hours by federal agents, and then put on a flight back to Athens. Professor Milios was scheduled to deliver a paper at Stony Brook's Center for the Study of Working-Class Life on "How Class Works—2006." Even though he had traveled to the United States on at least six occasions prior to his being detained on June 8, 2006, he had never had any trouble entering the country. When Homeland Security was asked for a reason why it revoked his visa, it could not provide one.[36] Ramadan, Ari, Milios, and others are only the tip of the iceberg. The arbitrary way in which recognized international public intellectuals and committed scholars were denied visas by the U.S. government serves as a chilling reminder not only that international knowledge production was being policed in an unprecedented fashion after 9/11 but also that the university can no longer defend such intrusions by appealing to the principle of academic freedom. Sadly, the government was not the only group restricting open inquiry, critical knowledge, and dissent in the United States.

The Attack on Middle Eastern Studies

Unlike the McCarthy era, when the government was the primary force behind attempts to squelch dissent and demonize academics who dared exercise their right of free speech, the current harassment of critical intellectuals after 9/11 was largely promoted by private advocacy groups. Media watchdogs, campus groups, and various payroll pundits not only held favor with the Bush administration but also received millions of dollars from right-wing foundations and were powerfully positioned to monitor and quarantine any vestige of independent thought in the academy. Since the events of 9/11, academics who challenged the political orthodoxy of the Bush administration were often subjected to intimidation and harassment by conservative politicians, ultra-conservative commentators, right-wing talk-show hosts, tabloid newspapers, Christian zealots, and conservative students, who often disrupted and reported on professors whom they considered too liberal. This was especially true for dissident professors who taught in the area of Middle Eastern studies. Joel Beinin, a renowned professor of Middle East history at Stanford University, described the evolution and growing influence of what he called the "American Likud"—those individuals and groups who transformed "uncritical support for Israel from a political position into a religious dogma enshrined in public policy" and who "worked tirelessly to delimit the boundaries of permissible discussion of the Middle East at colleges and universities."[37] In fact, the pattern of attack that emerged against academic critics of Israeli policies provided a standard model for the type of aggression used against oppositional academics in other fields. As Jonathan Cole points out, these attacks tended to follow a predictable path:

> A professor is singled out for criticism. This is followed by media coverage that carries the allegations to larger audiences. The coverage is often cursory and sometimes distorted. Some citizens conclude that the university harbors

extremists who subvert our national ideals. Pressed by irate
constituents, political leaders and alumni demand that the
university sanction or fire the professor. This is an all-too-
familiar story in our nation's history.[38]

A classic illustration of this type of intimidation can be seen
in the case of Joseph Massad, an assistant professor hired
in 1999 by Columbia University, who at the conclusion of
his first academic year was a finalist for the Van Doren
teaching award. While a number of area studies scholars,
including Hamid Dabashi, George Saliba, and Rashid
Khalidi, were subject to politically motivated harassment
at Columbia University, Joseph Massad's case received the
most public attention. Massad first came into the public eye
when he was featured in a twenty-five minute, pro-Israeli
film called *Columbia Unbecoming,* produced by the David
Project, an off-campus "Boston-based group that has ties
to the Israel on Campus Coalition, an organization whose
members include the American Israel Public Affairs Committee (AIPAC), the Anti-Defamation League (ADL) and the
American Jewish Committee."[39] In the film, a Jewish student and former Israeli solder, Tomy Schoenfeld, claimed
that Massad, in an off-campus lecture delivered in 2002,
responded to one of his questions with the comment: "How
many Palestinians have you killed?" Massad countered
that Schoenfeld was never one of his students, that he
had never taken a class with him, that the exchange never
took place, and that he had never met him.[40] The second
and most serious charge was made by a student who did
not appear in the film, but whose story was recounted by
someone else. Allegedly, "Massad angrily told a student, 'If
you're going to deny the atrocities being committed against
Palestinians, then you can get out of my classroom.' [T]he
charge was corroborated by one other student and one
auditor, but three other individuals present said they had
no recollection of the episode taking place, and it did not
appear in Massad's teaching evaluations."[41]
   Buckling under outside political pressures from what
John Mearsheimer and Stephen Walt called "the Israel

Lobby"[42]—the largely pro-Israel press such as the *Wall Street Journal, Daily News, New York Post, New York Sun,* as well as the Columbia University newspaper, the *Spectator,* and other organized groups and individuals who believed that area studies are hotbeds for anti-American and anti-Semitic sentiment—the Columbia University administration, despite the shabbiness of the charges directed against Massad, formed a faculty committee to look into allegations that he had intimidated students in his class. The Ad Hoc Grievance Committee cleared Massad and the Department of Middle East and Asian Languages and Cultures (MEALAC) of promoting anti-Semitism, intimidating Jewish students, and punishing pro-Israel students with poor grades, but it did conclude that some allegations against Massad were "credible," pointing specifically to the charge that he had asked a Jewish student to leave his class. Oddly, the report reached its decision knowing full well that the student, Deena Shanker, gave three different versions of the incident to the *New York Sun,* the *New York Times,* and the *Jerusalem Post,* that three students in the class had no recollection of the incident, and that Massad himself claimed the incident never took place—all significant revelations regarding Massad's case, to say the least. In addition to the fact that the panel was never able to reliably substantiate any acts of intimidation, twenty students who were present in Massad's class during the supposed incident sent a letter to the university administration stating that Shanker's accusations against Massad were "unequivocally false" and that the Ad Hoc Committee was "incorrect" to grant them any credibility.[43] The university chose not to respond to the letter. Massad told the *Jerusalem Post* that he had "never asked and would never ask any of my students to leave my class no matter what their comments and questions were."[44] Most of the allegations made by students against Massad either came from students not taking his classes or were never the subject of a formal complaint. Shanker's accusation was reported to the press three years after the incident allegedly took place and only *after* the release of the film *Columbia Unbecoming.*

In the aftermath of the publicity following the selective distribution of the discredited *Columbia Unbecoming* to the media (there was no single film but at least six versions and it has never been screened for the public), Massad was subject to a vicious media campaign waged against him by numerous right-wing newspapers such as the *Wall Street Journal,* the *Daily News,* and the *New York Sun.* The tabloid press attacked him incessantly, and pro-Israel students, who viewed any criticism of Israeli policies as anti-Semitic, met with other right-wing faculty at Columbia University to conspire to get Massad fired. Adam Federman, writing in *CounterPunch.org,* claimed that "[s]hortly after the allegations in the film were publicized, Massad received an email from Columbia associate clinical professor of medicine Moshe Rubin, telling him to 'Go back to Arab land where Jew hating is condoned. Get the hell out of America. You are a disgrace and a pathetic typical Arab liar.'"[45] The attack on Massad generated national attention and triggered a number of follow-up stories in the *Chronicle of Higher Education* and *New York Times.* The effects of such media sensationalism reached a low point when Congressman Anthony D. Weiner, a New York Democrat, called upon Lee Bollinger, the president of Columbia University, to fire Professor Massad. Ironically, Weiner argued that firing Massad "would make a brave statement in support of tolerance and academic freedom."[46] Jonathan Cole offered this apt reply:

> Weiner's Orwellian ploy—of calling intolerance 'tolerance'— must be seen in a broader context. There is a growing effort to pressure universities to monitor classroom discussion, create speech codes, and more generally, enable disgruntled students to savage professors who express ideas they find disagreeable. There is an effort to transmogrify speech that some people find offensive into a type of action that is punishable.[47]

Subject to an ongoing campaign of intimidation and harassment, Massad has endured having his picture along with defamatory profiles posted on various right-wing websites, including *DiscovertheNetworks.org* and *Campus-Watch.org*. The latter provided links to a number of *New York Sun* articles by Alec Magnet, who endlessly vilified Massad in a lethal language that combined tabloid sensationalism and character assassination.[48] In addition, students with clear-cut, pro-Israel agendas repeatedly attended classes taught by Massad and other professors in the Department of Middle East and Asian Languages and Cultures in order to interrupt lectures and disrupt classroom debate. The Columbia administration noted in its *Ad Hoc Grievance Committee Report*[49] that "[t]estimony that we received indicated that in February 2002 Professor Massad had good reason to believe that a member of the Columbia faculty was monitoring his teaching and approaching his students, requesting them to provide information on his statements in class as part of a campaign against him."[50]

Joel Beinin insists that the Columbia investigation of Massad should never have taken place. He writes:

> It is unclear why students' emotional reaction to information or analysis presented in a classroom has any bearing on its factual accuracy or intellectual legitimacy. Undoubtedly, many white student supporters of Jim Crow practices at universities throughout the American South in the 1960s were distressed to learn that these practices were illegal and despised by many Americans. This did not make them any less so.... Politically motivated groups, using evidence that was not made available to the public, pressured a major university into investigating its faculty based on criteria completely alien to academic procedures. Most of those who complained about professors were not students in their classes (and some were not students at all). As the *Ad Hoc Report* notes, some faculty members apparently recruited students to spy on their colleagues. But this was of less concern to the New York media than Columbia's failure to prevent the teaching of courses critical of Israel, irrespective of the scholarly validity of the courses' content.[51]

What is truly amazing about Columbia University's response to Professor Massad is that it failed to recognize or mention that the real crisis involving Massad was not that students had complained about his ideas, but that he and other members of MEALAC were systematically being harassed by the popular press, conservative students, and right-wing pro-Israel groups such as Daniel Pipes's Campus Watch website, the David Project, and the Anti-Defamation League. Joan W. Scott of the American Association of Professors rightly argued that Columbia University completely missed an opportunity to define the real issue—namely, "the threat to the integrity of the university by the intervention of organized outside agitators who are disrupting classes and programs for ideological purposes."[52] Equally important, the report refused to acknowledge, as Eric Foner, a historian at Columbia pointed out, that "professors who do not treat students fairly should be reprimanded; but when students encounter ideas they disagree with, that does not constitute grounds for a complaint to the university."[53] In other words, what was at stake in this struggle was not Massad's political views but a highly organized campaign of intimidation and an all-out assault on academic freedom, critical scholarship, and the very idea of the university as a place to question and think,[54] along with a chilling silence regarding the utter necessity of teachers having control over the "very nature of university pedagogy and the production of scholarly knowledge."[55] That the stakes were much higher than Columbia University realized was made painfully clear when the *New York Times* published an editorial in which it claimed that the Ad Hoc Committee had appointed members "who expressed anti-Israel views," that the committee's mandate should have included the question of "anti-Israel bias," that the committee failed to "examine the quality and fairness of teaching," and that it should hire and fire faculty "with more determination and care."[56] In short, the *New York Times* told its readers that Columbia University should not only prevent bias from entering the classroom but also "follow up on complaints about politicized courses and lack of scholarly rigor as part of its effort to upgrade the department."[57] While no one should support academics who are unqualified to teach a particular subject, it is very dangerous indeed for the *New York Times* to imply that positions supported by scholarly evidence and expressed in the classroom, however critical of government policy, should be faulted for lacking scholarly rigor, and that "professors [should] follow what it defines as an acceptable, 'fair' pedagogical line."[58] The *New York Times* criticized the university not only for limiting its investigation to the charge of intimidation but also for refusing to address the content of Massad's teaching, which amounted to a call to monitor his subject matter—or presumably any professor's pedagogy—for allegedly anti-Israeli views. What made the editorial from a supposed bastion of left-liberal elitism all the more suspect was that it followed an op-ed piece in which *New York Times* columnist Thomas Friedman called upon the State Department to draw up a blacklist of those critics he called "excuse makers," alluding to anyone who believes that U.S. actions are at the root cause of contemporary global violence. According to Friedman, "These excuse makers are just one notch less despicable than the terrorists and also deserve to be exposed."[59] This kind of McCarthyite connection that collapses democratic dissent with terrorism has become so commonplace in the United States that it is openly championed by a famous columnist in one of the world's leading newspapers. Challenging the current conservative wisdom—that is, holding views at odds with official orthodoxy—has now become the grounds for being labeled un-American and/or anti-Semitic, made the subject of a coordinated smear campaign, put on a blacklist, or dismissed from one's job.[60]

Public efforts to malign Joseph Massad and his colleagues not only constituted a victory for right-wing groups such as the American Israel Public Affairs Committee, the Anti-Defamation League, and Campus Watch, they also legitimated a second wave of attacks against those professors who opposed Israeli government policy, and against all professors who dared to challenge the policies of the Bush administration, or any of its allies, or to criticize any aspect of the mythology of America as a bearer of unfettered democracy and the apogee of Western civilization itself.

How Many Ward Churchills?

The attack on Joseph Massad revealed the degree to which McCarthyite invective, combined with the financial resources of private advocacy groups, could silence and abuse academics who challenged the interrelated policies of the Israeli and U.S. governments. The attempts on the part of the University of Colorado to punish Ward Churchill for an article in which he compared some victims in the World Trade Center attack to "little Eichmanns"[61] provides yet another instance of the expanding web of attacks against leftist academics whose political views are publicly represented as symptomatic of most professors in academia. Even though Churchill's political ideology represented a very small number of faculty, his ill-conceived remarks outside of the classroom created a firestorm among conservatives, who used him in turn as a poster boy for broadening their efforts to transform the university. For instance, Newt Gingrich, former Speaker of the House, argued with reference to Churchill: "We are going to nail this guy and send the dominoes tumbling. And everybody who has an opinion out there and entire disciplines like ethnic studies and women's studies and cultural studies and queer studies that we don't like won't be there anymore."[62] Responding to the intense pressure placed on the University of Colorado at Boulder to fire Churchill, a faculty panel was formed to investigate the incident. Recognizing that Churchill could not be fired for his infamous remarks comparing some victims of the September 11 attacks to Nazi bureaucrats since such commentary was protected by the First Amendment, the panel searched for other acts of wrongdoing, which, in this case, eventually amounted to a charge of "research misconduct." John Wilson, who has published widely on the issue of academic freedom, argued that "research misconduct" was a loaded term and any committee invoking the charge to fire a professor in the humanities must provide a concise definition that distinguishes between incompetent research and the literal fabrication of data. Wilson believed that Churchill was accused of "making broad claims without adequate evidence,"[63] a far cry from what could reasonably be called research misconduct. Not only did the committee allege that such "misconduct" took place on the basis of a footnote reference, among other minor charges, but it proceeded to issue a "notice of intent to dismiss."[64] Churchill is expected to be fired.[65] Wilson further argued that "by stretching the meaning of 'research misconduct' far beyond its original definition, and by supporting the suspension and even dismissal of a tenured professor for his use of footnotes, the Colorado committee [was] opening the door to a vast new right-wing witch-hunt on college campuses that conservatives could easily exploit across the country."[66] Not only did the university bend to the concerted pressures of both various reactionary organizations and Colorado Governor Bill Owens, who was a right-wing activist for the conservative American Council of Trustees and Alumni, but it actually affirmed in its report that academics who take unpopular positions can expect "to have their scholarship as well as their politics scrutinized."[67] What is crucial about Churchill's case is that what was being investigated by the Colorado panel was work that had actually been in circulation for many years, but became the subject of a formal inquiry only after Churchill's ill-tempered comments about 9/11. Gingrich's view that the firing of Ward Churchill was only the first step in a purge of those departments, programs, and academics that "despise America" (by criticizing its government's policies) was echoed in the comments of some of the University of Colorado regents who, pondering Churchill's future, assented to Regent Tom Lucero's insistence that "[i]t naturally follows that I will be seeking justification for all departments and their academic value and merit to the university community. I want to scrutinize whether or not it is necessary to eliminate courses and departments of questionable merit."[68] This sent a chilling message to faculty in Colorado and across the nation, especially to young, nontenured faculty who were doing critical scholarship—a warning that was actually reinforced when the Colorado committee reminded Churchill that he might not have been investigated if he had just kept his head down and remained quiet: "Public figures who choose to speak out on controversial matters of public concern naturally attract more controversy and attention to their background and work than scholars quietly writing about more esoteric matters that are not the subject of political debate."[69]

While Gingrich was honest enough to reveal that Churchill was just a pawn in a much larger war being waged by right-wing extremists in order to divest the university of its critical intellectuals and critically oriented curricula, programs, and departments, the American Council of Trustees and Alumni produced a booklet titled *How Many Ward Churchills?* in which it dressed up its endemic paranoia, jingoistic patriotism, and anti-intellectualism in the guise of a scholarly study, concerned with "protecting" academic freedom. Anne D. Neal, the president of ACTA, wrote in the Foreword of the report that "[a]cademic freedom is bestowed on professors so that they can pursue truth wherever it may lead. But academic freedom is as much a responsibility as a right. It does not exempt the academy from outside scrutiny and criticism. The faculty's academic freedom should end at the point where professors abuse the special trust they are given to respect students' academic freedom to learn."[70] But the primary argument of *How Many Ward Churchills?* insisted that the space that separated most faculty from Ward Churchill was small indeed, and that colleges and universities now "risk losing their independence and the privilege they have traditionally enjoyed."[71] And how do we know that higher education has fallen into such dire straits? This apocalyptic change was revealed through an inane summary of course syllabi taken from various colleges that prove "professors are using their classrooms to push political agendas in the name of teaching students to think critically."[72] Courses that included discussions of gender, race, class discrimination, and whiteness as practices of exclusion were dismissed as distorting American history, by which Neal meant consensus history—a position made famous by the tireless efforts of Lynne Cheney, who repeatedly asserted that history should be celebratory even if it meant overlooking "internal conflicts and the non-white population."[73] Rather than discuss the intellectual relevance, moral principles, or pedagogical values of courses organized around the need to address human suffering, evil, violence, and social injustice, the ACTA report claimed that "[a]nger and blame are central components of the pedagogy of social justice."[74] In addition to listing course descriptions that symbolized the evils of the liberal arts curriculum, the report ironically insisted on scholarly rigor and then recapitulated uncritically the allegations made in the *Columbia Unbecoming* film against Joseph Massad (another Ward Churchill?) as if they were still pending investigation, in the full knowledge that the Columbia University Ad Hoc Committee had cleared MEALAC of all charges in its final report a year before ACTA released its screed. In the end, the listing of course descriptions was designed to alert administrators, governing boards, trustees, and tenure and hiring committees of the need to police instructors in the name of "impartiality." Presenting itself as a defender of academic freedom, ACTA actually wanted to monitor and police the academy, just as Homeland Security monitors the reading habits of library patrons and the National Security Agency spies on American citizens without first obtaining warrants.[75] More recently ACTA supported a bill passed by the Missouri House of Representatives stating its public universities must protect religious freedom and "the teaching that the Bible is literally true." Cary Nelson, the president of the American Association of University Professors, "called the bill ... 'one of the worst pieces of higher legislation in a century!'"[76]

ACTA is not a friend of the principle of academic freedom, nor is it comfortable with John Dewey's notion that education should be responsive to the deepest conflicts of our time, or Hannah Arendt's insistence that debate and a commitment to persuasion are the essence of a democratically oriented politics, if not pedagogy. In fact, ACTA's attempt to slander leftist and liberal academics by suggesting they were all replicas of Ward Churchill had little to do with supporting academic freedom or critical learning; instead, it represented another species of right-wing authoritarianism committed to nurturing anti-intellectualism and intolerance rather than defending the right of faculty to make their own informed pedagogical choices and not be penalized for doing so. ACTA actively supports policing classroom knowledge, monitoring curricula, and limiting the autonomy of teachers and students as part of its larger assault on academic freedom. In fact, since ACTA and other right-wing groups have little to say about the relationship between education and democracy, the only way they can imagine a pedagogy for social justice is as a form of proselytizing. And for all of the bluster about critical pedagogy as a form of indoctrination, ACTA and other like-minded organizations attacking the university have failed to theorize pedagogy in ways that would illuminate how power shapes and is reinvented in the interaction among teachers, texts, and students, and what it would mean to help students come to terms with their own power as individual and social agents willing to take risks, appropriate knowledge critically, and develop a vision of a just society, which, at the very least, should be a modest goal of higher education in a democracy. Put differently, right-wing attacks on the university are totally at odds with Robert Hass's insight that the job of education is inherently moral and political because its purpose is "to refresh the idea of justice going dead in us all the time."[77]

Extremist Attacks on the University: McCarthyism Without an Apology

The most recent challenges to academic freedom, liberal professors, and critical pedagogy have developed more capacious and systemic efforts to convince the American public, university alumni, trustees, and politicians that higher education is primarily under the control of liberals and left-wing academics who promote an anti-corporate and anti-American bias. And while the tactics to undermine academic freedom and critical education have grown more sophisticated, right-wing representations of the academy have become more shrill. For instance, James Pierson in the conservative *Weekly Standard* claimed that when 16 million students enter what he calls the "left-wing university," they will discover that "[t]he ideology of the left university is both anti-American and anticapitalist."[78] And for Roger Kimball, editor of the conservative journal *The New Criterion*, the university has been

> corrupted by the values of Woodstock ... that permeate our lives like a corrosive fog.... Why should parents fund the moral de-civilization of their children at the hands of tenured antinomians? Why should alumni generously support an alma mater whose political and educational principles nourish a world view that is not simply different from but diametrically opposed to the one they endorse? Why should trustees preside over an institution whose faculty systematically repudiates the pedagogical mission they, as trustees, have committed themselves to uphold? These are questions that should be asked early and asked often.[79]

Carol Swain, writing in the *Chronicle of Higher Education*, made the undocumented claim that the secularized, liberal elites who inhabit the university direct their animus toward "bright, conservative students [who] are victimized again and again by faculty members who use the power of grading to push them towards conformity."[80] Another example of the inflated rhetoric and distorted arguments of these kinds of attacks occurred when former Republican presidential candidate Reverend Pat Robertson interviewed David Horowitz on his *700 Club* television program in March 2006. Displaying characteristic anger toward the radical academy, Robertson proclaimed that there are at least "thirty to forty thousand" left-wing professors or, as he called them, "termites that have worked into the woodwork of our academic society and it's appalling.... They are racists, murderers, sexual deviants and supporters of Al-Qaeda—and they could be teaching your kids! These guys are out and out communists, they are propagandists of the first order. You don't want your child to be brainwashed by these radicals, you just don't want it to happen. Not only be brainwashed but beat up, they beat these people up, cower them into submission."[81] Not one to be outraged, Horowitz agreed with Robertson, adding:

It is an intellectual corruption, and it is really a political corruption that is bigger than the Enron scandal and much worse. Enron was about money. This is about young people's minds and the future of the country. I estimate that there are 50,000 to 60,000 radical professors who want the terrorists to win and us to lose the war on terror. They regard the terrorists as freedom fighters and America as an imperialist power that oppresses third-world people, and we are the root cause of the attacks on us.[82]

Progressive educators are now viewed as closeted versions of Ward Churchill, the "torn scab revealing a festering sore beneath,"[83] in need of outside regulation if not outright dismissal. Ironically, the rallying cry for a conservative project designed to legislate more outside control over teacher authority, enact laws to protect conservative students from pedagogical discomfort, and pass legislation that regulates the hiring process and provides an affirmative action program for conservative faculty—more big government—has been dressed up in the language of fairness and balance. Expropriating "key terms in the liberal lexicon, as if they were the only true champions of freedom and diversity on campuses,"[84] various right-wing individuals and groups target the so-called liberal university by claiming that its faculties are dominated by left-oriented professors and that conservative faculty and students often find themselves victimized in such narrow politicized institutions and classrooms.

David Horowitz remains one of the most powerful and well-known spokespersons leading this effort for "academic balance." A self-identified former left-wing radical who has since become a right-wing conservative, Horowitz is the president of the Center for the Study of Popular Culture and the ideological force behind the online magazine *FrontPageMag.com*. He is the author of over twenty books and founder of Students for Academic Freedom, a national watchdog group that monitors what professors say in their classrooms. He is also the creator of *DiscovertheNetworks. org*, an online database whose purpose is to "catalogue all the organizations and individuals that make up" what he loosely defines in sweeping monolithic terms as "the Left."[85] As one of the most forceful voices in the assault on higher education, Horowitz has used the appeal to intellectual diversity and academic freedom with great success to promote his Academic Bill of Rights (ABOR),[86] conduct smear campaigns through various websites and books, and try to convince state and federal politicians to pass his ABOR. According to Horowitz, the purpose of ABOR is to "codify the tradition of academic freedom; to emphasize the value of 'intellectual diversity' already implicit in the concept of academic freedom; and, most important, to enumerate the rights of students to not be indoctrinated or otherwise assaulted by political propagandists in the classroom or any educational setting."[87] Attempting to expose what he views as an imbalance among faculty and discrimination toward conservative students, Horowitz insists that the academy is largely controlled by left-wing radicals, who dominate the faculty, monopolize the slots given to guest speakers on campuses, and overly influence the growth of student organizations with a leftist agenda.

Even before Horowitz's campaign picked up speed, these kinds of claims regarding faculty political affiliations had been promoted by Republican politicians, reproduced in editorials, and increasingly presented in the dominant media as a matter of common sense, despite an endless number of studies that have proven they are methodologically flawed and statistically biased. For instance, a *Wall Street Journal* editorial in 2003 claimed that "Democrats outnumber Republicans by a 10–1 margin in a recent study of political affiliation at 32 leading American Universities." Unperturbed by the deeply flawed and ideologically driven nature of the report, nationally syndicated columnist George Will quipped that college campuses were increasingly "intellectually akin to North Korea."[88] The upshot of the alleged left-wing stranglehold on higher education in the words of some conservatives was the threatening not merely of the campuses but of American society itself. As Steven Warshawsky ominously intoned:

> The Left's domination of American higher education, from humble community colleges to Ivy League universities, has been repeatedly and convincingly demonstrated for nearly

two decades. The irrefutable evidence of this domination includes the overwhelming imbalance of Democrats versus Republicans on college faculties and administrations; the corresponding rise of major universities (e.g., Harvard and Berkeley) as the leading donors for Democratic Party candidates; the pervasiveness of "critical" pedagogical approaches that emphasize "inequality" and "oppression" based on race, sex, class, and sexuality; the denial of objective, universal standards of meaning and logic under the guise of "deconstructionism"; harassment of conservative students and organizations; and rampant political correctness. The result, as Allan Bloom, David Horowitz, and others have argued, is the ongoing transformation of the college experience into the main front of the radical political assault on American society itself.[89]

Horowitz's case for the Academic Bill of Rights rests on a series of faulty empirical studies, many conducted by right-wing associations.[90] The studies look compelling until they are more closely engaged.[91] The studies Horowitz cites rarely look at colleges, departments, or programs outside of the social sciences and humanities, thus excluding a large portion of the campus. For instance, these studies generally have nothing to say about the political affiliation of faculty in the schools of business, agriculture, education, computer science, medical sciences, and engineering. And yet, according to the *Princeton Review*, four of the top-ten most popular subjects are business administration and management, biology, nursing, and computer science, none of which is included in Horowitz's studies.[92] While it is very difficult to provide adequate statistics regarding the proportion of liberals to conservatives in academe, a University of California at Los Angeles report surveyed over 55,000 full-time faculty and administrators in 2002–2003 and found that "48 percent identified themselves as either liberal or far left; 34 percent as middle of the road, and only 18 percent as conservative or far right."[93] All in all, 52.3 percent of college faculty either considered themselves centrist or conservative. A 2006 study by the journal *Public Opinion Quarterly* argues that "recent trends suggest increased movement to the center, toward a more moderate faculty" and that there is "little danger that ... an increasingly liberal faculty has taken over universities."[94] But there is more at stake here than the reliability of statistical studies measuring the voting patterns, values, and political positions of faculty. There is also the issue of relevance and whether such studies tell us anything at all about what happens in college classrooms. What correlation is to be correctly assumed between a professor's voting patterns and how he or she teaches a class? Actually, none. How might such studies deal with people whose political positions are not so clear, as when an individual is socially conservative but economically radical? And are we to assume that there is a correlation between "one's ideological orientation and the quality of one's academic work"?[95] Then, of course, there's the question that the right-wing commissars refuse to acknowledge: Who is going to monitor and determine what the politics should be of a potentially new hire, existing faculty members, and departments? How does such a crude notion of politics mediate disciplinary wars between, for instance, those whose work is empirically driven and those who adhere to qualitative methods? And if balance implies that all positions are equal and deserve equal time in order not to appear biased, should universities give equal time to Holocaust deniers, to work that supported apartheid in South Africa, or to pro-slavery advocates, to name but a few? Moreover, as Russell Jacoby points out with a degree of irony, if political balance is so important, then why isn't it invoked in other commanding sectors of society? Jacoby comments:

> Conservatives complain relentlessly that they do not get a fair shake in the university, and they want parity—that is, more conservatives on faculties. Conservatives are lonely on American campuses as well as beleaguered and misunderstood. News that tenured poets vote Democratic or that Kerry received far more money from professors than Bush pains them. They want America's faculties to reflect America's political composition. Of course, they do not ad-

dress such imbalances in the police force, Pentagon, FBI, CIA and other government outfits where the stakes seem far higher and where, presumably, followers of Michael Moore are in short supply. If life were a big game of Monopoly, one might suggest a trade to these conservatives: You give us one Pentagon, one Department of State, Justice and Education, plus throw in the Supreme Court, and we will give you every damned English department you want.[96]

The issue of balance is also used to suggest that conservative students are relentlessly harassed, intimidated, or unfairly graded because of their political views, despite their growing presence on college campuses and the generous financial support they receive from over a dozen conservative institutions that "spend some $38-million annually pushing their agendas by bringing speakers to colleges and financing conservative student publications."[97] One place where such examples of alleged discrimination can be found is on the website of Horowitz's Students for Academic Freedom (SAF), whose credo is "You can't get a good education if they're only telling you half the story."[98] SAF has chapters on 150 campuses and maintains a website where students can register complaints. Most complaints express dissatisfaction with teacher comments or assigned readings that have a left-liberal orientation; rather than reflect harassment or discrimination, the complaints largely register student disagreement with the content of particular books or ideas. This is hardly a basis for charges of discrimination. Students complain, for instance, about reading lists that include books by Howard Zinn, Cornel West, or Barbara Ehrenreich. Others protest classroom screenings of Michael Moore's *Fahrenheit 9/11, Super Size Me,* or *Wal-Mart: The High Cost of Low Living.* One student felt offended because a teacher in an introduction to international relations course asked what the class thought of "U.S. plans to attack Iran"? The nature of the pedagogical offense was twofold: The question allegedly revealed the teacher's "liberal bias" and created a hostile climate for the conservative complainant, who also took umbrage at the teacher's decision to ignore another student's dead-end assertion that planning wars was just what the "U.S. military intelligence community does." Other students echoed similarly besieged sensibilities: "This class was terrible. We were assigned 3 books, plus a course reader! I don't think that just because a professor thinks they have the right to assign anything they want that they should be able to force us to read so much. In fact, I think the professor found out my religious and political beliefs and this is why he assigned so much reading."[99] In a course on civil liberties at the University of Portland, a student complained on the SAF website that she felt intimidated because a professor had raised an issue concerning the political acuity of the American public given "the fact that the Administration had manipulated intelligence leading us into war,"[100] the implication being that the professor had somehow maligned American patriotic values. Another student felt harassed because she had to read a text in class titled *Fast Food Nation,* which is faulted for arguing in favor of government regulation of the food industry. And this is labeled as "left indoctrination."[101] Professor Ann Marie B. Bahr has chronicled her accounts of right-wing students' refusals to read two books assigned in her course, "Religion in American Culture," on the grounds that the books "were biased against evangelicals."[102] Russell Jacoby has argued that virtually all of the complaints "reported to the Academic Freedom Abuse center deal with leftist political comments or leftist assigned readings. To use the idiom of right-wing commentators, we see here the emergence of crybaby conservatives, who demand a judicial remedy, guaranteed safety and representation."[103]

What is disturbing about these instances is that aggrieved students and their sympathizers appear entirely indifferent to the degree to which they not only enact a political intrusion into the classroom but also undermine the concept of informed authority, teacher expertise, and professional academic standards that provide the basis for what is taught in classrooms, the approval of courses, and who is hired to teach such courses. The complaints by conservative students often share the premise that because they are "consumers" of education, they have a right to demand what should be taught, as if knowledge is simply a commodity to be purchased according to one's taste. Academic standards, norms of evidence, reasoning, and the assumption that professors earn a certain amount of authority because they are familiar with a research tradition and its methodologies, significant scholarship, and history are entirely removed from such complaints, leaving the presupposition that students have the right to listen only to ideas they agree with and to select their own classroom reading materials.[104] Because students disagree with an unsettling idea does not mean that they have the authority, expertise, education, or power to dictate for all their classmates what should be stated, discussed, or taught in a classroom. There is no language here for conservative students to become conscious of their own ignorance, engage unexamined assumptions, or recognize the limits of knowledge and the need to question official notions of truth and power. Efforts to derail scholarly inquiry and professorial authority also raise questions about the very purpose of education. As Professor Rashid Khalidi points out:

> If students were coming to be told ideas that they arrived at the university with they would be getting nothing of value here. If they were not to be challenged, if they were not to be forced to rethink the things that they come here as 18 year olds ... with, what for heaven's sake would be the point of a university? What would in heaven's name be the point of teaching? We would just arrive with monolithic conventional ideas, and we would leave with monolithic conventional ideas. This is why academic freedom is absolutely vital.[105]

The complaints recorded by Students for Academic Freedom, as well as those used by Horowitz, are almost entirely anecdotal and rarely are pursued through university grievance protocols. Moreover, such stories gain their credibility merely by being articulated, without any substantial proof or evidence. In fact, when pressed before a Pennsylvania congressional board that was investigating whether charges of widespread political bias in higher education had any merit, Horowitz admitted that some of the more notorious accusations he had constantly invoked in his speeches and writings were actually false. For example, the story of classroom bias based on a Penn State professor showing *Fahrenheit 9/11* in class proved fictional, and yet it was the very story that inspired the Pennsylvania hearing.[106] After the Pennsylvania legislature passed HR 177, which is a version of Horowitz's Academic Bill of Rights, Penn State was asked to submit a "list of all of the complaints it had received in the past five years that dealt with the issue of academic freedom. In a university of more than 80,000 students, during a period when more than 177,000 courses were taught, only 13 complaints had been filed ... and at least three of the 13 complaints seem to show students accusing their professors of being too conservative, rather than too liberal."[107] So much for Penn State sledge-hammering its conservative students into submission. In fact, when the Pennsylvania House of Representative's legislative panel examining whether the rights of students were being violated because of their political views issued its final report, it rejected Horowitz's arguments about large-scale discrimination against conservative students. Moreover, it stripped Horowitz's testimony from the final report and stated that it did not find any evidence of widespread oppression directed at students, specifically because of their political beliefs. Horowitz responded to the findings by blaming the Democrats and the unions and insisted that a "'cabal' of faculty leaders had convinced 'weak-spined Republicans' (who controlled the committee) to go along with the 'theft.'"[108]

Even more telling is Horowitz's attempt to document in his book, *The Professors,* the charge that academics indoctrinate their students with political views. The book is an appalling mix of falsehoods, lies, misrepresentations, and unsubstantiated anecdotes. Not only does Horowitz fail to include the words of even one conservative academic, but many quotes about "dangerous" professors are incorrect or taken out of context, and many professors are condemned simply for what they teach, as Horowitz actually has little or no ammunition against *how* they teach. For example, Professor Lewis Gordon is criticized for including "contributions from Africana and Eastern thought" in his course on existentialism.[109] In "Facts

Count," a critical and detailed study of the Free Exchange on Campus organization, Horowitz's book is shown to contain endless "inaccuracies, distortions, and manipulations of fact—including false statements, mischaracterizations of professors' views, broad claims unsupported by facts and selective omissions of information that does not fit his argument."[110] Horowitz, in spite of what he claims, is not opposed to all professors bringing their politics into the classroom, just those who happen to have left-oriented political positions. I think Neil Gross is entirely correct in arguing that "*The Professors* is not an objective account written from the standpoint of Social Science. Horowitz's book is a one-sided screed operating under the conceit of neutrality that mimics in form and content the kind of knee-jerk politics he mocks. What really rankles Horowitz aren't professors who bring their politics into the classroom, but professors who hold political views different from his own."[111] Horowitz's endless invective against critical intellectuals, all of whom he seems to consider left-wing, is perfectly captured in a comment he made on Dr. Laura's talk show in which he told the listening audience that "campus leftists hate America more than the terrorists."[112]

As Stanley Fish has argued, "balance" is a flawed concept and should be understood as a political tactic rather than an academic value.[113] As a tactic, its purpose is, not simply to get more conservatives teaching in English Departments, promote intellectual diversity, or protect conservative students from the horrors of left-wing indoctrination, but to call into question the viability of academic integrity, eliminate critical scholarship, and undermine the university as a public sphere that educates students as critically engaged and responsible citizens in the larger global context. The concept of balance demeans teacher authority by suggesting that a political litmus test is the most appropriate consideration for teaching, and it devalues students by suggesting that they are happy robots, interested not in thinking but in merely acquiring skills for jobs. In this view, students are infantilized; they are rendered incapable of thinking critically or engaging knowledge that unsettles their worldviews, and too weak to resist ideas that challenge their commonsense understanding of the world. Balance is often invoked to suggest that students who have to face troubling questions and ideas are being victimized rather than engaged as thoughtful agents—the foundation for any viable critical pedagogical experience. As Juan Cole points out, balance and fairness are not the point of pedagogy—the real goal is to get students to think independently and critically. He writes:

> The fact is that you will never get agreement on such matters of opinion, and no university teacher I know seeks such agreement. The point of teaching a course is to expose students to ideas and arguments that are new to them and to help them think critically about controversial issues. Nothing pleases teachers more than to see students craft their own, original arguments, based on solid evidence, that dispute the point of view presented in class lectures.... University teaching is not about fairness, and there is nobody capable of imposing "fair" views on teachers. It is about provoking students to think analytically and synthetically, and to reason on their own. In the assigned texts, in class discussion, and in lectures, the students are exposed to a wide range of views, whether fair or unfair.[114]

"Balance" for many conservatives has become code for monitoring pedagogical exchange, matched by a call for government intervention. For example, a Senate committee in Arizona passed a bill in which faculty could be fined up to $500 for "advocating one side of a social, political, or cultural issue that is a matter of partisan controversy." The Republican majority leader insisted it had nothing to do with violating academic freedom. As he put it with no irony intended, "You can speak about any subject you want, just don't take a position."[115] Balance in the current attack on higher education is used as a rhetorical tool by right-wing conservatives and Christian evangelicals whose worldviews are dominated by fixed dualisms and an ideological rigidity that resents questioning; it is more intent on censoring unpopular views than on engaging them. In this context, balance becomes an ideological weapon to denounce liberal thought, denigrate critical thinking, and vanquish a cast of diabolical enemies, conveniently lumped together as radical and un-American. It is difficult to understand what positive function the call to intellectual diversity and balance can have when its interlocutors presume that liberal academics are equated with an evil menace let loose on university campuses to do the work of the devil.

But intellectual integrity and critical learning are not what is really at stake here. As Horowitz travels extensively around the United States meeting with friendly Republican politicians at the state and federal levels of government, urging them to investigate cases of political bias and to enact his ABOR, he continues to insist that neither his motives nor his project is political. His ABOR has attracted a great deal of attention from various state representatives and has resulted in some alarming bills making the rounds through various stages of legislative review. For instance, Arizona Senate Bill 1331 "[r]equires universities and community colleges to provide a student with alternative coursework if the student deems regular course work to be personally offensive."[116] And Larry Mumper, a senator from Marion, Ohio, introduced Senate Bill 20, an academic bill of rights in which all public and private Ohio colleges would be required to generate "curricula and reading lists [that] provide students with dissenting sources and viewpoints."[117] When Mumper was asked by the press how he might rationalize this government intrusion into the classroom, he stated that "'80 percent or so of professors are Democrats, liberals or socialists or card-carrying Communists,' as if for a moment he forgot what decade he lived in."[118] It gets worse. Florida legislators are considering a bill inspired by the ABOR that would, according to the *Independent Florida Alligator,* "stamp out 'leftist totalitarianism' by 'dictator professors' in the classrooms of Florida's universities."[119] Sponsored by Republican Dennis Baxley, the bill, similar to the one making the rounds in several other states, would provide students with the right to sue their professors if they believe that their conservative views are disrespected in class. According to Paul Krugman, writing in the *New York Times,* "Mr. Baxley says that he is taking on 'leftists' struggling against 'mainstream society,' professors who act as 'dictators' and turn the classroom into a 'totalitarian niche.' His prime example of academic totalitarianism? When professors say that evolution is a fact."[120] Suggesting a return to an updated, if not bizarre, version of red-baiting, the discourse that informs these bills is not limited to the half-baked ideas of dim-witted, anti-intellectual politicians. At the federal level, the ABOR is making its way through various House and Senate Committees with the firm backing of a number of politicians. For instance, Senator Lamar Alexander has argued that the "biggest obstacle to increased federal support for higher education is left-wing political bias on college faculties,"[121] signaling that the ABOR was really part of a larger conservative political project to pressure schools to either get rid of teachers who introduce controversial ideas in their classrooms or be prepared to face funding cuts. The bill has also been endorsed by Karl Rove and the former House Majority Leader, Tom DeLay. A version of Horowitz's ABOR has been passed in the House of Representatives and is being considered with slight revisions in the Senate.[122] It has a good chance of being passed by Congress, though with the control of both houses of Congress having been taken over by the Democratic Party in 2006, the bill may receive stiff opposition from the majority party. At the same time, it is worth noting that a Democratic Congress will do little to change the deeper dynamics already set in motion by the neoconservatives in relation to higher education.

As I have stated previously, in spite of Horowitz's claim that the ABOR is not a political document, his activities are sponsored entirely by right-wing organizations such as the Sarah Scaife Foundation and the Lynde and Harry Bradley Foundation. Kathy Kelly writing in *CounterPunch. org* claimed that Horowitz's various projects received $13.7 million through 2003,[123] while Jennifer Jacobson reporting on Horowitz in the *Chronicle of Higher Education* stated that the Center for the Study of Popular Culture alone received $3.2 million in 2003.[124] Horowitz has repeatedly argued that the ABOR is purely voluntary, but this position is at odds with much of what he has articulated in a number of publications, talks, and interviews. For instance, in a December 2003 speech at the University of Montana, he declared, "We want every university in the country to have an Academic Bill of Rights and see it enforced." Rob Chaney, a writer for the *Montana Missoulian* reported, "Horowitz said campuses should screen their reading lists for bias, break up the 'Star Chamber' secrecy of hiring and tenure decisions, and monitor classrooms for imbalance of opinions or divergence from core class concepts."[125] But there is more at stake here than the contradiction between Horowitz's claim of the alleged neutrality of the Academic Bill of Rights and his attempts to get legislative backing to enforce it; there is also the endless stream of vicious attacks on anyone who does critical work in the academy, his consistent calls for censorship, and his ongoing use of McCarthyite slander to vilify professors who actively engage in addressing problems in the larger society.

Horowitz and his allies care little about balance as a principle, whether it be in hiring faculty or promoting open inquiry in the classroom; they seem far more concerned with intimidating, shaming, and bullying as part of a broader effort to control all social institutions not entirely committed to the values of conservative Republicans, market-driven evangelicals, or Christian fundamentalists. The call for balance by conservatives such as Horowitz, the Students for Academic Freedom, and ACTA is a red herring whose aim is not to expand critical learning but to shut it down, to mute criticism rather than endorse it as central to any viable notion of politics, education, and citizenship. All one has to do is read the apocalyptic rhetoric, which amounts to a holy war against academe, to recognize that this group hates any vestige of thought that is truly open to the play of multiple viewpoints and free inquiry and conscious of the need to ask difficult questions about the consequences of knowledge to promote the social good. Its primary aim, in fact, is to "narrow the political spectrum and move the entire political discourse to the right."[126] Horowitz, Anne D. Neal, and their ilk insist that only liberals bring their political views to the classroom while conservative views are somehow apolitical. In the end, as Ellen Willis has pointed out, the appeal to balance by Horowitz and his ideological cohorts simply becomes a rhetorical and political ploy designed to encourage the intimidation of "offending liberal professors by students or infiltrators who monitor their class and [put] pressure on legislative officials, donors, and trustees to influence faculty hiring decisions and the curriculum."[127]

How does one take seriously Horowitz's call for fairness when he labels the American Library Association in his online magazine as "a terrorist sanctuary,"[128] or describes Noam Chomsky, whom the *New Yorker* named "one of the greatest minds of the 20th century,"[129] as "demonic and seditious" and claims the purpose of his work is "to incite believers to provide aid and comfort to the enemies of the U.S."?[130] Horowitz's characterization of university professors as members of a "privileged elite that work between six to nine hours a week, eight months a year for an annual salary of about $150,000" displays an ignorance so profound that it is laughable.[131] Anyone familiar with higher education knows that faculty salaries are not keeping up with inflation, faculty benefits are shrinking, and half the faculty members in the United States hold part-time positions.[132] Indeed, what is one to make of Horowitz's online "A Guide to the Political Left," in which the mild-mannered film critic Roger Ebert occupies the same ideological ground as Omar Abdel Rahman, the mastermind of the 1993 World Trade Center bombing? Can one really believe that Horowitz is a voice for open inquiry when he portrays as activists for "left-wing agendas and causes" the late Peter Jennings, Supreme Court Justice Ruth B. Ginsburg, Garrison Keillor, and Katie Couric? Or when he labels Cornel West, Cindy Sheehan, and Dennis Kucinich "anti-American radicals" and former President Bill Clinton a leftist?[133] But Horowitz does more than engage in crude smear tactics reminiscent of the McCarthy era; he has no trouble calling for the banning of books and academic programs whose ideologies offend him. He has called for the banning of Barbara Ehrenreich's renowned *Nickel and Dimed* from student reading lists and has argued both that "Peace Studies programs in America . . . teach students to identify with America's terrorist enemies and to identify America as a 'Great Satan,'" and that such programs should be shut down.[134] He has also denounced women's studies programs as a violation of academic freedom because they "express a goal of educating students about 'how and why gender inequality developed and is maintained in the United States and in our global society,' [and argued that they] 'should be banned.'"[135] Most disturbingly, he has promoted a campaign for publishing the "addresses of editors and reporters of the *Times*," whom he views as being at war with the United States.[136] And the authoritarian drumbeat of this self-righteous pundit dressed up in the discourse of liberal plurality and academic freedom seems to continue with greater fury in every successive article, interview, and speech that he gives.[137] What is one to make of Horowitz's call for academic freedom and balance when he has not only accused critics of Bush's foreign and domestic policies of being guilty of treason but also accompanied such accusations with the promotion of publishing the addresses of those accused of such acts? Constitutional law attorney Glenn Greenwald puts such actions in their rightful political context with this comment:

> As people like Horowitz [know]—and just as my most extremist former White Supremacist clients well knew—if you throw burning matches at gasoline enough times, an explosion is inevitable. The rhetoric of treason—accusing individuals and organizations of aiding and abetting our nation's enemies and even waging war on this country—is a lit match. After all, the widely accepted penalty for traitors is execution, which is why it is such an inflammatory yet increasingly common accusation being hurled by the Right against their domestic 'enemies' (for precisely the same reason, the favorite accusation of the World Church of the Creator was to label someone a 'race traitor,' since everyone knows what should be done with traitors).[138]

The Necessity of Critical Pedagogy

Thinking is not the intellectual reproduction of what already exists anyway. As long as it doesn't break off, thinking has a secure hold on possibility. Its insatiable aspect, its aversion to being quickly and easily satis-

fied, refuses the foolish wisdom of resignation. The
utopian moment in thinking is stronger the less it . . .
objectifies itself into a utopia and hence sabotages its
realization. Open thinking points beyond itself.[139]

The attack against Middle Eastern studies as well as other
engaged areas of the social sciences and humanities has
opened the door to a whole new level of assault on academic
freedom, teacher authority, and critical pedagogy.[140] These
attacks, as I have pointed out, are much more widespread
and, in my estimation, much more dangerous than the
McCarthyite campaign several decades ago. Trading upon
the ongoing corporatization of the university, its increasing reliance on nongovernment financial resources, and its
vulnerability to outside criticism, a number of right-wing
advocacy groups are now targeting higher education, alleg-
ing it is not only a breeding ground for cultivating anti-Israel
and anti-capital sentiments but also a hotbed of politicized
pedagogical encounters considered both discriminatory
against conservative students and un-American in their
critical orientation. Invoking academic freedom is crucial
for maintaining the university as democratic public sphere,
but it is equally essential to defend critical pedagogy as a
condition of civic responsibility and teaching as a deliberate
act of intervening in the world as part of the goal of encour-
aging students to think about justice and to question "the
ostensibly unquestionable premises of our way of life."[141]

While most defenders of the university as a democratic
public sphere rightly argue that the right-wing assault on
the academy levels a serious threat to academic freedom,
they have largely ignored the crucial issue that the very
nature of pedagogy as a political, moral, and critical practice
is at stake, particularly the role it plays in presupposing a
view of the world that is more just, democratic, and free from
human suffering.[142] Robert Ivie has argued rightly that academic freedom in its basic form "means unfettered scholarly
inquiry, a scholar's fundamental right of research, publication, and instruction free of institutional constraint."[143] But
it is pedagogy that begs a more spirited defense as well as
analysis so that it can be protected against the challenges

that Horowitz, ACTA, SAF, Campus Watch, and others are initiating against what actually takes place in classrooms devoted to critical engagement, dialogue, research, and debate. Pedagogy at its best is about neither training nor political indoctrination; instead, it is about a political and moral practice that provides the knowledge, skills, and social relations that enable students to expand the possibilities of what it means to be critical citizens while using their knowledge and skills to deepen and extend their participation in a substantive and inclusive democracy. Rather than assume the mantle of a false impartiality, pedagogy recognizes that education and teaching involve the crucial act of intervening in the world and the recognition that human life is conditioned, not determined. The responsibility of pedagogy amounts to more than becoming the instrument of official power or an apologist for the existing order. Critical pedagogy attempts to understand how power works through the production, distribution, and consumption of knowledge within particular institutional contexts and seeks to constitute students as particular subjects and social agents. It is also invested in both the practice of self-criticism about the values that inform our teaching and a critical self-consciousness regarding what it means to equip students with analytical skills to be self-reflective about the knowledge and values they confront in classrooms.

What makes critical pedagogy so dangerous to Christian evangelicals, neoconservatives, and right-wing nationalists in the United States is that central to its very definition is the task of educating students to become critical agents who actively question and negotiate the relationships between theory and practice, critical analysis and common sense, and learning and social change. Critical pedagogy opens up a space where students should be able to come to terms with their own power as critical agents; it provides a sphere where the unconditional freedom to question and assert is central to the purpose of the university, if not to democracy itself.[144] And as a political and moral practice, pedagogy should "make evident the multiplicity and complexity of history," as a narrative to enter into critical dialogue with rather than to accept unquestioningly. Similarly, such a pedagogy should cultivate in students a healthy skepticism about power, a "willingness to temper any reverence for authority with a sense of critical awareness."[145] As a performative practice, pedagogy should provide the conditions for students to be able to reflectively frame their own relationship to the ongoing project of an unfinished democracy. It is precisely this relationship between democracy and pedagogy that is so threatening to conservatives such as Horowitz. Pedagogy always represents a commitment to the future, and it remains the task of educators to make sure that the future points the way to a more socially just world, a world in which the discourses of critique and possibility in conjunction with the values of reason, freedom, and equality function to alter, as part of a broader democratic project, the grounds upon which life is lived. This is hardly a prescription for political indoctrination, but it is a project that gives education its most valued purpose and meaning, which in part is "to encourage human agency, not mold it in the manner of Pygmalion."[146] It is also a position that threatens right-wing private advocacy groups, neoconservative politicians, and conservative extremists because they recognize that such a pedagogical commitment goes to the very heart of what it means to address real inequalities of power at the social level and to conceive of education as a project for democracy and critical citizenship while at the same time foregrounding a series of important and often ignored questions such as Why do we (as educators) do what we do the way we do it? Whose interests does higher education serve? How might it be possible to understand and engage the diverse contexts in which education takes place? In spite of the right-wing view that equates indoctrination with any suggestion of politics, critical pedagogy is not simply concerned with offering students new ways to think critically and act with authority as agents in the classroom; it is also concerned with providing students with the skills and knowledge necessary for them to expand their capacities both to question deep-seated assumptions and myths that legitimate the most archaic and disempowering social practices that structure every aspect of society and to take responsibility for intervening in the world they inhabit. Education is not neutral, but that does not mean it is merely a form of indoctrination. On the contrary, as a practice that attempts to expand the capacities necessary for human agency and hence the possibilities for democracy itself, the university must nourish those pedagogical practices that promote "a concern with keeping the forever unexhausted and unfulfilled human potential open, fighting back all attempts to foreclose and pre-empt the further unravelling of human possibilities, prodding human society to go on questioning itself and preventing that questioning from ever stalling or being declared finished."[147] In other words, critical pedagogy forges both critique and agency through a language of skepticism and possibility and a culture of openness, debate, and engagement—all elements that are now at risk in the latest and most dangerous attack on higher education.

The attack on pedagogy is, in part, an attempt to deskill teachers and dismantle teacher authority. Teachers can make a claim to being fair, but not to being either neutral or impartial. Teacher authority can never be neutral, nor can it be assessed in terms that are narrowly ideological. It is always broadly political and interventionist in terms of the knowledge-effects it produces, the classroom experiences it organizes, and the future it presupposes in the countless ways in which it addresses the world. Teacher authority at its best means taking a stand without standing still. It suggests that as educators we make a sincere effort to be self-reflective about the value-laden nature of our authority while taking on the fundamental task of educating students to take responsibility for the direction of society. Rather than shrink from our political responsibility as educators, we should embrace one of pedagogy's most fundamental goals: to teach students to believe that democracy is desirable and possible. Connecting education to the possibility of a better world is not a prescription for indoctrination; rather, it marks the distinction between the academic as a technician and the teacher as a self-reflective educator who is more than the instrument of a safely approved and officially sanctioned worldview. Pedagogy at its best does not avoid commitment, it makes it possible!

The authority that enables academics to teach emerges out of the education, knowledge, research, professional rituals, and scholarly experiences that they bring to their field of expertise and classroom teaching. Such authority provides the space and experience in which pedagogy goes beyond providing the conditions for the simple acts of knowing and understanding and includes the cultivation of the very power of self-definition and critical agency. But teacher authority cannot be grounded exclusively in the rituals of professional academic standards. Learning occurs in a space in which commitment and passion provide students with a sense of what it means to link knowledge to a sense of direction. Teaching is a practice rooted in an ethico-political vision that attempts to take students beyond the world they already know, in a way that does not insist on a particular fixed set of altered meanings. In this context, teacher authority rests on pedagogical practices that reject the role of students as passive recipients of familiar knowledge and view them instead as producers of knowledge, who not only critically engage diverse ideas but also transform and act on them.[148] Pedagogy is the space that provides a moral and political referent for understanding how what we do in the classroom is linked to wider social, political, and economic forces.

It is impossible to separate what we do in the classroom from the economic and political conditions that shape our work, and that means that pedagogy has to be understood as a form of academic labor in which questions of time, autonomy, freedom, and power become as central to the classroom as what is taught. As a referent for engaging fundamental questions about democracy, pedagogy gestures to important questions about the political, institutional, and structural conditions that allow teachers to produce curricula, collaborate with colleagues, engage in research, and connect their work to broader public issues. Pedagogy is not about balance, a merely methodological consideration;

on the contrary, as Cornelius Castoriadis reminds us, if education is not to become "the political equivalent of a religious ritual,"[149] it must do everything possible to provide students with the knowledge and competencies they need to learn how to deliberate, make judgments, and exercise choice, particularly as the latter is brought to bear on critical activities that offer the possibility of democratic change. Democracy cannot work if citizens are not autonomous, self-judging, curious, reflective, and independent—qualities that are indispensable for students if they are going to make vital judgments and choices about participating in and shaping decisions that affect everyday life, institutional reform, and governmental policy. Hence, pedagogy becomes the cornerstone of democracy in that it provides the very foundation for students to learn not merely how to be governed but also how to be capable of governing.

One gets the sense that conservative educators from Lynne Cheney to Ann D. Neal to David Horowitz believe that there is no place in the classroom for politics, worldly concerns, social issues, and questions about how to lessen human suffering. In this discourse, the classroom becomes an unworldly counterpart to the gated community, a space for conformity in which the meaning of education is largely reduced to respecting students' "comfort zones" and to perpetuating current governmental and social practices, however corrupt and anti-democratic. This is a form of education, as Howard Zinn notes, where scholars "publish while others perish."[150] This is not education; it is a flight from self and society. Its outcome is not a student who feels a responsibility to others and who feels that her presence in the world matters, but one who feels the presence of difference and critical thinking as an unbearable burden to be contained or expelled. The importance of academics as engaged intellectuals, the necessity of making education worldly and pedagogy a moral and political practice, has been captured in a different context by Edward Said in his discussion of the role of the public intellectual. He wrote:

So in the end it is the intellectual as a representative figure that matters—someone who visibly represents a standpoint of some kind, and someone who makes articulate representations to his or her public despite all sorts of barriers. My argument is that intellectuals are individuals with a vocation for the art of representing.... And that vocation is important to the extent that it is publicly recognizable and involves both commitment and risk, boldness and vulnerability.... The intellectual ... is neither a pacifier nor a consensus-builder, but someone whose whole being is staked on a critical sense, a sense of being unwilling to accept easy formulas, or ready-made clichés, or the smooth, ever-so-accommodating confirmations of what the powerful or conventional have to say, and what they do. Not just passively unwilling, but actively willing to say so in public.[151]

Given the seriousness of the current attack on higher education by an alliance of diverse right-wing forces, it is difficult to understand why liberals, progressives, and left-oriented educators have been relatively silent in the face of this assault. There is much more at stake in this attack on the university than the issue of academic freedom. First and foremost is the concerted attempt by right-wing extremists and corporate interests to strip the professoriate of any authority, render critical pedagogy as merely an instrumental task, eliminate tenure as a protection for teacher authority, and remove critical reason from any vestige of civic courage, engaged citizenship, and social responsibility. The three academic unions have a combined membership of almost 200,000, including graduate students and adjuncts, and yet they have barely stirred. In part, they are quiet because they are under the illusion that tenure will protect them, or they believe the attack on academic freedom has little to do with how they perform their academic labor. They are wrong on both counts, and unless the unions and progressives mobilize to protect the institutionalized relationships between democracy and pedagogy, teacher authority and classroom autonomy, they will be at the mercy of a right-wing revolution that views democracy as an excess and the university as a threat.

In short, the current assault on the academy is an attack, not only on the conditions that make critical pedagogy possible, but also on what it might mean to raise questions about the real problems facing higher education today, which include the increasing role of adjunct faculty, the instrumentalization of knowledge, the rise of an expanding national security state, the hijacking of the university by corporate interests, and the increasing attempts by right-wing extremists to turn education into job training or into an extended exercise in patriotic xenophobia. All of these conditions undermine the idea of the university as a place to think, to engage knowledge critically, to make judgments, and to assume responsibility for what it means to know something and to understand the consequences of such knowledge for the larger world. While Hannah Arendt did not address directly the importance of critical pedagogy, she understood that in its absence monstrous deeds, often committed on a gigantic scale, had less to do with some grand notion of evil than with a "quite authentic inability to think."[152] For Arendt, the absence of the faculty of thinking, making judgments, and assuming responsibility constituted the conditions not merely for stupidity but for a type of evil capable of monstrous crimes, and surely the precondition for a politics exemplified in old and new forms of totalitarianism. The current right-wing assault on higher education is in reality an attack on the most rudimentary conditions of politics—given its lack of respect for critical thought, judgment, dialogue, and imagination itself. In fact, right-wing notions of teaching and learning constitute a kind of anti-politics, one that substitutes balance for critical engagement, conformity for dialogue, and ideological inflexibility for judgment. Such attacks should be named for what they are—affirmations of thoughtlessness, antidotes to the difficult process of self- and social criticism, and acts of conformity as a substitute for risk taking.[151] Pedagogy must be understood as central to any discourse about academic freedom, but, more important, it must be understood as the most crucial referent we have for understanding politics and defending the university as one of the very few remaining democratic public spheres in the United States today.

Notes

1. This chapter is a revised version of "Academic Freedom Under Fire: The Case for Critical Pedagogy," *College Literature* 33:4 (Fall 2006), pp. 1–42.
. Cited in Jonathan R. Cole, "Academic Freedom Under Fire," *Daedalus* (Spring 2005), available online at http://www.findarticles.com/p/articles/mi_qa3671/is_200504/ai_n13641838.

2. Edward Said, *Humanism and Democratic Criticism* (New York: Columbia University Press, 2004), p. 22. I take up the legacy and role of higher education as a democratic public sphere in more detail in Henry A. Giroux and Susan Searls Giroux, *Take Back Higher Education: Race, Youth, and the Crisis of Democracy in the Post–Civil Rights Era* (New York: Palgrave, 2006).

3. Said, *Humanism*, p. 72.

4. For an excellent analysis of this attack, see Beshara Doumani, "Between Coercion and Privatization: Academic Freedom in the Twenty-First Century," in *Academic Freedom After September 11*, ed. Beshara Doumani (Cambridge, MA: Zone Books, 2006), pp. 11–57; and Evan Gerstmann and Matthew J. Streb, *Academic Freedom at the Dawn of a New Century: How Terrorism, Governments, and Culture Wars Impact Free Speech* (Stanford: Stanford University Press, 2006). A sustained and informative discussion of academic freedom after 9/11 can be found in Tom Abowd, Fida Adely, Lori Allen, Laura Bier, and Amahl Bishara et al., *Academic Freedom and Professional Responsibility After 9/11: A Handbook for Scholars and Teachers* (New York: Task Force on Middle East Anthropology, 2006), available online at http://www.meanthro.org/Handbook-1.pdf; see also AAUP, "Academic Freedom and National Security in a Time of Crisis," *Academe* 89:6 (2003), available online at www.aaup.org/AAUP/About/committees/committee+repts/cristime.htm; and Johathon R. Cole, "Academic Freedom Under Fire," *Daedalus* 134:2 (2005), pp. 1–23. For a diverse discussion of academic freedom in America, see Louis Menand, ed., *The Future of Academic Freedom* (Chicago: University of Chicago Press, 1996).

5. Richard Hofstadter, *Anti-Intellectualism in American Life* (New York: Vintage Books, 1962).

6. Ellen Willis, "The Pernicious Concept of 'Balance,'" *Chronicle of Higher Education* 52: 3 (September 9, 2005), p. B11.

7. Susan Searls Giroux and I have addressed this issue in Giroux and Giroux, *Take Back Higher Education.* See also Henry A. Giroux, *The Abandoned Generation* (New York: Palgrave, 2005).

8. Cole, "Academic Freedom Under Fire."

9. Ellen W. Schrecker, *No Ivory Tower: McCarthyism and the Universities* (New York: Oxford University Press, 1988); Ellen W. Schrecker, *Many Are the Crimes: McCarthyism in America* (Princeton: Princeton University Press, 1988).

10. Ellen Schrecker, "The New McCarthyism in Academe," *Thought & Action* (Fall 2005), pp. 103–104.

11. Cited in John C. Ensslin, "Hoffman Warns CU faculty of 'New McCarthyism.' But President Notes Obligation to Probe Churchill's Record," *Rocky Mountain News* (March 4, 2005), available online at http://www.rockymountainnews.com//drmn/education/article/0,1299,DRMN_957_3594209,00. html.

12. Ellen Schrecker, "Worse Than McCarthy," *Chronicle of Higher Education* 52:23 (February 10, 2006), p. B20.

13. Doumani, "Between Coercion and Privatization," pp. 14–15.

14. Jerry L. Martin and Anne D. Neal, *Defending Civilization: How Our Universities Are Failing America and What Can be Done About It, ACTA Report,* November 2001, p. 1, available online at http://www.la.utexas.edu/~chenry/2001LynnCheneyjsg01ax1. pdf. This statement was deleted from the revised February 2002 version of the report available on the ACTA website, http://www. goacta.org/publications/Reports/defciv.pdf.

15. Lewis F. Powell, Jr., "The Powell Memo," *ReclaimDemocracy.org* (August 23, 1971), available online at http://reclaimdemocracy.org/corporate_accountability/powell_memo_lewis. html.

16. Ibid.

17. Ibid.

18. See Michael P. Crozier, Samuel. J. Huntington, and J. Watanuki, *The Crisis of Democracy: Report on the Governability of Democracies to the Trilateral Commission* (New York: New York University Press, 1975).

19. Powell, "The Powell Memo."

20. Lewis H. Lapham, "Tentacles of Rage—The Republican Propaganda Mill, a Brief History," *Harper's Magazine* (September 2004), p. 32.

21. Dave Johnson, "Who's Behind the Attack on Liberal Professors?" *History News Network* (February 10, 2005), available online at http://hnn.us/articles/printfriendly/1244.html.

22. Ibid.

23. Alan Jones, "Connecting the Dots," *Inside Higher Ed* (June 16, 2006), available online at http://insidehighered.com/views/2006/06/16/jones.

24. Lapham, "Tentacles of Rage," p. 38.

25. See http://www.targetofopportunity.com/enemy_targets.htm.

26. Doumani, "Between Coercion and Privatization," pp. 15–16.

27. Bob Libal, "An Interview with Robert Jensen: The Right's Assault on the Academy," *CounterPunch.org* (July 5, 2005), available online at http://www.counterpunch.org/libal07052005.html.

28. I take up this issue in great detail in Henry A. Giroux, *Against the New Authoritarianism* (Winnipeg: Arbeiter Ring Press, 2005). See also Chris Hedges, *American Fascists: The Christian Right and the War on America* (New York: The Free Press, 2007); and Joe Conason, *It Can Happen Here: Star-Spangled Fascism in Bush's America* (New York: St. Martin's Press, 2007).

29. Jonathan R. Cole, "The New McCarthyism," *Chronicle of Higher Education* 52:3 (September 9, 2005), p. B7.

30. Ibid.

31. Annie Shuppy, "U.S. Denies a Visa to Swiss Muslim Scholar Who Was Barred in 2004," *Chronicle of Higher Education* (September 26, 2006), available online at http://chronicle.com/daily/2006/09/2006092603n.htm.

32. Tariq Ramadan, "Why I'm Banned in the USA," *Washington Post* (October 1, 2006), p. B1.

33. Bruce Craig, "Scholars Become Targets of the Patriot Act," *American Historical Society* (April 2006), available online at http://www.historians.org/perspectives/issues/2006/0604new1.dfm.

34. Burton Bollag, "U.of Nebraska Sues Government, Accusing It of Stalling on Visa Request for Bolivian Historian," *Chronicle of Higher Education*" (March 6, 2007), available online at http://chronicle.com/weekly/v53/i28/28a04201.htm.

35. Ibid.

36. Burton Bollag, "Greek Professor Traveling to Academic Conference at SUNY Is Turned Away at U.S. Border," *Chronicle of Higher Education* (June 22, 2006), available online at http://chronicle.com/daily/2006/06/2006062202n.htm.

37. Joel Beinin, "The New McCarthyism: Policing Thought About the Middle East," in *Academic Freedom After September 11,* ed. Beshara Doumani (New York: Zone Books, 2006), p. 241.

38. Cole, "Academic Freedom Under Fire."

39. Scott Sherman, "The Mideast Comes to Columbia," *The Nation* (April 4, 2005), p. 18.

40. Massad has forcefully refuted the claims made in the film in his statement to the Ad Hoc Grievance Committee. See Joseph Massad, "Statement to the Ad Hoc Committee" (March 14, 2005), available online at http://electronicintifada.net/downloads/pdf/ JosephMassadStatement.pdf.

41. Juan Cole, "The New McCarthyism," *Salon.com* (April 23, 2005), available online at http://www.commondreams.org/ views05/0423-20.htm.

42. John Mearsheimer and Stephen Walt, "The Israel Lobby," *London Review of Books* 28:6 (March 2006), available online at http://ksgnotes1.harvard.edu/Research/wpaper.nsf/rwp/ RWP06-011/$File/rwp_06_011_walt.pdf. See also Michael Massing, "The Storm over the Israel Lobby," *New York Review of Books* (June 8, 2006), pp. 64–69, 73. Massing is critical of Mearsheimer and Walt's depiction of the Israel Lobby. For an insightful understanding on putting the United States's relationship with the lobby in perspective, see Joseph Massad, "Blaming the Lobby," *Al-Ahram* (March 23–29, 2006), available online at http://weekly.ahram. org.eg/2006/787/op35.htm. One group that monitors attempts to stifle debates about U.S.-Israeli foreign policy can be found at Muzzle Watch, available online at http://www.muzzlewatch. org/.

43. This letter is available online at http://censoringthought. org/twentystudentpetition.html.

44. Cited in Sherman, "The Mideast comes to Columbia," p. 22.

45. Adam Federman, "Columbia Profs Smeared as Anti-Semites," *CounterPunch.org* (November 9, 2004), available online at http://www.counterpunch.org/federman11092004.html.

46. Cited in Cole, "Academic Freedom Under Fire."

47. Ibid.

48. Some of the more recent *New York Sun* links are Alec Magnet, "Former Columbia Student: Massad's Bullying, Anti-Israel Stance Led Her to Drop Out" (January 13, 2006), available online at http://www.nysun.com/article/2583; Alex Magnet, "Massad Wins Promotion at Columbia" (February 7, 2006), available online

at http://www.nysun.com/article/27126; and Alec Magnet, "Nine Professors at Columbia Are 'Dangerous'" (February 21, 2006), available online at http://www.nysun.com/pf.php?id=27850.

49. Columbia University, *Ad Hoc Grievance Report* (March 28, 2005), available online at http://www.columbia.edu/cu/news/05/03/ad_hoc_grievance_committee_report.html.

50. Cited in Cole, "The New McCarthyism."

51. Beinin, "The New McCarthyism," pp. 258–259.

52. Cited in Jon Wiener, "When Students Complain About Professors, Who Gets to Define the Controversy?" *Chronicle of Higher Education* (May 13, 2005), available online at http://chronicle.com/weekly/v51/i36/36b01201.htm.

53. Foner's letter to the *New York Times* is paraphrased in ibid.

54. For a brilliant defense of academic freedom and the unconditional freedom to question, see Jacques Derrida, "The Future of the Profession or the Unconditional University," in *Derrida Down Under,* ed. Laurence Simmons and Heather Worth (Auckland, New Zealand: Dunmore Press, 2001), pp. 233–247.

55. Joseph Massad, "Targeting the University," *Al-Ahram Weekly* 745 (June 2–8, 2005), available online at http://weekly.ahram.org.eg/2005/745/op2.htm.

56. Editorial, "Intimidation at Columbia," *New York Times* (April 7, 2005), p. A27.

57. Ibid.

58. Cole, "The New McCarthyism."

59. Thomas Friedman, "Giving the Hatemongers No Place to Hide," *New York Times* (July 22, 2005), available online at http://www.nytimes.com/2005/07/22/opinion/22friedman.html?ex=1279684800&en=17fb5beb19b09d86&ei=5090&partner=rssuserland&emc=rss.

60. For instance, when it became public knowledge that Juan Cole, a prolific and esteemed scholar, professor of history at the University of Michigan, and president of the Middle Eastern Association, was being considered for a joint appointment in sociology and history at Yale, he became the subject of an intense smear campaign by conservatives waged in the *New York Sun,* the *Wall Street Journal, National Review,* and elsewhere. Cole's crime is that he is a severe critic of the Bush administration and of Israel. The pressure appears to have paid off. Despite the approval of Cole's appointment at both department levels and his reputation as one of the preeminent historians of the Middle East, Yale rejected his appointment. Cole

responded to the decision by stating that "[t]hese vicious attacks on my character and my views are riddled with wild inaccuracies" and that such criticisms were "motivated by a desire to punish me for daring to stand up for Palestinian rights, criticize Israeli policy, criticize Bush administration policies and, in general, being a liberal Democrat." Cited in Scott Jaschik, "Blackballed at Yale," *Inside Higher Ed* (June 5, 2006), available online at http://insidehighered.com/news/2006/06/05/cole. For an extensive analysis of the Cole affair, see Philip Weiss, "Burning Cole," *The Nation* (July 3, 2006), available online at http://www.thenation.com/doc/20060703/weiss. A notorious and well-publicized example of such an attack took place when the internationally renown critic of the Israeli government Professor Norman Finkelstein went up for tenure at DePaul University in Chicago in 2007. Alan Dershowitz, a law professor at Harvard and an indefatigable defender of Israel, not only directly contacted the president of DePaul along with the chairman of the political science department, he also sent a barrage of e-mail messages and packets of information to faculty and administrators in an attempt to derail Professor Finkelstein's bid for tenure. Nonplussed by charges by DePaul's Arts and Sciences' Faculty Governance Council over his attempts to violate the integrity and independence of the university tenure process, Dershowitz alarmingly argued that his efforts were "neither ideological nor personal," a claim that is as disingenuous as his shabby attempts at labeling Finkelstein anti-Semitic in order to discredit his work and undermine his application for tenure. See Patricia Cohen, "A Bitter Spat over Ideas, Israel and Tenure, New York Times (April 12, 2007), p. B1.

61. Ward Churchill, "'Some People Push Back': On the Justice of Roosting Chickens" (September 11, 2001), available online at http://www.kersplebedeb.com/mystuff/s11/churchill.html.

62. Cited in Scott Smallwood, "Ward Churchill Gets a Warm Welcome in Speech in U. Of Hawaii," *Chronicle of Higher Education* (February 24, 2005), available online at http://chronicle.com/daily/2005/02/2005022402.

63. John K. Wilson, "The Footnote Police vs. Ward Churchill," *Inside Higher Ed* (May 19, 2006), available online at http://www.insidehighered.com/views/2006/05/19/wilson.

64. See "Recommendation of Interim Chancellor Phil DiStefano with regard to Investigation of Research Misconduct," *University of Colorado News Report* (June 26, 2006), available online at http://www.colorado.edu/news/reports/churchill/distefano062606.html.

65. See Scott Smallwood, "U. of Colorado Begins Process to Fire Ward Churchill," *Chronicle of Higher Education* (June 27, 2006), available online at http://chronicle.com/daily/2006/06/2006062704n.htm.

66. Wilson, "The Footnote Police vs. Ward Churchill."

67. Dennis Baron, "Churchill Fallout: It's About Academic Freedom," *Inside Higher Ed* (May 26, 2006), available online at http://www.insidehighered.com/views/2006/05/26/baron.

68. Cited in Ellen Schrecker, "The New McCarthyism in Academe," pp. 105–106.

69. Baron, "Churchill Fallout."

70. Anne D. Neal et al., *How Many Ward Churchills?: A Study by the American Council of Trustees and Alumni* (Washington, DC: American Council of Trustees and Alumni, May 2006).

71. Ibid., p. 22.

72. Ibid., p. 2.

73. Ellen Schrecker, cited in Justin M. Park, "Under Attack: Free Speech on Campus," *Clamor* 34 (September/October 2005), available online at http://www.refuseandresist.org/culture/art.php?aid=2207.

74. Neal et al., *How Many Ward Churchills?* p. 12.

75. In a conversation with Roger Bowen, who heads the American Association of University Professors, Anne Neal defended the publication of *How Many Ward Churchills?* by arguing that the study simply presents to the public an example of faculty course descriptions. Of course, she failed to mention that all of the faculty "exposed" are on the left. And in response to Bowen's pointing out that she states in the document "we want to expose faculty who use words like social justice," she simply laughed. See "Anne Neal vs. Roger Bowen," *Chronicle of Higher Education* (March 9, 2007), p. A9.

76. Scott Jaschik, "Intellectual Diversity or Intellectual Insult," *Inside Higher Ed* (April 16, 2007), available online at http://insidehighered.com/layout/set/print/news/2007/04/16/missouri.

77. Cited in Sarah Pollock, "Robert Hass," *Mother Jones* (March/April 1992), p. 22.

78. James Pierson, "The Left University," *The Weekly Standard* 11:3 (October 3, 2005), available online at http://www.weeklystandard.com/Content/Public/Articles/000/000/006/120xbklj.asp.

79. Roger Kimball, "Rethinking the University: 'Battle Plan,'" *The New Criterion* 23 (May 2005), available online at http://www.newcriterion.com/archive/23/may05/universe.htm.

80. Carol M. Swain, "Religious, Philosophical, and Socioeconomic Diversity," *Chronicle of Higher Education* 52:3 (September 9, 2005), pp. B12.

81. CBN News, transcript of an interview with David Horowitz, "The 101 Most Dangerous Professors in America," *CBN News.com* (March 22, 2006), available online at http://cbn.com/cbnnews/commentary/060322a.aspx.

82. Ibid.

83. Approvingly cited in Kimball, "Rethinking the University."

84. Jonathan Cole, "Academic Freedom Under Fire."

85. Cited in Jennifer Jacobson, "What Makes David Run," *Chronicle of Higher Education* (May 6, 2005), p. A9.

86. The Academic Bill of Rights is available online at http://www.studentsforacademicfreedom.org/abor.html.

87. David Horowitz, "In Defense of Intellectual Diversity," *Chronicle of Higher Education* 50:23 (February 13, 2004), p. B12.

88. Cited in Martin Plissner, "Flunking Statistics," *The American Prospect* 13:23 (December 30, 2002), available online at http://www.prospect.org/print-friendly/print/V13/23/plissner-m.html.

89. Steven M. Warshawsky, "Reclaiming Higher Education from the Left," *The American Thinker* (June 24, 2006), available online at http://www.americanthinker.com/articles.php?article_id=4859.

90. See, for instance, John K. Wilson, *Patriotic Correctness: Academic Freedom and Its Enemies* (Boulder, CO: Paradigm Publishers, 2006); Russell Jacoby, "The New PC: Crybaby Conservatives," *The Nation* (April 4, 2006), pp. 11–15; Plissner, "Flunking Statistics"; and Yoshie, "Conservatives: Underrepresented in Academia?" *Critical Montages* Blog (April 2, 2005), available online at http://montages.blogspot.com/2005/04/conservatives-under-represented-in.html.

91. See Lionel Lewis's response to Anne D. Neal in "Political Bias on Campus," *Academe* (May 5, 2005), available online at http://www.aaup.org/publications/Academe/2005/05/mj/05mjlte.htm.

92. Gary Younge, "Silence in Class," *The Guardian* (April 3, 2006), available online at http://www.guardian.co.uk/usa/story/0,,1746227,00.html.

93. Jennifer Jacobson, "Conservatives in a Liberal Landscape," *Chronicle of Higher Education* 51:5 (September 24, 2004), pp. A8–A11.

94. John F. Zipp and Ruddy Fenwick, "Is the Academy a Liberal Hegemony? The Political Orientation and Educational Values of Professors," *Public Opinion Quarterly* 70:3 (2006), available online at http://poq.oxfordjournals.org/cgi/content/full/70/3/304?ijkey=dVt13UcYfsj5AyF&keytype=ref#SEC5.

95. Stanley Fish, "On Balance," *Chronicle of Higher Education* (April 1, 2005), available online at http://chronicle.com/jobs/2005/04/2005040101c.htm.

96. Jacoby, "The New PC," p. 13.

97. Jacobson, "Conservatives in a Liberal Landscape," p. A10. Kelly Field has reported in the *Chronicle of Higher Education* that conservative organizations have created "1,060 groups and newspapers on 443 campuses" as of 2006. See Kelly Field, "Recruiting for the Right," *Chronicle of Higher Education* (January 12, 2007), pp. A33–A34.

98. The Students for Academic Freedom website address is http://www.studentsforacademicfreedom.org.

99. The "SAF Complaint Center" can be found at http://www.studentsforacademicfreedom.org/comp/default.asp.

100. Ibid.

101. Robert Ivie, "Academic Freedom and Political Heresy," *IU Progressive Faculty Coalition Forum* (October 3, 2005), available online at http://www.indiana.edu/~ivieweb/academicfreedom.htm.

102. Ann Marie B. Bahr, "The Right to Tell the Truth," *Chronicle of Higher Education* (May 6, 2005), available online at http://chronicle.com/weekly/v51/i35/35b00501.htm.

103. Jacoby, "The New PC," pp. 4–5.

104. David Hollinger provides an interesting argument against academic balance and for the importance of professionalism in giving students the benefit of years of research, writing, and teaching. See David A. Hollinger, "What Does It Mean to Be 'Balanced' in Academia?" *History News Network* (February 28, 2005), available online at http://hnn.us/articles/10194.html.

105. Cited in Amy Goodman, "Columbia U. Professor Rashid Khalidi: Freedom of Speech and Academic Freedom Are Necessary for Unpopular and Difficult Ideas," *DemocracyNow.org* (April 6, 2005), available online at http://www.democracynow.org/article.pl?sid=05/04/06/1421213.

106. Adam J. Jentleson and Jamie Horwitz, "Statement by Megan Fitzgerals Representing the Free Exchange on Campus Coalition on 'Academic Freedom' Conference in Washington, D.C. April 6–7," *Center for Campus Free Speech* (April 6, 2006),

available online at http://www.campusspeech.org/speech.
asp?id2=23418.

107. Dan Morrell, "A Question of Balance," *The Penn Stater*
(January/February 2006), p. 32.

108. Scott Jaschik, "From Bad to Worse for David Horowitz,"
Inside Higher Ed (November 22, 2006), available online at http://
insidehighered.com/news/2006/11/22/tabor. Some universities
have been favorably influenced by Horowitz's position, and, in the
case of CUNY, proposals have been made by the administration
to set up new procedures for handling student complaints that
are vague by suggesting that whenever intellectual disagree-
ments occur in a classroom, rather than be subject to dialogue
and debate, they should be treated as a practice to be monitored
by students and subject to an official report or complaint, ultimately to be handled by administrative committees. If the basis
for such a procedure is vague, the implications it has for stripping
the classroom of any critical content is quite serious. How is the
classroom altered when students are led to believe that having
their ideas challenged constitutes a practice serious enough for
administrative action and judicial review? One outcome is that
such procedures have less to do with safeguarding students than
with policing classroom and intimidating teachers who might fear
being subject to an administrative review every time they say
something that might offend "the comfort zone" of a particular
student. See Scott Jaschik, "Students' Complaints, Professors'
Rights," *Inside Higher Ed* (January 18, 2007), available online at
http://insidehighered.com/news/2007/01/18/cuny.

109. David Horowitz, *The Professors: The 101 Most Dangerous Academics in America* (Washington, DC: Regnery Publishing,
2006), p. 200.

110. Free Exchange on Campus, "Facts Count: An Analysis of
David Horowitz's *The Professors: The 101 Most Dangerous Academics in America*," May 2006, p. 1. This report is available online at
http://www.freeexchangeoncampus.org/index.php?option=com_
docman&Itemid=25&task=view_category&catid=12&order=dmda
te_published&ascdesc=DESC.

111. Neil Gross, "Right, Left, and Wrong: David Horowitz's
Latest Attack on America's Left-Leaning College Professors Doesn't
Add Up," *Boston Globe* (February 26, 2006), p. D10.

112. Cited in Bill Berkowitz, "Horowitz's Campus Jihads,"
Dissident Voice (October 9–19, 2004), pp. 1–6, available online at
http://www.dissidentvoice.org/Oct04/Berkowitz1009.htm.

113. Fish, "On Balance."

114. Jonathan Cole, "The New McCarthyism."

115. Scott Jaschik, "$500 Fines for Political Profs," Inside Higher Ed (February 19, 2007), available online at http://inside-highered.com/layout/set/print/news/2007/02/19/ariz.

116. Arizona State Senate, "Senate Fact Sheet for S.B. 1331" (February 13, 2006), available online at http://www.azleg.state.az.us/FormatDocument.asp?inDoc=/legtext/47leg/2r/summary/s.1331hed.doc.htm. For an excellent analysis of the bill, see Scott Jaschik, "Avoid Whatever Offends You," *Inside Higher Ed* (February 17, 2006), available online at http://www.inside-highered.com/news/2006/02/17/ariz.

117. Kevin Mattson, "A Student Bill of Fights," *The Nation* (April 4, 2005), p. 16.

118. Matson, "A Student Bill of Fights."

119. James Vanlandingham, "Capital Bill Aims to Control 'Leftist Profs': The Law Would Let Students Sue for Untolerated Beliefs," *Independent Florida Alligator* (March 23, 2005), available online at http://www.alligator.org/pt2/050323freedom.php.

120. Paul Krugman, "An Academic Question," *New York Times* (April 5, 2005), p. A27.

121. Cited in Kelly Field, "'Political Rigidity' in Academe Undermines Federal Support for Higher Education, Senator Tells Commission," *Chronicle of Higher Education* (December 12, 2005), available online at http://chronicle.com/daily/2005/12/2005121201n.htm.

122. In the House of Representatives, ABOR was taken up as HR 3077, which was part of HR 609. It is Title VI of the Higher Education Act, which is why it is also called "Title VI" in some discussions. This house version is also called the "College Access and Opportunity Act." It has been recommended with some significant revisions to the Senate as S 1614. For a summary of the differences, see the AAUP website, which can be found at http://aaup.org/govrel/hea/index.htm.

123. Kathy Kelly, "Undermining Civil Society," *CounterPunch. org* (April 11, 2005), available online at http://www.counterpunch.org/rooij04112005.html.

124. Jacobson, "What Makes David Run," p. A12. See also Johnson, "Who's Behind the Attack on Liberal Professors?"

125. Rob Chaney, "Free Schools: David Horowitz Visits Montana," *The Missoulian* (December 2003), available online at http://www.studentsforacademicfreedom.org/archive/december2003/Missoulian120303.htm.

126. Kelly, "Undermining Civil Society."

127. Willis, "The Pernicious Concept of Balance."

128. Cited in Leslie Rose, "David Horowitz: Battering Ram for Bush Regime," *Revolution Online* (August 28, 2005), available online at http://rwor.org/a/013/horowitz-battering-ram.htm.

129. Larissa MacFarquhar, "The Devil's Accountant," *New Yorker* (March 31, 2003), available online at http://www.analphilosopher.com/files/MacFarquhar,_The_Devil's_Accountant_(2003).pdf.

130. David Horowitz, *Unholy Alliance: Radical Islam and the American Left* (New York: National Book Network, 2004), p. 56.

131. Cited in Mattson, "A Student Bill of Rights," p. 18.

132. The Annual Report on the Economic Status of the Profession 2005–2006, "The Devaluing of Higher Education," *Academe* (March–April 2006), pp. 24–34.

133. This self-righteous shame and smear list can be found online at http://www.discoverthenetworks.com/individual.asp.

134. David Horowitz, "One Man's Terrorist … ," in *Campus Support for Terrorism,* ed. Horowitz and Ben Johnson (Los Angeles: Center for the Support for the Study of Popular Culture, 2004), pp. 19–20.

135. Wilson, "The Footnote Police vs. Ward Churchill."

136. Glenn Greenwald, "Far-Right Thugs Go Mainstream," *Alternet* (July 11, 2006), available online at http://www.alternet.org/story/38679/.

137. See, for example, David Horowitz, "The *NY Times* Points Cranks, Radicals, Al-Quaeda Operatives and Would-Be Assassins to the Summer Homes of Cheney and Rumsfeld," *Front Page Mag.com* (June 30, 2006), available online at http://www.frontpagemag.com/blog/BlogEntry.asp?ID=676.

138. Greenwald, "Far Right Thugs Go Mainstream."

139. Theodor W. Adorno, *The Culture Industry: Selected Essays on Mass Culture,* ed. J. M. Bernstein (New York: Routledge, 1991), p. 292.

140. See Beinin, "The New McCarthyism."

141. Zygmunt Bauman, *Globalization* (New York: Columbia University Press, 1998), p. 5.

142. I have taken up the issues of critical pedagogy, democracy, and schooling in a number of books. See, most recently, Henry A. Giroux, *Border Crossings* (New York: Routledge, 2005); *America on the Edge* (New York: Palgrave, 2006); *The Giroux Reader,* ed. Christopher Robbins (Boulder, CO: Paradigm Publishers, 2006); and Henry A. Giroux and Susan Searls Giroux, *Take Back Higher Education* (New York: Palgrave, 2006).

143. Ivie, "Academic Freedom and Political Heresy."

144. Derrida, "The Future of the Profession or the Unconditional University," p. 233.

145. Edward Said, *Reflections on Exile and Other Essays* (Cambridge, MA: Harvard University Press, 2001), p. 501.

146. Stanley Aronowitz, "Introduction," in Paulo Freire, *Pedagogy of Freedom* (Boulder, CO: Rowman and Littlefield, 1998), pp. 10–11.

147. Zygmunt Bauman and Keith Tester, *Conversations with Zygmunt Bauman* (Cambridge, UK: Polity Press, 2001), p. 4.

148. Chandra Mohanty, "On Race and Voice: Challenges for Liberal Education in the 1990s," *Cultural Critique* (Winter 1989–1990), p. 192.

149. Cornelius Castoriadis, "Democracy as Procedure and Democracy as Regime," *Constellations* 4:1 (1997), p. 5.

150. Howard Zinn, *On History* (New York: Seven Stories Press, 2001), p. 178.

151. Edward Said, *Representations of the Intellectual* (New York: Pantheon, 1994), pp. 12–13, 22–23.

152. Hannah Arendt, *Responsibility and Judgment*, ed. Jerome Kohn (New York: Shocken, 2003), p. 159.

153. These themes in Arendt's work are explored in detail in Elizabeth Young-Bruehl, *Why Arendt Matters* (New Haven: Yale University Press, 2006).

◇

4

Breaking the Chains

A Strategy to Retake the University

There is a time when the operation of the machine becomes so odious, makes you so sick at heart, that you can't take part; you can't even passively take part, and you've got to put your bodies upon the gears and upon the wheels, upon the levers, upon all the apparatus, and you've got to make it stop. And you've got to indicate to the people who run it, to the peopole who own it, that unless you're free, the machine will be prevented from working at all.

—*Mario Savio*

As higher education is reduced in its ability to resist the ongoing pressures of militarization, the dominating influence of corporate power, and the right-wing assault on academic freedom, it becomes more difficult for faculty, students, and administrators to address pressing social and ethical issues. Disengaged citizens provide fodder for a growing cynicism and disinvestment in the university as a public good at a time when there is an increasing awareness of corporate corruption, financial mismanagement, and systemic greed, as well as the recognition that a democracy of critical citizens is being quickly replaced by an ersatz democracy of ardent consumers, silent "patriots," and warrior soldiers. In the vocabulary of neoliberalism, the public collapses into the personal, and the personal becomes "the only politics there is, the only politics with a tangible referent or emotional valence."[1] The market now

200

foregrounds private interests while hiding public concerns, all the while dissolving any vestige of the public good and bonds of sociality and reciprocity. This suggests a perilous turn in American society, one that threatens our understanding of democracy as fundamental to our basic rights and freedoms and demands ways in which we can rethink and re-appropriate the meaning, purpose, and future of higher education. Situated within a broader context of issues concerned with social responsibility, politics, and the dignity of human life, higher education must be engaged as a public sphere that offers students the opportunity to involve themselves in the deepest problems of society and to acquire the knowledge, skills, and ethical vocabulary necessary for modes of critical dialogue and forms of broadened civic participation. Crucial toward this end is the development of educational conditions for students to come to terms with their own sense of power and public voice as individual and social agents by enabling them to examine and frame critically what they learn in the classroom as part of a broader understanding of what it means to live in a global democracy. Students need to learn how to be responsible for their own ideas, take intellectual risks, develop a sense of respect for others different from themselves, and think critically in order to shape the conditions that influence how they participate in a wider democratic culture. At the very least, as Eric Gould has argued, a democratic education must do three things:

> First, it must be an education for democracy, for the greater good of a just society—but it cannot assume that society is, a priori, just. Second, it must argue for its means as well as its ends. It must derive from the history of ideas, from long-standing democratic values and practices which include the ability to argue and critique but also to tolerate ambiguity. And third, it must participate in the democratic social process, displaying not only a moral preference for recognizing the rights of others and accepting them, too, but for encouraging argument and cultural critique. In short, a university education is a democratic education because it mediates liberal democracy and the cultural contradictions of capitalism.[2]

But more is needed than defending higher education as a vital sphere in which to develop and nourish the proper balance between democratic values and the ideology of militarization, between identities founded on democratic principles and identities steeped in a form of competitive, self-interested individualism that celebrates its own material and ideological advantages. And more is needed than defining the culture of questioning as the most fundamental pedagogical consequence of how we educate young people. Given the current assault on critical educators in light of the tragic events of September 11, 2001, and the conservative backlash against higher education waged by the Bush administration and its diverse group of secular and religious allies, it is politically crucial that educators at all levels of involvement in the academy be defended as public intellectuals who provide an indispensable service to the nation. Such an appeal can be made not in the name of professionalism but in terms of the civic benefits provided by such intellectuals and the vigorous models of scholarship and pedagogy that they offer their students. Scholars such as Howard Zinn, Noam Chomsky, Stanley Aronowitz, Edward Said, Judith Butler, and the late Pierre Bourdieu and Jacques Derrida have argued that intellectuals need to create new ways for doing politics by investing in pedagogical strategies that emphasize a relentless critique of the abuses of authority and power, on the one hand, and a discourse of possibility that performatively engages the promise of a democracy to come, on the other. All of these public intellectuals have urged academics to use their skills and knowledge to break out of the microcosm of academia, combine scholarship with commitment, and "enter into sustained and vigorous exchange with the outside world (especially with unions, grassroots organizations, and issue-oriented activist groups) instead of being content with waging the 'political' battles, at once intimate and ultimate, and always a bit unreal, of the scholastic universe."[3]

Organizing against the military-industrial-academic complex suggests criticizing the dominant trends in American society toward militarization, ideological conformity, and the power of capital and the market to shape all aspects of society. At stake here is the challenge to formulate a new understanding of higher education and its connection to both the common good and a new model of democratic politics. Democracy involves an informed citizenry and some level of shared beliefs about what it means to expand and deepen the locations, forms of knowledge, values, identities, and social relations in which democracy is both learned and experienced. In part, this suggests not only that understanding and responsibility are crucial to learning and civic action but also that pedagogy has a normative function as part of its project to provide the conditions for students to address "the kind of social order responsible for unhappiness, human suffering, and the [obligation] to help those in danger."[4]

The most important challenges facing higher education are not merely technical, instrumental, economic, or military in nature. In fact, the greatest challenge facing higher education centers on the collective task of developing a politics that extends beyond nation-state and reclaiming the academy as a democratic public sphere willing to confront the myriad global problems that produce needless human suffering, obscene forms of inequality, ongoing exploitation of marginalized groups, rapidly expanding masses of disposable human beings, increasing forms of social exclusion, and new forms of authoritarianism. Higher education is a moral and political enterprise that must struggle against all forms of dogmatism, commit itself to the most meaningful principles of an inclusive democracy, exercise a rigorous practice of self-criticism, and provide a vision of the future in which students can function as informed, critical citizens capable of actively participating, shaping, and governing a world that takes seriously the relationship between education and democracy.

If the university is to emphasize a discourse of enlightenment, ethics, vision, and democratic politics over the language of militarization, political orthodoxy, and market fundamentalism, it is crucial that academics and their allies fight to protect the jobs of full-time faculty, turning adjunct jobs into full-time positions, expanding benefits to part-time workers, and putting power into the hands of faculty and students. Protecting the jobs of full-time faculty means ensuring that they have the right to academic freedom, are paid a decent wage, and play an important role in governing the university. A weak faculty translates into a faculty without rights or power, one that is governed by fear rather than by shared responsibilities and is susceptible to labor-bashing tactics such as increased workloads, contract labor, and the suppression of dissent. Adjunct or part-time educators must be given the opportunity to break the cycle of exploitative labor and, within a short period of time, be considered for full-time positions with full benefits and the power to influence governance policies. Within the universities and colleges today, power is top-heavy, largely controlled by trustees and administrators and removed from those who actually do the work of the university—namely, the faculty, staff, and students. Moreover, the struggle against corporatization, conformity, and militarization must consider addressing the often exploitative conditions under which many graduate students work, constituting a de facto army of service workers who are underpaid, overworked, and shorn of any real power or benefits. At the same time, the issue of what constitutes ethical research in the university must be more closely understood as a matter of politics and power, one that both recognizes and refuses to enter into relations with those anti-democratic forces willing to corporatize many functions of the university, impose a code of silence on researchers, decouple matters of excellence from equity, and militarize knowledge. The current pressures remove the university from its traditional obligation to teach students how to think critically, connect self-knowledge to larger social issues, take risks, develop a sense of social responsibility, and learn how to make official power accountable.

The challenge for faculty in higher education is both structural and ideological. On the structural side, faculty, students, and staff need to organize labor movements and unions to challenge the emerging military-industrial-academic complex. Universities have enormous resources that can be mobilized to oppress faculty, exploit staff, and deny the rights of students to a decent education. To fight against such power demands labor and student movements capable of exercising enormous power collectively in both influencing and shaping academic policies. Such movements can connect to local communities, reach out to national and international organizations, and develop multiple strategies for taking back the universities from the corporations and reclaiming the private and public forces that now support militarization, a weak citizenry, and empire-building. I want to stress here the need for multiple interventions, extending from taking control of academic departments to organizing larger faculty structures and organizations. At best, faculty and students should unionize whenever they can in order to speak with a collective voice and the power of collective opposition.

There is also the crucial issue of how faculty can find ways to contribute their knowledge and skills to an understanding of how corporate and military values, identities, and practices create the conditions for both devaluing critical learning and undermining viable forms of political agency. Within the last few years, activism on and off campuses has picked up and spawned a number of student actions, including protests against sweatshops and resistance to the increasing militarization of the university. Such movements offer instances of collective resistance to the increasing separation of corporations from traditional politics and public obligations, while rejecting right-wing efforts "to displace political sovereignty with the sovereignty of the market, as if the latter has a mind and morality of its own."[5] Samuel Weber suggested that what seems to be involved in this process of displacement is "a fundamental and political redefinition of the social value of public services in general, and of universities and education in particular."[6] The challenge here is for faculty to learn as much as possible from these student movements about what it means to deepen and expand the struggle for establishing pedagogical approaches and social movements that can be used to mediate the fundamental tension between the public values of higher education and the commercial values of corporate culture, on the one hand, and fight against the more crucial assaults waged against the welfare state, public services, and public goods, on the other. If the forces of corporate and military culture are to be challenged, educators must consider enlisting the help of diverse communities, interests, foundations, social movements, and other forces to ensure that public institutions of higher learning are adequately funded so that they will not have to rely on corporate sponsorship, funding by defense and intelligence agencies, and the arms industries.

As public intellectuals, academics can learn from such struggles by turning the university into a vibrant critical site of learning and an unconditional site of pedagogical and political resistance—a space where students can figure out what is true, just, responsible, meaningful, and possible not only as a measure of individual success but also as part of the struggle to nurture a thriving democracy. The power of the dominant order resides not merely in the economic realm or in material relations of power but also in the realm of ideas and culture. That is why intellectuals must take sides, speak out, and engage in the hard work of debunking corporate culture's assault on teaching and learning. They must orient their teaching toward social change, connect learning to public life, link knowledge to the operations of power, and allow issues of human rights and crimes against humanity in their diverse forms to occupy a space of critical and open discussion in the classroom. This also means stepping out of the classroom and working with others to create public spaces where it becomes possible not only to "shift the way people think about the moment, but potentially to energize them to do something differently in that moment,"[7] to link one's critical imagination with the possibility of activism in the public sphere. Pedagogy is a border space that should enable students to confront ethically and politically the connecting tissue of thought and experience, theory and praxis, ideas and public life. Rather than merely confirm what students already know, any viable space of pedagogy must unsettle common sense with the power of sustained theoretical analysis. As an attempt to connect the worldly space of criticism with the democratic values that make such criticism possible, pedagogy refuses to treat theory as an end in itself by supposing it can understand social problems without "contesting their manifestation in the polity."[8]

It is in the spirit of such a critique and act of resistance that educators need to break with what Pierre Bourdieu described as a "new faith in the historical inevitability professed by the theorists of [neo]liberalism" in order to "invent new forms of collective political work"[9] capable not only of confronting the march of corporate and military power but also of thinking beyond a war on terrorism and the policing and surveillance of all aspects of everyday life, all of which seems to have no end in sight. This will not be an easy task, but it is a necessary one if democracy is to be won back from the reign of financial markets, the Darwinian values of an unbridled capitalism, and the ideological and material forces driving the increasing power of the national security state. Academics can contribute to such a struggle by, among other things, defending higher education for its contribution to the quality of public life, fighting through organized resistance for the crucial role that higher education can exercise pedagogically in asserting the primacy of democratic values over commercial interests, and struggling collectively through a powerful union movement to preserve the institutional and ideological conditions necessary to provide both faculty and students with the capacities they need for civic courage and engaged critical citizenship. John Dewey once claimed that "democracy needs to be reborn in each generation, and education is its midwife."[10] We live at a time when education needs to be reborn if democracy is to survive in both the United States and the world at large. And there is more at stake here than a legitimation crisis over how to define the relationship between higher education and the public good, though this problem should not be underestimated. What is crucial to recognize is that at a moment when critical thinking, informed dialogue, and rigorous accountability are urgently needed in America, these valued elements of citizenship are now under assault in the classrooms of higher education by right-wing extremists who view such practices as un-American and, in doing so, exhibit a deep hatred for the fundamentals of a real democracy. There is a further need to acknowledge that higher education is faring poorly in the context of a galloping neoliberalism that sells off public goods and subordinates all noncommodified democratic values to the dictates of the market. Nor is it doing well against the overdetermined designs of the national security state to trade off individual freedoms, if not democracy itself, for individual security and personal safety at home while ruthlessly spreading democracy abroad with occupying armies, bombs, and high-tech weaponry.

If solutions to the problems facing higher education are to be effective, then they cannot be abstracted from the growing inequality between the rich and the poor that is taking place at a global level. This type of rabid capitalism must be confronted both at home and abroad on multiple levels, including the ideological, cultural, economic, and political. Stuart Tannock is right to insist that "[i]f we are to develop a comprehensive vision of how higher education should serve the public good, we must ... make sure that when we speak of inequality, we are thinking of it at a worldwide level. And we must, hard as this is to conceptualize, include in our vision of the 'public' and the 'public good' the college- and non-college-educated not just of our own country but across the planet."[11] Such a struggle suggests, in part, that educators and others must organize collectively to oppose the creeping privatization of the university, close the college/noncollege wage-gap, protect academic freedom, preserve strong tenure contracts, appoint the growing army of part-time academics to full-time tenure-track positions, advocate for engaged scholarship, make critical education central to any understanding of classroom pedagogy, and create an international organization in defense of all forms of education as a public good essential to the very meaning of global democracy. Equally important is the need to transform the fight against militarization and the war in Iraq into a struggle for higher education as a project for democracy. One possibility is the demand that higher education be made accessible to every student in this country who wants to pursue such an education. If this government can spend billions of dollars on weapons of war, and a war that has made the world unsafe for democracy, it surely can embrace a redemptive politics by reallocating defense funds for educational needs, providing a combination of grants, scholarships, and no-interest loans to every student in America who qualifies for such aid. Such resistance demands a new political discourse, one that takes power seriously, understands politics as a matter of critique and possibility, reclaims democracy as a progressive and ongoing struggle, and builds social movements to provide a viable politics with organizational force and substance. This may sound particularly utopian in an age of widespread cynicism and despair; yet hope is a precondition not only for merging matters of agency and social responsibility but also for imagining a future that does not repeat the present.

This book addresses three diverse but connected forms of assault on higher education and freedom in the United States. Militarization views higher education as central to providing the identities, subject positions, knowledge, human resources, and legitimating ideologies that place it securely within the grip of the national security state. Corporatization enables a view of the university as an adjunct for the business world, resulting in the relegation of higher learning either to the status of the ornamental or, by largely dispensing with any viable notion of critical education, to an instrumental task at best and a form of training at worst. A caricature of principled conservatism, the new ideological fundamentalism, in its political, market, and religious versions, views democracy as a deficit and the university as both a weak link in the war on terrorism and an obstacle to banishing all remnants of enlightenment rationality—with its legacy of critique, dialogue, thoughtfulness, responsibility, and judgment—in favor of a no-holds-barred Americanism. All of these anti-democratic ideas and social movements contribute to what Hannah Arendt once called "dark times"—a period in which the public realm has lost "the power of illumination."[12] Genuine politics begins to disappear as people methodically lose those freedoms and rights that enable them to speak, act, dissent, and exercise both their individual right to resistance and a shared sense of collective responsibility. While higher education is only one site, it is one of the most crucial institutional and political spaces where democratic subjects can be shaped, democratic relations can be experienced, and anti-democratic forms of power can be identified and critically engaged. It is also one of the few spaces left where young people can think critically about the knowledge they gain, learn values that refuse to reduce the obligations of citizenship to either consumerism or the dictates of the national security state, and develop the language and skills necessary to defend those institutions and social relations that are vital to a substantive democracy. As Arendt insisted, a meaningful conception of politics appears only when concrete spaces exist for people to come together to talk, think critically, and act on their capacities for empathy, judgment, and social responsibility. Under such circumstances, the academy, faithful to its role as a crucial democratic public sphere, offers "a hope that makes all hoping possible"[13] while also offering a space both to resist the "dark times" in which we now live and to embrace the possibility of a future forged in the civic struggles requisite for a viable democracy.

Notes

1. Jean Comaroff and John L. Comaroff, "Millennial Capitalism: First Thoughts on a Second Coming," *Public Culture* 12:2 (2000), pp. 305–306.

2. Eric Gould, *The University in a Corporate Culture* (New Haven: Yale University Press, 2003), p. 225.

3. Pierre Bourdieu, "For a Scholarship with Commitment," *Profession* (2000), p. 44.

4. Zygmunt Bauman, *Liquid Modernity* (London: Polity Press, 2000), p. 215.

5. Comaroff and Comaroff, "Millennial Capitalism," p. 332.

6. Cited in Roger Simon, "The University: A Place to Think?"

in *Beyond the Corporate University*, ed. Henry A. Giroux and Kostas Myrsiades (Lanham, MD: Rowman and Littlefield, 2001), pp. 47–48.

7. Lani Guinier and Anna Deavere Smith, "A Conversation Between Lani Guinier and Anna Deavere Smith: 'Rethinking Power, Rethinking Theater,'" *Theater* 31:3 (Winter 2002), pp. 34–35.

8. John Brenkman, "Extreme Criticism," in *What's Left of Theory?* ed. Judith Butler, John Guillory, and Kendall Thomas (New York: Routledge, 2000), p. 130.

9. Pierre Bourdieu, *Acts of Resistance* (New York: The New Press, 1999), p. 26.

10. Cited in Elizabeth L. Hollander, "The Engaged University," *Academe* (July/August 2000), available online at http://www.aaup.org/publications/Academe/2000/00ja/JA00Holl.htm.

11. Stuart Tannock, "Higher Education, Inequality, and the Public Good," *Dissent* (Spring 2006), p. 50.

12. Hannah Arendt, *Men in Dark Times* (New York: Harcourt Brace, 1983), pp. 4–5.

13. Zygmunt Bauman, *Liquid Life* (London: Polity Press, 2005), p. 151.

◇

Index

◊

About the Author

Henry A. Giroux is an American-born educator who currently holds the Global TV Network Chair in the Department
of English and Cultural Studies at McMaster University in
Canada.

His most recent books include: *America on the Edge*
(2006); *The Giroux Reader* (2006); *Beyond the Spectacle of
Terrorism* (2006); *Stormy Weather: Katrina and the Politics
of Disposability* (2006), *Take Back Higher Education* (coauthored with Susan Searls Giroux, 2004); *The Terror
of Neoliberalism* (2004); and *The Abandoned Generation:
Democracy Beyond the Culture of Fear* (2003).

Giroux's primary research areas are critical pedagogy,
media studies, cultural studies, youth studies, social theory,
and the politics of public and higher education.